Indiana Academy of Science

Founded 1885

ða

1986 Officers

ða

E. Campaigne, *President*
Stanley L. Burden, *President-Elect*
Duvall A. Jones, *Treasurer*
Richard L. Conklin, *Secretary*

Ernest M. Shull

The
Butterflies
of
INDIANA

Published by the Indiana Academy of Science
Distributed by Indiana University Press,
Bloomington & Indianapolis

Manufactured in Japan

Library of Congress Cataloging-in-Publication Data

Shull, Ernest M.
  The butterflies of Indiana.

  Bibliography: p.
  Includes index.
    1. Butterflies—Indiana—Identification.
  2. Butterflies—Indiana. 3. Insects—Identification.
  4. Insects—Indiana—Identification. I. Title.
  QL551.I6S58 1987   595.78'90954   86-46216
  ISBN 0-253-31292-2

  1 2 3 4 5 91 90 89 88 87

Contents

Foreword

Few organisms have attracted as much attention among amateur and professional collectors alike as butterflies. Nearly every schoolchild has tried his or her hand at making a "bug collection" which is sure to contain some butterflies. Major university and museum collections may contain millions of butterflies from all over the world.

Almost as numerous as the butterflies themselves are books about butterflies. Why another one? The only previous attempt to present a major treatment of the butterflies of Indiana was nearly a century ago. Changes in nomenclature, the discovery of new species in Indiana, and more comprehensive distribution records certainly justify this new study. Brilliant color photographs illustrate every species of butterfly found in Indiana, with upper and lower views of both male and female specimens in species exhibiting sexual dimorphism and pictures of the many variations of color patterns found among the natural populations.

This book is designed as a manual to aid the collector and student in identifying the butterflies presently known to occur in Indiana. In addition, the author presents comprehensive life histories for each species based on his own extensive field observations over many years as well as his knowledge of the vast literature on the butterflies of the world. Two unique contributions to our understanding of the biology of butterflies are detailed in this present volume. Never before has so much detailed information on the mating habits of butterflies been presented in a single volume. Shull has recorded in great detail every observation of mating butterflies, including not only the date but the time of day, air temperature, and often the plant species on which the copulating butterflies were resting. A second feature of this book is the extensive listing of larval foodplants for each species as known.

Ernest M. Shull is a naturalist in the best of the nineteenth-century tradition. An ordained minister, a long-time missionary in India, and a professor of sociology at St. Francis College in Fort Wayne, Shull has pursued his lifelong study of butterflies as a most dedicated and thoroughly scientific amateur. He has collected countless thousands of butterflies, both in America and India (and elsewhere). He has donated tens of thousands of his specimens to some of the largest museum and private collections in America. He has consulted with the leading specialists in the various groups of butterflies in America. This book is his *magnum opus,* so to speak, the crowning achievement of his lifetime "hobby" of collecting these jewels of the sky.

In the early part of this century, the major publisher of studies on the flora and fauna of Indiana was the Indiana Department of Geology and Natural History. After about 1920 a few books of this sort were published by the Department of Conservation, but there was a long interval when few taxonomic studies on Indiana biota were issued. In 1969 the Indiana Academy of Science initiated a series to accommodate authors who had written monographs in this subject area. To date, the Academy has published books on mammals, reptiles and amphibians, and mammalian ectoparasites. It is a great pleasure to be able to present to the public this monograph on the butterflies of Indiana.

It is also a privilege and a pleasure to share with the Indiana University Press in this joint publishing effort. In recent years, the Indiana University Press has become quite active in publishing books on Indiana plants and animals. We of the Indiana Academy of Science are honored to have this book accepted by the Indiana University Press as one of their publications.

As editor, I want to thank Dr. James Clark, Indiana Department of Natural Resources, Dr. Frank N. Young, Indiana University, and especially Dr. Lee D. Miller of the Allyn Museum of Entomology, Sarasota, Florida, for reading the manuscript and offering many helpful suggestions and corrections. Mr. Gerald P. Abel of the Bass Photo Company in Indianapolis took the beautiful color photographs that appear in this book. I would also like to express my gratitude to Mr. John Gallman, Director of the Indiana University Press, and his staff for providing us this opportunity to publish this book.

William R. Eberly
Editor of Special Publications
Indiana Academy of Science

Part One

The Butterflies
of Indiana

Introduction

The knowledge of Indiana butterflies has been accumulating slowly. There have been only three checklists published that covered the entire state. Before 1972, only two major annotated lists of butterflies had been published, one by Blatchley (1892) and the other by Montgomery (1931), but only Blatchley included the skippers known to occur in Indiana. The most recent comprehensive list, "Annotated List of the Butterflies of Indiana" (Shull and Badger, 1972), was published by the Lepidopterists' Society.

Numerous partial treatments and regional papers were published by Blatchley in the *Indiana Farmer* and the *Hoosier Naturalist* (1886−87). In 1936 Hall's paper "The Occurrence of Unusual Rhopalocera in Indiana" appeared in the *Proceedings of the Indiana Academy of Science*. Masters and Masters (1969) dealt specifically with the butterflies of Perry County but added a list of the skippers then found throughout the state. Price and Shull (1969) reported the uncommon species of northeastern Indiana. Other important writings, although limited in scope, are included in the bibliography.

The entomologists at Purdue University and Indiana University have concentrated their efforts primarily on teaching and research on the insects considered agricultural pests; however, both institutions are building worldwide collections of Lepidoptera.

In recent years many new species of Lepidoptera (especially those considered essentially western species) have been collected in Indiana. Several forms once considered subspecies have been separated into distinct species. Many aspects of the nomenclature of the butterflies are in a great state of flux. Efforts are being made not only to stabilize scientific and common names, but to make classification more uniform throughout the world. There will probably be a debate lasting for many years about which system of classification is the best.

In this present work I have chosen to follow Miller and Brown (1981) in their *Catalog/Checklist of the Butterflies of America North of Mexico*. These authors recognize two superfamilies, Hesperioidea (the skippers) and Papilionoidea (all other butterflies), in contrast to a few authors who divide the latter group into several superfamilies.

The state of Indiana, customarily considered a flat agricultural area, in reality combines a number of different and interesting biogeographic regions with a variety of natural habitats holding a very diversified flora and fauna. Briefly, these are the northeastern lakes and bogs, the northeastern and central plains, the southeastern lowlands and flats, the south-central hills, the Ohio-Wabash

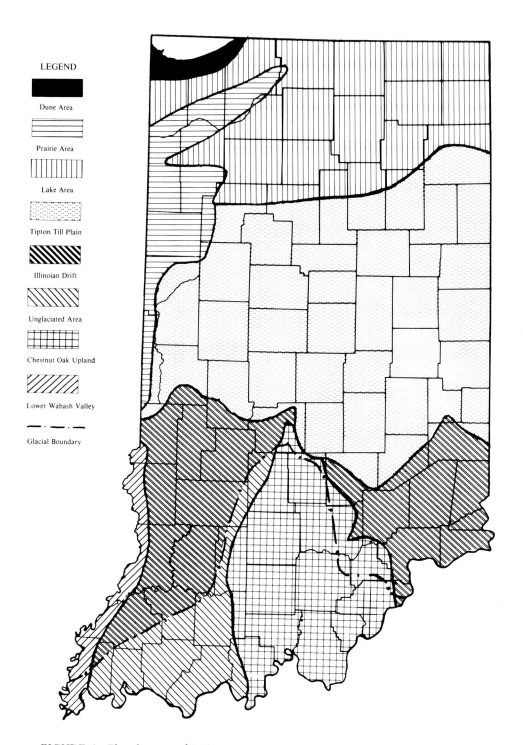

LEGEND

Dune Area

Prairie Area

Lake Area

Tipton Till Plain

Illinoian Drift

Unglaciated Area

Chestnut Oak Upland

Lower Wabash Valley

Glacial Boundary

FIGURE 1. Floral areas of Indiana

River lowlands, the intrusion of the prairie and the Kankakee sand area from Illinois, and the northwestern snow belt extending south and west of Lake Michigan and including the typical Lake Michigan dune country. Thus Indiana provides a rich and varied area for collecting and research by professional and amateur entomologists.

An area of research needing much more attention is the close interrelationship between butterflies and their larval foodplants. Ehrlich and Raven (1965) published a worldwide study entitled "Butterflies and Plants: A Study in Co-evolution," but specific studies for Indiana are lacking. Since the publication of *The Vascular Plants of Indiana: A Computer Based Checklist* by Crovello, Keller, and Kartesz (1983), the determination of the larval foodplants of the butterflies of Indiana can be more accurate. However, not all the foodplants listed in the present work are found in the state.

Portions of the state have not been adequately covered to present complete butterfly distribution records, even though the dot maps for each species/subspecies reflect much data. These maps are based on data found in the published records, along with many new county records presented here. Inadequately covered are the central western prairie areas for the skippers surviving from the western prairies, the south central areas from Spring Mill State Park south including French Lick, and the southeastern counties adjoining Kentucky and Ohio. Some of the areas have only been spot-checked; more intensive research might add other species. Although the southwestern counties have proved comparatively unrewarding, on occasion they yield southern species wandering northwards when conditions are favorable.

I have been studying Lepidoptera sporadically in the state from 1932 to 1946 and regularly from 1964 to the present. Specimens have been collected in each of the 92 counties. Most of these have been deposited in the American Museum of Natural History, but some have been donated to the United States National Museum and to several college and university museums. Of the estimated 30,000 butterflies and moths I have collected in Indiana, about 7,000 remain in my personal collection. Almost all the known literature has been examined. It hardly needs to be said that much more fieldwork needs to be done.

It is hoped that this monograph will be helpful to collectors and researchers of this state as well as in the contiguous states and elsewhere. Many of the subjects included here will be of universal interest.

The author has received much encouragement and help from the officers and other members of the Lepidopterists' Society, particularly for publishing the Shull and Badger list of the butterflies of Indiana (1972) and for the annual season summaries that report the state and county records each year.

For many years the Indiana Department of Natural Resources, especially the

Division of State Parks and the Division of Nature Preserves, has issued me permits to research and photograph the Lepidoptera in these restricted and protected areas. Without their generous help, a comprehensive picture of the butterfly fauna would have been impossible.

Another major source of help has been three grants from the Research Grants Committee of the Indiana Academy of Science. The first two grants made it possible to study and collect specimens in every county of the state, and the third grant made it possible to photograph the butterflies in color.

For help in various ways—identification, reprints, county records, specimens, general suggestions, and encouragement—I want to thank the following: Richard T. Arbogast, F. Sidney Badger, John M. Burns, Lee A. Casebere, Francis S. Chew, Harry K. Clench, Julian P. Donahue, Robert E. Dolphin, John C. Downey, William R. Eberly, Paul R. Ehrlich, H. A. Freeman, Ronald R. Gatrelle, George L. Godfrey, L. Paul Grey, David F. Hardwick, John Richard Heitzman, David F. Hess, Roderick R. Irwin, Alexander B. Klots, Irwin Leeuw, John H. Masters, William W. McGuire, Lee D. Miller, Marc C. Minno, Jack R. Munsee, Mogens C. Nielsen, Emerson R. Niswander, Paul A. Opler, Philip A. Orpurt, Cyril F. dos Passos, Jerry A. Powell, Homer F. Price, Charles F. Remington, Frederick H. Rindge, John Richard Schrock, James A. Shields, David M. Wright, and Harold L. Zimmack.

To my frequent collecting companion and good friend David L. Eiler, I wish to give special thanks for permission to photograph a few of his specimens.

Lastly, I owe a debt of gratitude to Lee D. Miller, Curator of the Allyn Museum of Entomology, for reading my manuscript. However, I assume responsibility for any errors that may appear in this writing.

The Biology of Butterflies

Butterflies are insects that show complete metamorphosis in their life cycle. The egg hatches into a larval stage which forms a pupa (chrysalis) from which the adult eventually emerges. Eggs are usually laid on or near the larval food-plants. Usually the food needs of the larva are met by very specific plants or groups of plants. Most commonly, the pupal stage is the form that survives through the winter season, but in some species the adults hibernate or migrate to warmer climates.

It is not the intent of this book to deal with all aspects of the biology of butterflies. The reader is directed to such works as Howe (1975), Klots (1951, 1957), Pyle (1981), and many others for this kind of information. However, several topics are of special importance in the present work.

The Color Patterns of Butterflies

Butterflies are flying gems of exquisite beauty and design. The wing patterns, mosaics of tiny scales, give butterflies their most prominent characteristic—color. In the 100,000 or more species of Lepidoptera already classified, no two species are exactly alike; however, a few of the closely related, dull-colored species are occasionally difficult to identify with certainty. For such specimens, one should consult the experts who study the genitalia and may have large collections with which to compare the freaks, aberrant forms, and atypical specimens.

H. Frederik Nijhout's study "The Color Patterns of Butterflies and Moths" (1981) explains the phenomenon of color. In butterflies a few of the most vivid colors are due to the structural arrangements of the tiny scales (a powdery substance on the wings that can easily be rubbed off with a finger during capture or mounting), and not color due largely to chemical pigments as in the Luna moth, whose green color fades with long exposure to light.

The iridescent or metallic colors—all blues and greens on the wings of butterflies—are structural. These colors come about through the interference or scattering of light, a phenomenon known as diffraction. When the wing of a butterfly is examined with a high-powered microscope, the color pattern is seen to be determined by the tiled mosaic or structural arrangement of the scales, each scale being of a single color. As Nijhout points out, "Fine gradations in color and hue are achieved by variations in the ratios of the different scales. . . ."

The forewing of the American Buckeye has scales made up of four colors: red, buff, black, and brown. The whiteness in the large eyespot (ocellus) is due to the reflection of light by tiny air bubbles inside the scales. Under microscopic examination three shades of brown scales can be detected on the Buckeye's wing pattern. Even the buff and red scales have the same pigment as do the brown. With its wings closed, the colors are concealed, affording protection from predators. Thus, the color patterns of butterflies are of two major kinds, one due to pigments and the other to structural patterns of the scales.

In the satyrids (basically brown butterflies) the various shades of tan, gray, brown, black, brownish red, and yellowish brown are all probably due to a pigment called melanin within the scales. During the flight period, the color of satyrids appears to fade from exposure to sunlight. Another category of pigments consists of the pterins, which account for many of the bright reds, yellows, and oranges, and even whites. A number of unidentified pigments have been detected in a few species of butterflies.

Two species captured in Indiana (and perhaps others), the Tawny-edged Skipper (*Polites themistocles*) and the Pearl Crescent (*Phyciodes tharos tharos*), show more extensive melanism than is found in the general populations of those species. Specimens of unusual color patterns should always be reported.

The spectacular colors and elaborate patterns on the wings, formed by circles and rings of pigments and by the structural arrangement of the scales and veins, have not only given butterflies breathtaking beauty but have helped these lowly creatures survive by imitating or mimicking objects or other organisms and by blending in with the background environment. Likewise, the design or outline of the wings adds endless variety, helping with identification and providing protection for many of the species. Butterflies may resemble dead leaves in shape and color; the large eyespots of some frighten away predators; the smaller ocelli and contrasting colors display bright areas and shadows when the butterfly opens and closes its wings, thereby confusing its natural enemies. The angular wings of *Polygonia,* the small sex dot in the discal area of the wings of male hairstreaks, the tails on many of the swallowtails, and many other contour and color variations contribute to the butterfly's natural survival ability.

Batesian and Müllerian Mimicry

In 1862 Henry W. Bates, after eleven years of study in the Amazon Basin of Brazil, published his theory of mimicry in an article entitled, "The Naturalist on the Amazon." This classic of natural history was published in the *Transactions of the Linnean Society of London.* He theorized that edible species of butterflies mimic the bright warning color of the inedible (bad-tasting) species. The species may be inedible to predators (birds, mice, and other creatures) primarily because the larvae of certain butterflies feed on plants which make the bodies of the adult butterflies distasteful. The inedible species were known as models and the very similar edible species were called mimics. Bates's explanation came to be called Batesian mimicry.

Among the butterflies of Indiana, there are two classic examples of Batesian mimicry. Perhaps the best known is the Monarch (the model) and its mimic, the Viceroy (details are recorded under number 149 in the annotated listing of Indiana butterflies which follows). Another example is the Pipevine Swallowtail (the model) which has five mimics (details under species number 54). Species need not belong to the same family in order to establish the model-mimic relationship.

Müllerian mimicry is largely a tropical phenomenon. Fritz Müller noted that many unrelated but distasteful species closely resemble each other. Thus the protected (inedible) species, by mimicking each other, attain an appearance of a group uniformity. Among such a group, the warning patterns consist of only a few usually very striking color patterns. Thus, a large group of inedible species is protected from predators. Even if a few of the many inedible species are tasted by the predators, the remaining individuals of the uniform group will be further protected.

In most cases, these theories of mimicry, when tested in the laboratory, are supported by a large body of evidence.

Butterfly Migration

Some species of butterflies migrate hundreds, or even thousands, of miles from their birthplace. Migrating species seldom stop during the day for food or mating, but many species stop their unidirectional flight for rest at night. Butterflies may migrate in small numbers or in flights estimated in the millions.

The Monarch or Milkweed Butterfly (*Danaus plexippus*) is Indiana's most famous traveler. Its strong veins, especially the costal forewing vein, make the Monarch easy to mark or tag so that its changes in location are easily recorded. Other migrating species mentioned in this monograph are the Cloudless Giant Sulphur (*Phoebis sennae eubule*), the very rare Orange-banded Sulphur (*Phoebis philea*), the Mexican Sulphur (*Eurema mexicana*), the Little Sulphur (*Pyrisitia lisa lisa*), the Dwarf Yellow (*Nathalis iole*), the Painted Lady (*Vanessa cardui*), the Buckeye (*Junonia coenia*), and the rare Gulf Fritillary (*Agraulis vanillae nigrior*).

Although the Cabbage White (*Artogeia rapae*) is widely known as a migrant, records of its migration in Indiana seem to be lacking. The Mustard White

(*Artogeia napi*) is highly migratory, but the subspecies *oleracea* found in Indiana seems to be nonmigratory.

According to C. B. Williams (1930, 1937) about 250 species of butterflies are known to migrate. A higher percentage of tropical or subtropical butterflies migrate than do those found in other climates.

In the fall season several species of skippers immigrate into Indiana from the prairie and neighboring states. Large aggregates of a single species do not constitute a migration; however, such concentrations should be watched for some sudden dispersal movement developing into a migration. Population pressures may cause some species to migrate. It is likely that other Indiana species migrate, for many migrations go undetected.

Sap-feeding Butterflies in Indiana

Since October 1967 I have been recording the species of butterflies and other insects which have been observed feeding on sap oozing from breaks and perforations in the bark of various kinds of trees. This report is limited to the butterflies.

On 1–4 October 1967 sap was oozing from holes made in the trunk of a White Oak tree (*Quercus alba*) in a woods at Silver Lake in Kosciusko County. The holes were made by wood-boring beetles. Three nymphalid butterflies were feeding on the sap, a substance no doubt high in food nutrients. These species were observed daily: *Polygonia interrogationis, Polygonia comma,* and *Polygonia satyrus.* On 14 September 1971 *Polygonia progne* was captured when feeding on sap on the trunk of a White Oak in the same woods.

On 30 May 1977 the following butterflies were feeding on sap oozing from a low branch of a willow (*Salix*) in a wet meadow at North Manchester, Wabash County: *Polygonia interrogationis, Vanessa atalanta rubria, Nymphalis antiopa antiopa,* and *Asterocampa celtis.*

On 24 June 1977 five nymphalid species and one satyrid were feeding on sap oozing from *Salix* branches: *Polygonia interrogationis, Polygonia comma* and its dry season form "*dryas,*" *Vanessa atalanta rubria, Basilarchia arthemis astyanax, Nymphalis antiopa antiopa,* and the satyrid *Megisto cymela cymela.* The temperature was 88° F and the humidity was high that day in North Manchester, Wabash County.

On 17 April 1979 at Silver Lake (Kosciusko County) four nymphalid species were found on oozing sap and smears of sap on Bigtooth Aspen (*Populus grandidentata*): *Nymphalis antiopa antiopa, Aglais milberti milberti, Vanessa atalanta rubria,* and *Polygonia comma.* Several individuals of each species were captured and others were flying nearby, no doubt attracted by the pungent odor of the sap.

On 28 June 1980, on a single clump of *Salix* growing in a North Manchester wet meadow, I found an amazing number of wasps, flies, Nessus Sphinx, gnats, and butterflies feeding on the sap. According to Dr. Philip Orpurt of Manchester College (personal communication) the sap may have contained a form of yeast, but no direct chemical analysis was made. The butterflies observed included *Basilarchia arthemis astyanax, Basilarchia archippus archippus, Nymphalis antiopa antiopa, Polygonia comma, Vanessa atalanta rubria, Polygonia interrogationis, Asterocampa celtis,* and *Megisto cymela cymela.* On 7 July 1980 on the same bush I found *Polygonia comma, Satyrodes eurydice eurydice,* and *Megisto cymela cymela.* Dozens of Hop Merchants (*Polygonia comma*) were vying for feeding places on the trees. Still on the same tree on 8 August 1980 I found *Nymphalis antiopa antiopa, Cercyonis pegala alope,* and *Asterocampa clyton.*

A few of the above nymphalids, especially the early spring species, are attracted by maple sap running into containers on tapped trees.

Sugaring for moths has been practiced for many years. W. J. Holland's smear mixture consisted of four pounds of sugar, a bottle of stale beer, and a little rum. After the mixture has been stirred well, brush it on the trunks of trees. This semi-intoxicating mixture not only attracts moths at night, but many butterflies during the day.

The following formula works even better: two pounds of brown sugar, one pint of beer, several tablespoons of Karo white syrup, and a half-dozen crushed, ripe bananas. Mix the brew well, let it ferment for a few days and then apply it with a brush to the trunks of trees or even on the walls of an old building. Collecting will be very rewarding almost any time of the day for butterflies and at dusk or night for moths.

It is likely that there is much more to this sap-feeding by the butterflies than just an occasional meal. The rich nutrients found in the various kinds of sap probably make it possible for many species to lengthen their flying periods in the fall, long after most nectar-producing flowers have seeded. As late as November, several species of *Polygonia* have been seen feeding on rotten apples and other fruits. Late in the season these hibernating species depend on sap, not nectar.

Quercus sap contains sucrose, a good food nutrient, and amino acids. Dr. David Wright says, "My amino acid analysis of the sap shows many amino acids in good quantity. These basic building blocks of structural and enzymatic proteins would be necessary for long-lived lepidoptera" (personal communication, 14 January 1980). The phenomenon of sap-feeding no doubt has many biological implications for the survival of butterflies and for the distribution of populations, especially of the nymphalids. This is a challenging area for research.

Collecting Butterflies

Equipment

Biological supply companies, the larger museums of natural history, 4-H clubs, and a few of the larger universities either sell entomological equipment or publish information on collecting insects. In Indiana, Purdue University, through its Cooperative Extension Service, publishes a pamphlet entitled "How to collect, preserve and identify insects" (Sanders, Lehker, and Matthew, 1980). Another popular treatment of insects that contains much information on collecting and mounting insects is *How to Know the Insects* (Jaques, 1947). These and other sources should be consulted for information on collecting and preparing butterflies.

In addition to the standard collecting nets, the pocket net, with a 5-inch aluminum handle and a 12-inch collapsible spiral rim, can be opened at the flash of a wing. The three-piece telescopic-handled net can, in a few seconds, extend the collector's reach about ten feet.

Specimens can be kept in a relaxed condition indefinitely for convenient mounting by using 4-chloro-3 methylphenol crystals, a chemical available from biological supply companies. A large-mouthed jar with a self-sealing lid, such as some peanut butter jars, works well. To prepare a relaxant jar, sprinkle one tablespoon of the 4-chloro-3 methylphenol crystals in the bottom of the jar; then cover the crystals with five or six thicknesses of paper toweling cut to fit snugly. To activate the chemical, dampen the toweling with water and close the lid tightly. The jar is ready to use when a film of moisture collects on the inside of the glass. After placing the specimens in individual glassine envelopes, drop them into the relaxant jar. Direct contact with the chemical will spoil the insects. Avoid touching or breathing the relaxant chemical. The crystals can be reactivated, as needed, by adding a few drops of water.

Many collectors are using Safety Solvent (a substitute for carbon tetrachloride) as a safer killing agent than cyanide. It can be purchased in most drug stores. To prepare an insect-killing jar, select a small or medium-sized jar with a tight-fitting lid, one that will fit into your carrying bag or knapsack. Cut a thin sponge the size of the jar and glue it inside to the bottom. Just before going to collect, drop approximately a teaspoon of the Safety Solvent fluid onto the sponge. Freshly captured insects can be put into the jar immediately. Keep the jar closed when not in use. When opening the jar, be sure there is adequate ventilation since this substance is poisonous.

The standard spreading board, with its adjustable groove to accommodate insects of varying body size, is preferred by most collectors. Specimens pinned and dried in this manner are mounted in trays or boxes, pinned to a softer material on the bottom of the tray. However, Riker mounts have some advantages for display and lecture purposes. In Riker mounts the specimens are placed on cotton directly under glass; this protects the specimen (especially the antennae) during transport. A good method of preparing specimens for Riker mounts is to use soft cardboard instead of wood mounting blocks. Stick the insect pin through the thorax from the ventral side, open the wings with a scalpel or forceps, and then place the dorsal side of the butterfly next to the cardboard. The wings should now be spread in the same manner as used on the spreading board, except that two additional strips of paper should form an X over the thorax and close to the pin in order that the pin can be removed while the thorax is still soft. It is easier to mount micro-lepidoptera on soft cardboard than on the hard spreading board. Also, Riker mounts of a uniform size are easily stored. For scientific study and research, however, the standard pinning method, using the spreading board, should be used.

When collecting, always carry a pocket notebook for recording the date and place of capture, including the nearest city, the county and state, and the altitude if known. Without this minimal data, the specimens have little scientific value. Common and scientific names and the name of the collector should be included in the final labeling.

Collecting in Indiana

The total number of species of butterflies reported for individual counties varies from 4 in Boone, Greene, and Ripley counties to 104 in Wabash County (see Figure 2). To a large extent this reflects the intensity of collecting in the various counties more than the real differences in the butterfly fauna among the counties. Areas with fewer than 20 or 30 reported species should receive more intensive study in the future.

How many butterfly species can be collected in a single day? Any day in which a collector nets forty or more species is exceptional, because that number represents nearly half of the average number of species found in the entire season. A few of my own high records follow:

26 July 1969	Camp Mack, Kosciusko Co.	40
18 June 1970	Kosciusko Co.	40
23 June 1970	Wabash and Kosciusko cos.	40
25 June 1970	Wabash and Kosciusko cos.	50

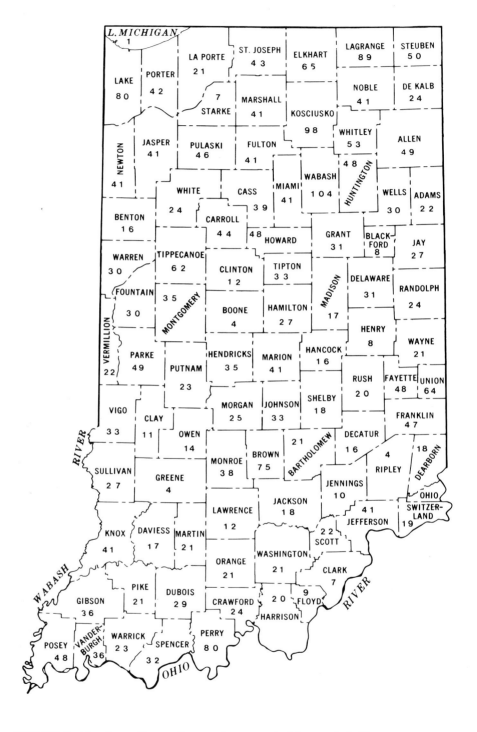

FIGURE 2. Number of butterfly species recorded for each Indiana county

26 June 1971	Wabash and Kosciusko cos.	46
2 July 1971	Wabash and Kosciusko cos.	43
12 July 1971	Wabash and Kosciusko cos.	41
21 July 1971	Camp Mack, Kosciusko Co.	41
31 July 1971	Wabash and Kosciusko cos.	45
1 August 1971	Silver Lake, Kosciusko Co.	41
1 July 1975	Allen, Steuben, and LaGrange cos.	41
15 July 1975	Wabash, Kosciusko, and LaGrange cos.	41
25 July 1975	Wabash and Kosciusko cos.	40
5 July 1977	Wabash Co.	42
13 July 1977	Cedar Lake and Mongo in LaGrange Co. and Silver Lake in Kosciusko Co.	54
28 June 1978	Wabash and Kosciusko cos.	44
4 July 1978	LaGrange and Kosciusko cos.	45
11 July 1978	Kosciusko and LaGrange cos.	48
20 July 1978	LaGrange and Kosciusko cos.	43
25 July 1978	LaGrange and Kosciusko cos.	46
8 August 1978	LaGrange, Kosciusko, and Wabash cos.	40

From 1967 to 1983 the peak periods for collecting were from late June to mid-August. The author has collected more frequently in the northeastern counties. However, many southern counties offer splendid collecting opportunities. The northwestern and southwestern counties are frequently rewarding, but not in terms of the variety of species.

When temperatures reach the high fifties and sixties, hibernating species may appear on any day of the year. Some early spring and late fall species will not be present during the summer months.

How many species may be collected in a year? The following information from the author's collection notes may be of interest to the reader:

1967	77 species total	1975	89
1968	79	1976	61
1969	77	1977	89
1970	86	1978	91
1971	83	1979	94
1972	78	1981	93
1973	78	1982	78
1974	69	1983	80

The desire to watch, touch, collect, and learn more about the crawling, walking, and flying creatures around us is a natural desire in most children until this curiosity is discouraged by adults. I was one of the fortunate ones, for my father says that from the time I was four, he used to keep an eye on me as I followed the horse-drawn plow, picking up all sorts of fascinating creatures and stuffing them into my pockets to carry home to show Mother and my nine older brothers and sisters.

When I was five, Mother made me my first butterfly net from an old window curtain. Then, a few years later, removing her canned fruit and vegetables from a long table under the windows in the basement, she provided space for me to start the "Shull Natural History Museum." Kind people through the years donated specimens to my museum; there was even an African leopard from Nigeria, presented to me by a returning missionary who stayed at our house one weekend.

Since that time my fascination with nature, instead of diminishing, has become an exciting hobby, offering me an opportunity to collect officially for various museums and to meet scientists, philosophers, and national leaders in many places. It has also led to confrontations with cobras, swarms of bees, monsoon floods, and avalanches as well as malaria-carrying mosquitoes, ticks, leeches, poison sumac, poison ivy, and deerflies—all a part of the "joys" of a nature hobby.

My wife, Lois, and my children, Linda, Jim, and Dan, who share my enthusiasm and have themselves become collectors, agree that the 9000 or so specimens which I still keep here in our house no doubt make ours the "buggiest" house in town.

Classification and Identification

Classification

Many beginning butterfly collectors are thoroughly confused by the language of classification. The proper names of species of butterflies (and all other kinds of living organisms) as well as other categories of groups in the classification scheme are written in Latin and appear in printed form in italics. The full name of a species consists of two words, of which the first only is capitalized. If a species has been divided into subspecific forms, a third word is added to the proper name. Thus the full name of the Black Swallowtail found in Indiana is *Papilio polyxenes asterius* while the Silver-spotted Skipper is *Epargyreus clarus clarus*.

A whole series of categories represents closely or distantly related forms. A genus includes very closely related species. A family includes a number of genera which have many characteristics in common. All the butterflies (as well as the closely related moths) belong to the same order, Lepidoptera, which is only one of many orders of insects. Insects and their relatives the spiders and crayfish and many other similar animals belong to the same phylum, Arthropoda, which along with many other phyla is a part of the Animal Kingdom (Animalia). Often these categories are subdivided into "super" or "sub" categories.

The complete classification of two butterflies, the Black Swallowtail and the Silver-spotted Skipper, illustrates the system presently in use by lepidopterists.

Black Swallowtail

Kingdom	Animalia
Phylum	Arthropoda
Class	Insecta
Order	Lepidoptera
Superfamily	Papilionoidea
Family	Papilionidae
Subfamily	Papilioninae
Tribe	Papilionini
Genus	*Papilio*
Species	*polyxenes*

Subspecies	*asterius*
Full name	*Papilio polyxenes asterius*

Silver-spotted Skipper

Kingdom	Animalia
Phylum	Arthropoda
Class	Insecta
Order	Lepidoptera
Superfamily	Hesperioidea
Family	Hesperiidae
Subfamily	Pyrginae
Genus	*Epargyreus*
Species	*clarus*
Subspecies	*clarus*
Full name	*Epargyreus clarus clarus*

There are more than 120,000 species of Lepidoptera (butterflies, moths, and skippers) known in the world. Moths outnumber butterflies about seven to one. No attempt has been made yet to determine the number of moths that are found in Indiana, but the present study lists 149 species of butterflies and skippers found in our state.

Identification

One of the most obvious ways of identifying butterflies once they are captured and properly mounted is to compare your specimens with photographs of named species in this book·or similar manuals available for this area (e.g., Howe, 1975 or Pyle, 1981). The next step is to turn to the text and read the descriptive notes on the species. This process should enable the beginning collector to identify a large number of the most common forms found in Indiana. However, you will soon discover that some genera and even some families contain a great number of species that are very similar in appearance.

The specialist will then turn to the study of certain anatomical features that are very specific in separating one species from another. One very important morphological feature that is often used in taxonomic studies is the form of the male sex organs (the genitalia) located at the end of the abdomen. Nothing is included in the present study about the nature of the genitalia because of the highly technical nature of this information.

Another, somewhat easier morphological concept to master is the nature of

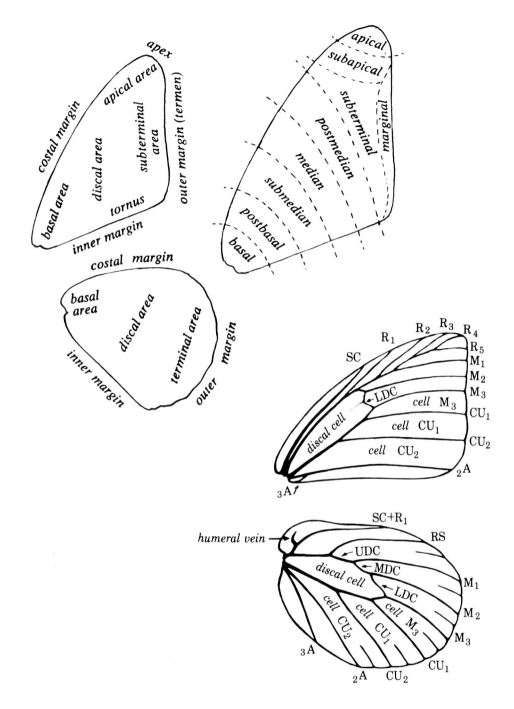

FIGURE 3. Terminology used in identifying areas
of wings and naming veins

the vein structure in the wings of the butterflies. Figure 3 illustrates the names of the veins of a "generalized" butterfly, as well as the names of the cells (the spaces between veins).

The strongest and most anterior vein on the forewing (FW) is the subcosta (SC). The radical veins (R_1, R_2, R_3, R_4, R_5), the median veins (M_1, M_2, M_3), the cubitus veins (Cu_1, Cu_2), and the second anal vein all end on the outer margin of the wing. The shape and size of the discal cell is important to note in the identification of some species. All of the veins with the exception of the subcosta and the anal veins arise from the discal cell. There are, of course, some exceptions. Some skippers have a vestigial third anal vein (3A) as do the papilionids.

Venation in the hindwing (HW) is noticeably different from that in the FW. Arising from the anterior end of the discal cell, the subcosta and the first radius ($SC + R_1$) are fused. This is followed by the radial sector (RS) which is equivalent to the R_2 to the R_5 on the FW. This is followed by the M_1, M_2, M_3, and Cu_1 and Cu_2. The short humeral vein (h) arises from $SC + R_1$, near the basal margin.

Sometimes the wing venation patterns are useful in separating families as well as genera. Shown in Figure 4 are the venation patterns for some selected families and specific genera.

Sooner or later every collector will need to consult a more advanced collector somewhere or even a specialist in a particular family or genus. It will sometimes be helpful to send specimens to one of the major museums for verification by comparison with named specimens. A list of the museums that have major collections of lepidoptera is included here. Be sure to write before sending any specimens.

Museums and Collections

The large institutions listed here are centers for research, publishers of invaluable literature (bulletins, novitates, annals, and special publications), protectors of specimens of former and present times, and they offer grants and study opportunities for qualified persons.

Opposite:
FIGURE 4. Wing vein patterns for selected butterfly genuses.
> A. *Epargyreus* (Hesperiidae); B. *Erynnis* (Hesperiidae); C. *Hesperia* (Hesperiidae); D. *Papilio* (Papilionidae); E. *Colias* (Pieridae); F. *Artogeia* (Pieridae); G. *Danaus* (Danaidae); H. *Euptychia* (Satyridae); I. *Heliconius* (Heliconiidae); J. *Speyeria* (Nymphalidae); K. *Calephelis* (Riodinidae); L. *Lycaena* (Lycaenidae).

Conservation and the Endangered Species Act

The Endangered Species Act of 1973, with its 1978 and 1982 amendments, seeks to prevent man-caused extinction of animal and plant species and to promote conservation of endangered and threatened species. Endangered species are those facing extinction; threatened species are those likely to become endangered in the near future if their ecosystems are not protected. Unquestionably, the greatest threat to the survival of butterfly species and/or subspecies is not overcollecting of the adults, which mate soon after emerging from the pupa and have a short flight period, but destruction of the natural habitats through construction of buildings and highways, drainage of wetlands, filling of lake margins, unwise farming practices, unscientific cutting of forests, overgrazing, spraying of chemicals without knowledge of long-term ecological effects, and fires.

Permits are required for collecting in Indiana state parks and preserves. The following sites with their rare-in-Indiana species need protection if these butterflies are to survive in Indiana. This responsibility rests largely with the Indiana Department of Natural Resources.

The Pigeon River Fish and Game Area, LaGrange County, which contains the largest stand of tamarack in Indiana, supports the Mustard White (*Artogeia napi oleracea*), the Swamp Metalmark (*Calephelis muticum*), the Creole Pearly Eye (*Enodia creola*), and the Appalachian Eyed Brown (*Satyrodes appalachia leeuwi*).

The Cedar Lake bogs, LaGrange County, with their floating gardens and very rare Mitchell's Satyr (*Neonympha mitchellii*), should be preserved; however, the inaccessibility of the area where *mitchellii* breeds affords some protection.

The Hoosier Prairie Preserve, Lake County, is a major habitat of the Karner Blue (*Lycaeides melissa samuelis*). A few Karner Blues can still be found in the South City Park in Griffith, Lake Co., but the overuse of recreational vehicles in the park is damaging this habitat.

The Bog Copper (*Epidemia epixanthe*) is a species restricted to acid bogs and boggy marshes. If this species still occurs in Indiana, it will likely be found in the Binkley Bog in Steuben County, the Pinhook Bog in LaPorte County, and the Cedar Lake bogs in LaGrange County. Wild cranberries, the foodplant of *epixanthe* larvae, grow in all these places.

Violations of the Endangered Species Act are punishable by a fine of up to $10,000 and/or a year in prison. For further information about the Act and its provisions for collecting, transporting, and exchanging specimens, write to the

Director of Endangered Species, U.S. Fish and Wildlife Service, Washington, D.C., 20240.

A "grandfather clause" excludes specimens taken prior to passage of the 1973 Act. Persons engaged in scientific research will not normally have difficulty securing a permit to collect a limited number of rare species, especially if the majority of the specimens are donated to one of the larger institutions of natural history.

Another law that may affect a few lepidopterists is the Convention on International Trade in Endangered Species of Wild Fauna and Flora (CITES). The United States is a signatory to this treaty. If a collector wants to import certain endangered species, or even common species for commercial purposes, an export permit from the country where the specimens were collected should be secured. Such permits are increasingly difficult to obtain.

Part Two

Species Accounts –
The Skippers

Superfamily Hesperioidea Latreille

ஐ

Family Hesperiidae Latreille

The skippers, or hesperids, are a very large, worldwide group, characterized as having the head, thorax, and abdomen stout and massive, and the wings proportionally small. The antennae are far apart on top of the head. The club of the antenna is partly or wholly curved backward and hooklike. The recurved segment is called the apiculus. All the veins of the FW arise from the discal cell. These veins are simple and unbranched. The flight of hesperids is swift and darting, hence the name "skipper." They show little of the slower, erratic flight of the regular butterflies.

I say "regular butterflies" because Ehrlich and Ehrlich do not include the skippers in their book, *How to Know the Butterflies* (1961). The Ehrlichs refer to the butterflies as Papilionoidea, the skippers as Hesperioidea, and to the moths as the "Rest of the Lepidoptera." Current entomologists are reverting to the traditional system of placing the skippers with the butterflies; therefore, I am placing the butterflies of Indiana into two superfamilies, skippers (Hesperioidea) and all other butterflies (Papilionoidea).

The author agrees with Evans (1951–55), Voss (1952), Miller and Brown (1981) and Ferris and Brown (1981) that the structural and behavioral variations among the skippers are relatively slight and sufficiently clinal to permit the group to be considered as a single family, Hesperiidae. Miller and Brown (1981) divide the family Hesperiidae into five subfamilies—Pyrrhopyginae, Pyrginae, Heteropterinae, Hesperiinae, and Megathyminae. They have suppressed the former family Megathyminidae (Giant Skippers). Two subfamilies, Pyrginae and Hesperiinae, are found in Indiana.

In general, skippers are small to medium-sized butterflies, many of which are dull-colored. They account for more than one-third of the butterfly species officially reported in Indiana. Skippers are often difficult to catch, to handle alive without damaging them, to mount, and to identify correctly. In fact, even the experts cannot identify every individual specimen referred to them. When in doubt about identification, it is best to consult the specialists for each group. For example, the expert for the genus *Erynnis* is Dr. John M. Burns, Associate Curator of the National Museum of Natural History in Washington, D.C.

Skippers are usually diurnal, flying during the daylight hours; however, a few species are crepuscular, active in the twilight. The pupa is usually enclosed in a loose cocoon. The larvae are external feeders on the leaves of plants, and most of them live in a rolled-up or folded leaf or a nest of leaves. More of the technical details of classification and of the life cycle—egg, larva, pupa, and adult (imago)—will be dealt with under each subfamily and each species/subspecies. The male genitalia (sex organs) of most species offer distinct characteristics, but this book will not picture these differences. In our eastern area, *The Hesperioidea of North America* by Lindsey, Bell, and Williams, Jr. (1931) illustrates the technical characters and the genitalia of most of the species discussed here. Modifications, of course, have been made and will continue to be made. Efforts are being made to find a more universal system of nomenclature.

Subfamily Pyrginae Burmeister

The subfamily Pyrginae contains 19 species in Indiana, and others may be added (see Hypothetical List). The members of this group vary from small to medium-sized and are colored dark brown or black with scant lighter markings. A few are checkered black and white. Still others have prominent translucent spots in the FW or silver patches across the VHW disc. Vein M_2 of the FW is only slightly curved at the base; it arises from the cell approximately midway between veins M_1 and M_3. The fore and midtibiae are unspined, and the hind tibiae have two pairs of spurs which on the males may have tufts of specialized hairs. In the males of some species (i.e., *Erynnis*) the main secondary character is a long costal fold on the dorsal border of the FW. These folds enclose the androconia (specialized sex cells).

After being collected, skippers must be treated carefully to preserve the antennae, legs, and palpi that are often necessary for the accurate determination of the species.

Genus *Epargyreus* Hübner

1. *Epargyreus clarus clarus* Cramer. Silver-spotted Skipper. Plate I.

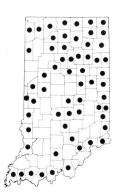

Description. The Silver-spotted Skipper is the largest and probably the most easily recognized skipper in the state. Indiana has only the nominate subspecies. Its wingspread (from wing tip to wing tip when properly mounted) varies from 1.75 to 2.5 inches (44–63 mm.), but occasionally larger specimens will be found. This species is a chocolate brown on the upper surface and has a distinctive band of golden-orange spots on the FW. The VHW has a large, irregular silver band across the middle area. The fringes on the borders of the wings are brown or buff and faintly checkered.

A similar species, *Achalarus lyciades* Geyer, has rounder wings and a large white VHW patch extending from the margin to about one-third of the wing's total area.

Distribution and Habitat. The Silver-spotted Skipper ranges from southern Canada south to South America; however, it may be uncommon, rare or absent in Texas and southern Florida. Eventually, it will probably be found in all 92 counties of Indiana. It seems to be more common in the northern part of the state than in our southern hills. Although it can be found almost anywhere, it inhabits fields and gardens from May to September and occasionally later. The "Silver-spot" is a strong flier, flitting from flower to flower. It likes to protect itself from the wind or rain by perching on the stem of the Blue Flag (*Iris versicolor*) just below the flowers.

Life Cycle. In *Butterflies of the Rocky Mountain States,* Ray E. Stanford (1981) states that larvae of the nominate subspecies eat woody legumes. Klots (1964) lists its foodplants as Locust (*Robinia*), *Wistaria,* Honey Locust (*Gleditsia*), *Acacia, Amorpha, Lespedeza, Apios,* and *Desmodium.* The yellow mature larva has a brownish red head, with two orange-red eyelike spots.

After ten years of observing the behavior of skippers, I have observed only one pair of the Silver-spotted Skipper *in copula* (15 August 1970; 10:40 A.M.; 72° F; North Manchester, Wabash County). The female, as in all hesperids, was the flight partner, meaning that the female carries the male with his wings closed. Although *Epargyreus clarus clarus* seems to have only one brood (univoltine) in Indiana, in much of its range it is multivoltine, having two or even three broods annually.

The Silver-spotted Skipper pupates in a loosely woven cocoon among fallen leaves and trash on the ground. It winters as a pupa and emerges as an adult (imago) in May.

Genus *Autochton* Hübner

2. *Autochton cellus* Boisduval and Leconte. Golden-banded Skipper. Plate I.

Description. The Golden-banded Skipper is a large brown skipper with a wingspread varying from 1.75 to 2.25 inches (44–56 mm.). The unbroken yellow or golden band across the FW and the whitish apical spots make this an attractive insect. The VHW has shades of dark and light brown transverse bands, lacking the white areas so typical of *Epargyreus clarus* and *Achalarus lyciades*. Indiana specimens are a more uniform chocolate or bronze above, not blackish as in specimens from other regions.

Distribution and Habitat. The species ranges from Central America north to New York and Ohio. It is rare northward and apparently absent from the Gulf states, but it occurs in Florida and Texas (Klots, 1964). Irwin and Downey (1973) collected it in Illinois in July 1966 but it was rare. The author's son, James D. Shull, netted one male, 7 June 1970, in Brown County State Park near Nashville, Indiana. On 7 July 1978 I collected another one in the same park. These were the first two specimens collected in Indiana. It was also found in Crawford County. Thus it is a rare and sporadic visitor to Indiana and Illinois. I have found it inhabiting open areas where there are flowers.

The flight of *A. cellus* is sluggish, not darting and rapid like that of *E. clarus*. It visits Hydrangea, Buttonbush, and Ironwood (*Verononia*) flowers. Many late summer and fall hesperids seem to prefer the Ironwood flowers.

PLATE I

Top row	Silver-spotted Skipper, *Epargyreus clarus clarus* UP♂. 28 May 1973, Silver Lake, Kosciusko Co., IN. *E. c. clarus* UN♂. 12 June 1984, North Manchester, Wabash Co., IN. *E. c. clarus* UP♀. 12 June 1969, North Manchester, Wabash Co., IN.
Second row	*E. c. clarus* UN♀. June 1973, North Manchester, Wabash Co., IN. Golden-banded Skipper, *Autochton cellus* UP♂. 7 July 1978, Brown County State Park, Nashville, IN. *A. cellus* UN♀. 7 June 1970, Brown County State Park, Nashville, IN.
Third row	Hoary Edge, *Achalarus lyciades* UP♂. 25 May 1976, Brown County State Park, Nashville, IN. *A. lyciades* UN♂. 2 June 1972, Silver Lake, Kosciusko Co., IN. *A. lyciades* UP♀. 7 June 1970, Brown County State Park, Nashville, IN.
Fourth row	*A. lyciades* UN♀. 7 June 1970, Brown County State Park, Nashville, IN. Southern Cloudywing, *Thorybes bathyllus* UP♂. 20 June 1969, Silver Lake, Kosciusko Co., IN. *T. bathyllus* UN♂. 1 August 1975, Mongo, LaGrange Co., IN.
Fifth row	*T. bathyllus* UP♀. 26 June 1967, North Manchester, Wabash Co., IN. *T. bathyllus* UN♀. 1 August 1975, Mongo, LaGrange Co., IN. Northern Cloudywing, *Thorybes pylades* UP♂. 18 June 1970, Silver Lake, Kosciusko Co., IN.

UN = under side
UP = upper side
Coll. = Collected by or from the collection of
Det. = Determined by

Life Cycle. The hemispherical eggs are usually deposited in strings of two to seven. The tiny eggs (less than 1 mm in diameter) are yellow when laid but turn brownish yellow before hatching. The larva is yellowish green and speckled with small yellow dots. It has a broad lateral line of sulphur yellow. The head is a reddish brown with two large yellowish spots in front. The larva lives in a nest of leaves fastened together with silk, emerging at night to feed on the Hog Peanut (*Amphicarpa pitcheri*) and perhaps *Breweria aquatica* (Convolvulaceae) in the eastern United States (Howe, 1975, and Klots, 1964).

The Golden-banded Skipper hibernates in the pupal stage and emerges as an adult in late May (Virginia), according to Klots. The imago appears in Indiana in July and August.

Genus *Achalarus* Scudder

3. *Achalarus lyciades* Geyer. Hoary Edge. Plate I.

Description. The Hoary Edge is a distinctive skipper and should not be confused with the Silver-spotted Skipper. The outer, broad whitish area on the VHW of *A. lyciades* makes identification easy. It is smaller than either *E. clarus* or *A. cellus,* with a wingspread of less than 1.5 to slightly over 1.75 inches (38–45 mm). The Hoary Edge is similar to *E. clarus* in that it is brown with hyaline orange spots, but its flight is not as powerful.

Distribution and Habitat. The Hoary Edge is an eastern species, ranging from New Hampshire west to Iowa and Minnesota and south to the Gulf states from Florida to northeastern and central Texas. In our northern Indiana counties it is common, uncommon, or absent in late May through July, but it is more common in the southern half of the state, appearing around mid-May. The Hoary Edge frequents the edges of woodlands by open fields, where its host plants and larval foodplants can be found.

Life Cycle. Howe (1975) describes the egg as being an opalescent, dull white (1 mm in diameter) with 13 to 15 vertical ridges connected by raised cross-striations. The first larval stage (instar) is green and spotted with pale green dots arranged in lines across the segments of the fold. The half-grown caterpillar is yellowish green and covered with tiny lemon dots, forming a lateral line on each side. The mature larva is dark green, having a green median line with a speckling of yellowish orange dots. The head is always black in these larval stages.

The larva feeds chiefly on the Tick Trefoils (*Desmodium*) and False Indigo (*Baptisia*), both common plants throughout Indiana. It possibly feeds on the Morning Glory (*Ipomoea*). Howe (1975) adds *Lespedeza hirta* and *L. toxana* to the above list. *A. lyciades* hibernates as a pupa and the adults appear sometime in May, depending on geographical and environmental factors. The pupa is pale brown, being darkest toward the head and lighter on the abdomen. Black dots are clustered in irregular patches on the head, with a few on the thorax, and form lines on the abdomen.

Genus *Thorybes* Scudder

4. *Thorybes bathyllus* J. E. Smith. Southern Cloudywing. Plate I.

Description. Like other cloudywings, this species is a medium-sized skipper, with the forewing rather broad and the hindwing rounded. The wingspread varies from 1.25 to 1.62 inches (32–41 mm). The male has no costal fold. The hyaline white spots of the FW are usually large, filling the spaces between the veins. The VHW marking is less distinct than in *T. pylades* and *T. confusis*.

Distribution and Habitat. This species ranges from Florida and Texas north to Massachusetts, Nebraska, and Wisconsin. In Indiana the largest populations are found in the northeastern and southern counties; however, it has been recorded in widely scattered parts of the state. Extensive collecting will likely add additional counties to its range.

It is fairly common from late May through July, frequenting flowers on woodland trails and along streams. Occasionally it may be found in open clover fields and along roadsides. Its flight is fast and erratic, and it often returns to the spot from which it was disturbed.

Life Cycle. The egg, according to Howe (1975), is hemispherical with 14 or 15 slender vertical ridges connected horizontally by numerous cross-striations.

The mature larva is mahogany brown with an olivaceous tinge. It is dotted with pale wartlets each bearing a short hair. The head of the larva is black and covered with golden brown hairs.

The chrysalis, which is stout and greenish brown, lives in a silky nest on the leaves of various foodplants which include the Wild Bean (*Strephostyles*), *Dolicholus tomentosus,* Goat's-rue (*Cracca ambigua*), Butterfly Pea (*Bradburya virginiana*), and others (Klots, 1964).

The Southern Cloudywing has one brood in our area. Like other skippers, it hibernates in the pupal stage.

5. *Thorybes pylades* Scudder. Northern Cloudywing. Plates I and II.

Description. The wingspread is similar to *T. bathyllus,* measuring from 1.25 to 1.75 inches (32–44 mm). It can be distinguished from the Southern Cloudywing by the smaller white spots in the FW, by the underside of the palpi being darker, and by the VHW markings being less distinct. The male *pylades* has a costal fold.

Distribution and Habitat. This species ranges from Quebec to British Columbia, southward throughout the United States into Baja California and Cen-

PLATE II

Top row Northern Cloudywing, *Thorybes pylades* UN♂. 26 June 1967, Silver Lake, Kosciusko Co., IN.
T. pylades UP♀. 12 June 1969, North Manchester, Wabash Co., IN.
T. pylades UN♀ 10 June 1973, Silver Lake, Kosciusko Co., IN.

Second Row Eastern Cloudywing, *Thorybes confusis* UP♂. 1 August 1975, Perry Co., IN. Det. J. M. Burns
Scalloped Sootywing, *Staphylus hayhurstii* UP♂. 29 July 1980, Gibson Co., IN.
S. hayhurstii UP♀. 29 July 1980, Gibson Co., IN.
Dreamy Duskywing, *Erynnis icelus* UP♂. 23 May 1979, Mongo, LaGrange Co., IN.

Third row *E. icelus* UN♂. 1 May 1979, Mongo, LaGrange Co., IN.
E. icelus UP♀. 29 April 1970, Silver Lake, Kosciusko Co., IN.
E. icelus UN♀. 22 May 1978, Silver Lake, Kosciusko Co., IN.
Sleepy Duskywing, *Erynnis brizo brizo* UP♂. 9 May 1979, Salamonie River State Forest, Lagro, Wabash Co., IN.

Fourth row *E. b. brizo* UN♂. 20 April 1969, North Manchester, Wabash Co., IN.
E. b. brizo UP♀. 3 May 1970, Silver Lake, Kosciusko Co., IN.
E. b. brizo UN♀. 9 May 1979, Salamonie River State Forest, Lagro, Wabash Co., IN.
Juvenal's Duskywing, *Erynnis juvenalis juvenalis* UP♂. 6 June 1975, Sidney, Kosciusko Co., IN. Det. J. M. Burns

Fifth row *E. j. juvenalis* UN♂. 14 May 1972, North Manchester, Wabash Co., IN.
E. j. juvenalis UP♀. 23 May 1975, Silver Lake, Kosciusko Co., IN. Det. J. M. Burns
Horace's Duskywing, *Erynnis horatius* UP♂. 13 June 1954, Kokomo, Howard Co., IN. Det. J. M. Burns
E. horatius UN♂. 5 April 1972, North Manchester, Wabash Co., IN.

Sixth row *E. horatius* UP♀. 5 July 1954, Burlington, Howard Co., IN. Det. J. M. Burns
E. horatius UN♀. 22 May 1978, Silver Lake, Kosciusko Co., IN.
Mottled Duskywing, *Erynnis martialis* UP♂. 1 August 1958, Lucas Co., OH.
E. martialis UP♀. 2 June 1955, Lucas Co., OH.

Seventh row Zarucco Duskywing, *Erynnis zarucco* UP♂. 26 July 1966, Hammond, LA. Det. H. A. Freeman
E. zarucco UP♀. 21 July 1959, Jacksonville, FL. Det. H. A. Freeman
Funeral Duskywing, *Erynnis funeralis* UP♂. 1 July 1975, Mongo, LaGrange Co., IN. Det. J. M. Burns
E. funeralis UN♂. 27 July 1973, Puebla Mts., Mexico.

tral Mexico. It is more common and widespread than *T. bathyllus.* In Indiana adults fly from mid-May to July and will probably be recorded throughout the state.

The Northern Cloudywing inhabits much the same areas as the other *Thorybes.* It is a very pugnacious species frequently seen driving other skippers from its territory.

Life Cycle. The egg is light green, becoming paler before hatching. The larva is green to purplish green and striped with black along the back. It has a salmon line running laterally on each side; below this line there is another less distinct line. As in *T. bathyllus,* the larval head is black. Klots (1964) states that the larvae probably feed on many Fabaceae, especially clovers (*Trifolium*), *Lespedeza,* and *Desmodium,* plants that are widespread in Indiana.

I have recorded five pairs *in copula:* 11 July 1969, 3:00 P.M., Silver Lake, Kosciusko County; 18 June 1970, two pairs, 1:20 P.M. and 2:25 P.M., Silver Lake, both pairs mating on a small woodland path in a raspberry patch; 23 June 1970, 2:35 P.M. and 25 June 1970, two more pairs mating on the ground in the same woods, Silver Lake. In every case the female was the flight partner (when the mating pairs were disturbed, the females carried the males). There may be one or two broods in Indiana. This species hibernates in the pupal stage.

6. *Thorybes confusis* Bell. Eastern Cloudywing. Plate II.

Description. The wingspread varies from 1.25 to 1.62 inches (32–41 mm). The identification of this confusing species is very difficult and should be verified by specialists. The male of *T. confusis* may be distinguished from the male of *T. pylades* by the absence of a costal fold on the forewing. In color and pattern both species are similar. The white spots forming the central band of the FW are differently shaped, especially the spot below the cell, which is long and aligned with the wingband. This spot may be lacking in some specimens. The markings of the VHW are more distinct than in *pylades.*

Distribution and Habitat. The Eastern Cloudywing ranges from Florida to Texas and north to Kansas, Missouri, Maryland, and Pennsylvania. Shull and Badger (1972) placed *T. confusis* on the hypothetical list for Indiana because Badger had collected a female on 17 June 1962 in Marshall County, but this record could not be confirmed. Marc Minno netted the first authentic Indiana specimen, a male, on 1 August 1975 in Perry County, a record confirmed by John Burns.

Life Cycle. No information is available concerning the larva and its foodplants. As nearly as can be determined, its life cycle has never been recorded.

Genus *Staphylus* Goodman and Salvin

7. *Staphylus hayhurstii* W. H. Edwards. Scalloped Sootywing. Plate II.

Description. Although *Staphylus hayhurstii* is considered to be a sub-species of *S. mazans* by some writers, I prefer to treat them as two distinct species. In color and pattern the two closely resemble each other, but the male genitalia are distinct. The Scalloped Sootywing formerly went by the name of Southern Sooty-Wing or Hayhurst's Sooty Wing.

The Scalloped Sootywing is a small, dark skipper measuring from 1 to 1.25 inches (25–34 mm) wingspread; a single wing varies from 11 to 15 mm. The male has a costal fold on the FW. It is the only Indiana skipper with the deep scallops or wavy margins on the HW.

Distribution and Habitat. The Scalloped Sootywing ranges from Pennsylvania to Colorado and south to central Texas and southern Florida. It has a wide range in Indiana, where it is uncommon in May, June, and July. Look for this skipper in moist and shady areas near its foodplants (*Chenopodium* and *Alternanthera*). On 28 July 1980 I collected several in Sullivan County and two more on 30 July 1980 in Spencer County, both late dates for the state. It can rarely be found along old railroad tracks, but it prefers small creeks running through wooded areas.

Life Cycle. Heitzman (1963) carefully worked out the life cycle of this species. The egg is an orange, somewhat flattened hemisphere, having irregular white vertical ridges. The first instar of the larva is orange; then with growth it fades into pale green with orange edges and a black head. The body is covered with white hairs, which are slightly longer on the last segment. The folds between the segments are pinkish green, the legs are cream, and the ventral abdomen and the prolegs are deep green. Its spiracles are creamy white and slightly raised.

The caterpillar in its final instar constructs a tent by folding a leaf together. There is a thin lining of silk over the pupa. It probably has two or three broods, but I have never found it mating in the state.

Genus *Erynnis* Schrank

The Duskywings are a large genus with ten species in Indiana. Many of them look alike, with individual and seasonal variations making positive identification difficult. They are mostly medium-sized, dark brownish to black above, and usually have a few whitish spots on the forewings. The males are generally darker with reduced whitish spots. Females usually have larger hyaline spots and more contrasting patterns. Males of our Indiana species have a costal fold on the FW and several species have a tibial tuft.

8. *Erynnis icelus* Scudder and Burgess. Dreamy Duskywing. Plate II.

Description. This species is smaller than *E. brizo,* with which it is easily confused, and has a wingspread of about 1 to 1.25 inches (25–32 mm). The upper FW lacks white spots, but it has a chainlike series of small, interrupted postmedian markings. The wings are short and more rounded than in *brizo.* The male has a tibial brush on the hind leg and the palp is very long. The tip of the antennal club is sharply pointed.

Distribution and Habitat. It ranges from British Columbia to Nova Scotia, south to Georgia, and west to Minnesota, New Mexico, and California. It is lacking in most of the southern Great Plains and Gulf states. It is more common in northern Indiana than the rest of the state; however, the county records are widely scattered. I have collected it from late April to August in our state. It is fairly common on woodland trails, along roads, and in open clearings, being more common in the early part of the season.

Life Cycle. According to Burns (1964), the leading *Erynnis* specialist, the larva feeds chiefly on *Salix* and *Populus* and apparently also on *Robinia pseudo-acacia* (Black Locust). It also feeds on Wild Indigo, Witch Hazel, and oaks. Klots (1964) says that the larva is stout and tapering. The prothorax is yellow, the remaining segments pale yellow with whitish granulations. There is a dark dorsal line on the abdominal segments, with a pale lateral stripe.

This species of *Erynnis* usually spends the winter in the mature larval stage. The pupa varies from a dark brown to greenish. Throughout its range it has only one brood per year.

9. *Erynnis brizo brizo* Boisduval and Leconte. Sleepy Duskywing. Plate II.

Description. This species is larger than *E. icelus,* having a wingspread of 1.1 to 1.62 inches (28–41 mm). The crescent, chainlike postmedial band of the FW is more distinct and complete than in *icelus.* The male is without the tibial tuft on the hind leg. Compared with *icelus* the palpi are short and the club of the antenna is stout with a blunt tip.

Distribution and Habitat. The nominate species occurs from Manitoba and Massachusetts south to northern Florida and eastern Texas. I collected several in Mexico. It is widely scattered throughout Indiana. It is common from April to June in the northern half of the state, but uncommon southward. It is very partial to scrub oaks, but it may also be found in our northern mixed forests and less commonly in the southern hills.

Life Cycle. At first the egg is green, but it turns pink before hatching. The larva is pale green with white specks, covered with short hairs, and has a head of red, yellow, or orange patterns. The chrysalis is brown or light green. Its larval foodplants consist of a variety of oaks (*Quercus*).

On 9 May 1978 I found a pair *in copula* at 10:00 A.M., 74° F, in the Salamonie River State Forest, Lagro, Wabash County. The pair was mating on the ground until disturbed, when the female flew a short distance carrying the male with his wings folded.

10. *Erynnis juvenalis juvenalis* Fabricius. Juvenal's Duskywing. Plate II.

Description. The nominate *E. juvenalis* is one of the larger members of the genus with a wingspread of 1.25 to 1.75 inches (32–45 mm). This species is frequently confused with *E. horatius,* but the fringes of the HW are brown and there are two conspicuous pale brown spots on the apical third of the VHW. The photographs show the differences in the spots on the FW. In the female Juvenal's Duskywing the spots are larger and more numerous.

Distribution and Habitat. It ranges from southern Canada west to the Rocky Mountains and south to Florida and Texas; however, it is absent in much of the Great Plains. It is widespread in Indiana from early May to June and occasionally later. It is a common skipper in our state.

This species prefers sunny open areas near the edge of woods, especially where there are oaks and chestnuts. It also inhabits woodland trails.

Life Cycle. The egg is so similar to the egg of *E. brizo* that it needs no further description. The mature light-green larva has white specks, thick hair, and a variegated head color of yellow, red, or orange. It winters as a mature larva. The chrysalis is dark green or brown. Its larval foodplants are Scrub Oak (*Quercus ilicifolia*), Black Oak (*Q. velutina*), Northern Red Oak (*Q. rubra*), and White Oak (*Q. alba*).

I have found two pairs *in copula*: 30 April 1976, 2:00 P.M., 65° F, Silver Lake, Kosciusko County; and 25 May 1978, 11:00 A.M., 78° F, Mongo, LaGrange County. The courtship of the last pair took less than one minute. Apparently the female had just released her pheromones (sex attractors) and the male found her ready to mate. The pair settled on a twig of a bush, turned their caudal portions toward each other, and joined in copulation. The female was the active flight partner. The species has one to two broods.

11. *Erynnis horatius* Scudder and Burgess. Horace's Duskywing. Plate II.

Description. This species is only slightly larger than *E. juvenalis,* having a wingspread of 1.25 to 1.75 inches (34–46 mm). It is more uniformly brown, with less contrast in the male brown markings than in the female. The female has larger hyaline spots on the FW. The HW spots are not as well defined in this species as they are in *juvenalis.* The Horace's Duskywing has brown fringes, not white.

Distribution and Habitat. It is widely distributed over the eastern United States, ranging from Massachusetts west to Minnesota and Colorado and south through Florida and Texas, but it is usually absent from the Great Plains. In Indiana I have collected specimens from mid-April to mid-August, especially in the northern counties. Recently (1980) I found this species in Jefferson and

Clark counties. Because *horatius* has often been confused with *juvenalis,* the dot map may not give an accurate picture of its distribution in the state.

Look for *horatius* on woodland trails and other sunny spots in clearings. Like many other animals, this species may be found where the meadow joins the woods.

Life Cycle. At first the egg is green, becoming pink as it matures. The grown larva is light green, hairy, and specked with white. It has red, yellow, and orange on the head. The larval foodplants of *horatius* are various species of oaks (*Quercus*), depending largely on the species of oaks found throughout the breeding areas.

On 30 April 1977 I found one pair *in copula:* 1:45 P.M., 66° F, Silver Lake, Kosciusko County. The pair was clinging near the top of a dead raspberry branch, about 2½ feet above the ground. The color patterns of the mating pair blended perfectly with the dead twig, providing a good example of protective coloration. This species probably has two broods in Indiana.

12. *Erynnis martialis* Scudder. Mottled Duskywing. Plate II.

Description. The wingspread of this species varies from 1 to 1.5 inches (25–37 mm). The upper wings have a somewhat lavender sheen with strongly mottled markings of black and brown. The VHW has a double row of submarginal pale spots, the inner series of spots consisting of blue-white crescents. The fringes of the HW are brown. The males lack tibial tufts and long wing hairs, thus resembling the females.

Distribution and Habitat. The Mottled Duskywing ranges over the eastern half of the United States from New England to western South Dakota and the eastern foothills of the Rocky Mountains, south to Georgia, Mississippi, and Texas. In Indiana this species has been reported mostly from the northwestern counties and from Wabash County. However, it generally occurs locally and rarely in hilly woodlands from late May or early June to late July.

Life Cycle. Little is known with certainty about the early stages of this species. Many of its larval foodplants suggested in the literature are dubious. At this time it is probably best to accept Burns's observation that *Ceanothus americanus* is at least one of the larval foodplants of *E. martialis.*

13. *Erynnis zarucco* Lucas. Zarucco Duskywing. Plate II.

Description. This dark brown species is very similar to *E. funeralis.* It has a wingspread of 1.1 to 1.75 inches (28–44 mm). The FW has very small hyaline spots; the pale patch in the end of the cell of the FW is conspicuous and the wing itself is narrower than in other *Erynnis* species. The Zarucco Duskywing has also been confused with *E. baptisiae* (Wild Indigo Duskywing) from which it can be distinguished by its more pointed FW and large triangular HW.

Distribution and Habitat. According to Howe (1975) this species occurs in the southeastern United States, Cuba, Hispaniola (Haiti/Dominican Republic), and possibly Puerto Rico. On the mainland it ranges from Florida north to New Jersey and perhaps Massachusetts and west to Louisiana, but northern records may be based on misidentifications.

Hall (1936) reported *E. zarucco* from Crawfordsville, Indiana, but some of his records are suspect, or impossible to confirm. Look for this species in open fields and roadsides where wildflowers grow.

Life Cycle. The larvae may feed on a large variety of legumes, but many of the reported plant records should not be trusted. Burns found larvae feeding on *Robinia.* Since the status of the Zarucco Duskywing is uncertain in Indiana, its larval foodplants for the state are unknown.

14. *Erynnis funeralis* Scudder and Burgess. Funeral Duskywing. Plates II and III.

Description. The wingspread varies from 1.1 to 1.75 inches (28–44 mm). It is the only Indiana species having distinct white fringes on the borders of the hindwings. The fringes of *E. juvenalis* are brown. Males have a hind tibial tuft.

Distribution and Habitat. Normally it ranges from California, Nevada, Utah, Colorado, and Kansas south to Argentina and Chile, but I collected a somewhat worn male on 1 July 1975 at Mongo, LaGrange County, Indiana, when it was resting on the ground in an area between the tamarack bog and a woods. This essentially western species was identified by John M. Burns, Associate Curator of Entomology of the National Museum of Natural History in Washington, D.C., where the specimen has been deposited. The Funeral Duskywing has been known to travel great distances, perhaps explaining the Indiana record.

Life Cycle. The larvae of *funeralis* and *zarucco* are both marked with a prominent longitudinal yellow line which is interrupted by a bright yellow spot on each abdominal segment. Burns has accepted the following larval foodplants: *Lotus scoparius, Olyneya tesota, Robinia neomexicana, Vicia taxana, Indigofera leptosepala, Geoffroca decorticans,* and possibly *Medicago sativa* and *Nemophila membranacea,* the last being a non-legume. Of these foodplants, only *Medicago* (alfalfa) is common in Indiana; therefore search alfalfa fields for *funeralis.* Its presence in Indiana is probably accidental.

15. *Erynnis lucilius* Scudder and Burgess. Columbine Duskywing. Plate III.

Description. The wingspread is usually less than one inch to about 1.25 inches (23–31 mm). *E. lucilius* is closely related to *baptisiae* and *persius;* however, the latter two species are usually larger and have longer wings. Again, it is best to have an *Erynnis* authority check your specimens. The Columbine Duskywing is a small, dark skipper with short, rounder wings. The dorsal FW is

PLATE III

Top row
Funeral Duskywing, *Erynnis funeralis* UP♂. 4 July 1968, Cave Creek Canyon, Chiricahua Mts., Cochise Co., AZ. Det. J. M. Burns
Columbine Duskywing, *Erynnis lucilius* UP♂. 3 May 1970, Silver Lake, Kosciusko Co., IN.
E. lucilius UN♂. 22 May 1978, Silver Lake, Kosciusko Co., IN.

Second row
Wild Indigo Duskywing, *Erynnis baptisiae* UP♂. 27 August 1970, Silver Lake, Kosciusko Co., IN.
E. baptisiae UP♀. 27 August 1970, Silver Lake, Kosciusko Co., IN. Det. H. A. Freeman
Persius Duskywing, *Eyrnnis persius* UP♂. 15 May 1955, Indiana Dunes State Park, Lake Co., IN. Det. J. M. Burns
E. persius UP♀. 1 May 1958, Indiana Dunes State Park, Lake Co., IN. Det. J. M. Burns

Third row
Common Checkered Skipper, *Pyrgus communis* UP♂. 30 September 1983, North Manchester, Wabash Co., IN.
P. communis UN♂. 22 September 1984, North Manchester, Wabash Co., IN.
P. communis UP♀. 5 September 1970, Silver Lake, Kosciusko Co., IN.
Common Sootywing, *Pholisora catullus* UP♂. 4 September 1970, Silver Lake, Kosciusko Co., IN.

Fourth row
P. catullus UN♂. 9 June 1969, Silver Lake, Kosciusko Co., IN.
P. catullus UP♀. 4 September 1970, Silver Lake, Kosciusko Co., IN.
P. catullus UN♀. 22 June 1967, Silver Lake, Kosciusko Co., IN.
Swarthy Skipper, *Nastra lherminier* UP♂. 5 August 1977, Brown County State Park, Nashville, IN.

Fifth row
N. lherminier UN♂. 10 August 1975, Brown County State Park, Nashville, IN.
Clouded Skipper, *Lerema accius* UP♂. 25 April 1973, Galveston, Galveston Co., TX.
L. accius UP♀. 15 April 1973, Buffalo, Leon Co., TX.
L. accius UN♀. 2 April 1974, Buffalo, Leon Co., TX.

Sixth row
Least Skipper, *Ancyloxypha numitor* UP♂. 9 June 1969, North Manchester, Wabash Co., IN.
A. numitor UN♂. 12 September 1984, North Manchester, Wabash Co., IN.
A. numitor UP♀. 9 June 1969, North Manchester, Wabash Co., IN.
A. numitor UN♀. 11 June 1969, North Manchester, Wabash Co., IN.
Poweshiek Skipper, *Oarisma powesheik* UP♂. 15 July 1971, Livingston, McDunn Co., MI. Det. M. C. Nielsen

Seventh row
European Skipper, *Thymelicus lineola* UP♂. 17 June 1969, North Manchester, Wabash Co., IN.
T. lineola UN♂. 19 June 1969, North Manchester, Wabash Co., IN.
T. lineola UP♀. 20 June 1969, Silver Lake, Kosciusko Co., IN.
Fiery Skipper, *Hylephila phyleus* UP♂. 11 August 1971, North Manchester, Wabash Co., IN.

blackish in the basal half and the outer half is pale brown, showing dark brown bands with several glassy white dots near the tip and margin. The hindwings have a brown fringe. Males sometimes resemble females in their wing markings.

Distribution and Habitat. It ranges from Quebec and Ontario, south to New Jersey and Pennsylvania, and west to Michigan and Minnesota. In Indiana I have found it mostly in the northeastern counties, with a few scattered records elsewhere. Blatchley (1891) found it in Putnam and Lake counties. More research is needed to determine its distribution in the state.

Usually it is not uncommon from late April to July, but some years populations are down and occasionally even absent. Look for *lucilius* near its foodplants, on sunny woodland paths, in ravines, and on shady slopes.

Life Cycle. The greenish egg becomes pink before hatching. The hairy young larva is pale greenish while mature caterpillars are light green with white specks. The head is patterned with red, yellow, or orange. The chrysalis is dark green or brown. *E. lucilius* overwinters in the mature larval stage. This species seldom flies far from its larval foodplants, which are the Wild Columbine (*Aquilegia canadensis*) and the Garden Columbine (*A. vulgaris*). Throughout its range it is multivoltine.

16. *Erynnis baptisiae* Forbes. Wild Indigo Duskywing. Plate III.

Description. The wingspread varies from 1.1 to 1.6 inches (28–44 mm). In the past it was confused with *E. persius* by many collectors. Klots maintains that the male genitalia offer no safe diagnosis—thus the only safe determination can be obtained by raising *baptisiae* on its foodplant. A few *baptisiae* are much like *lucilius;* others have a pale brown patch that is so characteristic of *zarucco.* Howe (1975) discusses the problems of identification very well. The HW of *baptisiae* is not enlarged and triangular, and the FW is not conspicuously pointed.

Distribution and Habitat. Its range extends from New England south to Florida and west to Nebraska, Kansas, Arkansas, and Texas. It has been recorded in only a few Indiana counties. I collected my first Wild Indigo Duskywing on 27 August 1970, a female, near its foodplant (*Baptisia tinctoria*) in a field just north of North Manchester in Kosciusko County. It was determined by H. A. Freeman. In Indiana the adults can be found from early spring through August, inhabiting brushy edges of woods and roadsides. It also likes barren and wasteland areas.

Life Cycle. The egg is green, becoming pinkish as it matures. The young larva is orange-white; the mature larva is hairy and light green with white specks. Its head is patterned in red, yellow, or orange. The chrysalis is dark green or brownish. Probably the only valid foodplants for this species are varieties of Wild Indigo (*Baptisia*). It winters as a mature larva and apparently is multivoltine.

17. *Erynnis persius* Scudder. Persius Duskywing. Plate III.

Description. The wingspread ranges from 1 to 1.37 inches (25–35 mm). Compared with the other *Erynnis* species, *Erynnis persius* is small to medium in size. Adults are usually dark brown with conspicuous but small subapical spots on the forewings. The males have a covering of elevated hairlike scales on the forewings, giving the wing a soft appearance that tends to blur the darker markings on the basal half of the wing. *Persius, lucilius,* and *baptisiae* do not have the two subapical pale brown spots on the VHW, a characteristic found in the *juvenalis* group; however, they do have a marginal and submarginal series of small pale spots on the VHW. Like the three species mentioned above, the males have a hair tuft on the hind tibia (Howe, 1975).

Distribution and Habitat. *E. persius* ranges from New England, possibly Quebec and Ontario, south in Appalachia to Tennessee and westward across the northern United States and southward in the Rocky Mountains to New Mexico and Arizona. Badger collected one in early May in the Dunes State Park, Lake County, which was identified by J. M. Burns. So far it has been recorded in only five Indiana counties. Its flight period is from April to June. It must be listed as rare in Indiana. It may be found in willow swamps and sandy aspen flats.

Life Cycle. Some of the data for this species are probably not reliable, but the larva is pale green and sprinkled with raised white dots, each bearing a short white hair. There is a narrow dark-green middorsal line and a thin yellowish white lateral line. The head is variable in color. In our area, the larvae feed on willow (*Salix*) and various species of *Populus*. The Persius Duskywing is univoltine.

Genus *Pyrgus* Hübner

Pyrgus is a very large genus of the Old World and the New World, ranging from the Arctic to Argentina and Chile. Taxonomy and nomenclature at the specific and infraspecific levels is difficult and still somewhat confused. Most of the Checkered Skippers in the United States can be distinguished by their checkered patterns.

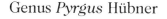

18. *Pyrgus communis* Grote. Common Checkered Skipper. Plate III.

Description. The Common Checkered Skipper has a wingspread from 1.0 inch (or less) to 1.25 inches (20–32 mm). Its forms in Indiana vary from very dark to light, the females generally averaging darker. Howe gives an excellent description of this species (1975, 518). Thus the pictures will suffice to identify our only Indiana species.

Distribution and Habitat. It ranges from Canada to Mexico and is well distributed from coast to coast. Although *communis* has been reported from only twenty-one counties in Indiana, the widely scattered records seem to indicate that more intensive collecting will add many more counties to the record. Usually it is fairly common from August to November; however, it may appear much earlier in the spring. Some years it is absent.

Look for this species almost anyplace, especially in pastures, along streams, roadsides, river banks, hills, valleys, and gardens in town.

Life Cycle. The egg changes from green to cream color before hatching. The larva is tan with a darker median line, brown and white lateral lines, and a black head. The chrysalis is greener toward its head and browner on its caudal portions. Adults are very aggressive, patrolling their own territories. Some sun themselves with their wings spread at their sides.

According to Klots (1964) the larval foodplants are Hollyhocks (*Althea*), Indian Mallow (*Abutilon*), and Wild Tea (*Sida*). It hibernates in the pupal stage or as a full-grown larva. The number of broods is not known.

Genus *Pholisora* Scudder

Pholisora is a small genus of small to medium-sized black skippers with long, forward-projecting palpi. The antennae are short and the club is curved like a sickle and tapered to a blunt point. Only one species of *Pholisora* is found in Indiana.

19. *Pholisora catullus* Fabricius. Common Sootywing. Plate III.

Description. The wingspread ranges from 0.9 to 1.25 inches (22–32 mm). The black or dark brown forewings are crossed by crescent-shaped rows of white spots which are occasionally present also on the hindwings. These minute white dots on the FW may be absent. Males have a costal fold. The fringes and HW may be browner than black.

Distribution and Habitat. It is distributed throughout North America between mid-Canada and New Mexico; however, it has not been found in Florida. In time the Common Sootywing will probably be recorded in every Indiana county. It is common from May to September in cultivated landscapes, parks, fields, and gardens. When disturbed, it usually flies away rapidly and erratically, keeping close to the ground and then returning to its territory.

Life Cycle. The tiny egg (about 0.5 mm in diameter) is yellowish to whitish. The larva is a pale green with straw-colored flecks, and the head is black. The half-grown larva, according to Howe, is pale yellowish green with two narrow lines laterally. The mature larva is dull pale green and flecked with pale dots. The head is now a blackish brown and covered with tawny hairs. The pupa is purplish brown with a glaucous bloom. Its foodplants are various Chenopodiaceae and Amaranthaceae. Klots (1964) lists Pigweed (*Chenopo-*

dium album), Tumbleweed (*Amaranthus graecizans*), and others of the above families as possible foodplants.

The Common Sootywing hibernates in a firm nest as a mature larva. In Indiana I have recorded four pairs *in copula*: 25 July 1969, 2:30 P.M., 4 October 1970, 12:40 P.M., 78° F, and 16 July 1971, 12:45 P.M., 80° F, all at Silver Lake, Kosciusko County, and all mating in an alfalfa field; 20 August 1979, 11:55 A.M., 80° F, Mongo, LaGrange County. In all cases the female was the flight partner. There are two broods in our area.

Subfamily Hesperiinae Latreille

The majority of Indiana skippers, presently 34 species, belong to the subfamily Hesperiinae, the Branded Skippers, and are small to medium-sized among the hesperids. Males often have a brand or stigma of specialized scales on the dorsal FW; they do not have the tibial tuft of hair or the costal fold as do many species of the subfamily Pyrginae. They have blunt, oppressed palpi and usually the antennal club ends in an abrupt, reflexed apiculus.

In most cases, the eggs appear to be rather smooth with a pitlike reticulation. For individual identification, a magnifying glass is useful. The head of the mature larva is relatively narrow and often subconical at the summit. The distribution of the Branded Skippers is worldwide.

Genus *Nastra* Evans

20. *Nastra lherminier* Latreille. Swarthy Skipper. Plate III.

Description. This rather small, nondescript brown skipper has a wingspread from 0.9 to 1.0 inch (22–25 mm). Usually the wings are without spots both above and below. Occasionally there are some paler areas below the end of the cell, but these are poorly developed (not hyaline spots). The veins of the HW are often a paler yellow.

Distribution and Habitat. This species ranges from New York to Florida and west to Missouri and Texas. It is uncommon and local throughout Indiana, for there are only scattered records. Masters and Masters (1969) found it not uncommon in Perry County. I have sometimes found it in Brown County. It is rare in Wabash and Kosciusko counties and absent from most other counties.

In Indiana I found more Swarthy Skippers in the fall from August to September, but occasionally it has been taken in the spring. Look for it in open fields and in thick grassy areas, especially in moist meadows near wooded areas.

Life Cycle. According to Lucien Harris, Jr. (1972) and Howe (1975), the life history of the Swarthy Skipper is unknown; however, its life cycle is partially described in Pyle (1981) who states that the egg is pearly white, the caterpillar is opaque white with a brown head, and the larval foodplant is Prairie Beardgrass (*Andropogon scoparius*). Throughout most of its wider range it has two broods, but mating data are lacking from Indiana.

Genus *Lerema* Scudder

21. *Lerema accius* J. E. Smith. Clouded Skipper. Plate III.

Description. This species is dark brown, almost blackish, having a series of three small white spots or specks on the FW; sometimes an additional two or more spots are present. The wingspread varies from 1.0 to 1.4 inches (25–35 mm). The stigma, sometimes faint, is gray or blackish and curved. On the female's FW the spots are larger. The underside of the HW is unmarked except for patterns of violet-gray which are distinctive of this species.

Distribution and Habitat. It ranges from New England to Florida westward to Illinois, Arkansas and Texas, and even to South America. Irwin and Downey (1973) still leave *L. accius* on their Illinois checklist because there is a record of a specimen collected in Carbondale, Jackson County, deposited in the American Museum of Natural History. Blatchley (1892) collected two worn specimens on 3 July 1886 in Monroe County. More recently (1956) Lee D. Miller collected several specimens in Warrick County (personal communication). It is hoped that new records will soon be found in southern Illinois and in Indiana. The Clouded Skipper, according to Howe, is scarce in its northern range and locally not uncommon in the southern states, where it may be taken from February to November. It occurs in open fields, meadows, and hilly glades.

Life Cycle. The egg measures about 1 mm in diameter and has netlike markings on the surface. The nearly white larva is mottled with fine lines and dots; the rings on the posterior half of each segment are unmottled and more prominent. The small white head is flattened dorsally and has a black band around the top and sides and three vertical streaks on the front. The chrysalis is slender, smooth, and greenish white, with the head terminating as a slender beak.

Howe (1975) summarizes the larval foodplants of *accius*: Woolly Beard Grass (*Erianthus alopecuroides*), St. Augustine Grass (*Stenotaphrum secundatum*), Indian Corn (*Zea mays*), and *Echinochloa poiretiana*.

In its southern range the Clouded Skipper is multivoltine, but mating records are completely lacking for Indiana.

Genus *Ancyloxypha* C. Felder

22. *Ancyloxypha numitor* Fabricius. Least Skipper. Plate III.

Description. The Least Skipper is a small brown skipper with a wingspread of .75 to 1 inch (19–25 mm). The extent of fulvous or tawny orange on the HW discal area varies considerably. In some specimens the FW is solidly black. The VFW is black except for yellow on the costa and apex; the VHW is a uniform bright yellow. The male and female are similarly marked, but the female has the greater wingspread.

Distribution and Habitat. It ranges throughout eastern North America from Nova Scotia and Quebec to Florida, westward to Alberta, eastern Colorado and New Mexico, Texas, and recently to northern Mexico. It is widely distributed throughout Indiana and should be found in many more counties.

This species has a weak flight, usually close to the ground among the tall grasses. It is also found along the edges of streams and lakes and on open patches of ground. In Indiana it occurs as an adult from May to mid-October.

Life Cycle. Howe (1975) says that the egg measures about 0.75 mm in diameter. At first the egg is bright yellow, soon acquiring patches of orange-red in a band around the middle. The first larval instar is pale yellow with a black head. The half-grown larva is straw to pale green and mottled with greenish white except on the middorsal line. The mature larva is light green with a dark brown head showing various white spots. The blunt-headed pupa is cream-colored with brown lines and patches. Its larval foodplants are various grasses.

I have found four pairs *in copula:* 22 September 1969, 1:25 P.M., 71° F, Silver Lake, Kosciusko County, in grass bordering a pond; 7 October 1970, 2:15 P.M., 90° F, Carroll County, in a wet, grassy field; 24 May 1977, 9:20 A.M., 80° F, North Manchester, Wabash County, resting on a blade of grass in a marshy field; and 28 July 1978, 1:30 P.M., 73° F, Lagro, Wabash County. Thus, the grasses found in wet places are more likely the preferred foodplants in Indiana. It is double- and possibly triple-brooded in Indiana.

Genus *Oarisma* Scudder

23. *Oarisma powesheik* Parker. PoweSheik Skipper. Plate III.

Description. This blackish skipper, with the costal area above the cell on the FW being a conspicuous orange, measures from less than one inch to 1.25 inches (24–32 mm). Its contrasting patterns of black and orange distinguish it from other species.

Distribution and Habitat. This species has been reported from Nebraska, the Dakotas, Iowa, and Illinois. There is only one record from Indiana. Blatchley (1891) says, "It is a western species, not before recorded east of Illinois. It occurs in small numbers about Whiting, Lake County." It is unlikely that he would have confused this distinctly marked skipper with any other species.

It was found along marshy lakeshores and wetlands in June and July, thus the drainage of the prairie wetlands probably accounts for its rarity. Reportedly this species is univoltine.

Life Cycle. Unrecorded.

Genus *Thymelicus* Hübner

24. *Thymelicus lineola* Ochsenheimer. European Skipper. Plate III.

Description. This is another of the lesser skippers with a wingspread of around 0.75 to slightly over 1 inch (20–25 mm). Its orange wings are bordered with black and have prominent dark veins. The small linear stigma of the FW points to the midthorax. The VHW is dusky or olive-orange, but the VHW is broadly orange.

Distribution and Habitat. This species was accidentally introduced into North America at London, Ontario, in 1910. Since then it has spread from New Brunswick to Michigan and south to Maryland, Kentucky, Wisconsin and Illinois. Shull and Badger (1972) were the first to report it from Indiana. It is widespread and may become an economic pest. It flies from late May through July and occasionally in August, frequenting grassy fields.

Life Cycle. The whitish eggs (each about 1 mm in diameter) are laid in strips of 30 to 40. The first instar larva is yellowish white with a black head. The half-grown larva is greenish with a dark middorsal stripe; the head is light brown with two whitish or yellowish patches. The mature larva is similar except that the yellowish patches on the head extend forward as longitudinal stripes down the front of the face. The yellowish green pupa has the same longitudinal yellowish striping as found in the larva. The thorax of the pupa is green, and on the front of the head there is a downward-curved horn. The larva eat Timothy (*Phleum pratense*), a common grass in Indiana. This species winters in the egg stage.

I have recorded four pairs *in copula:* 20 June 1969, 2:25 P.M., Silver Lake, Kosciusko County; 27 June 1970, 11:45 A.M., Mongo, LaGrange County; 26 June 1971, 1:00 P.M., 84° F, Silver Lake, Kosciusko County; and 3 June 1977, 11:00 A.M., 70° F, Silver Lake, Kosciusko County. This last mating pair was resting on Alfalfa (*Medicago sativa*). There is only one brood annually.

Genus *Hylephila* Billberg

25. *Hylephila phyleus* Drury. Fiery Skipper. Plates III and IV.

Description. The wingspread measures from 1 to about 1.25 inches (25–32 mm). The males are bright orange-yellow above except for the dark stigma and a large dash between the stigma and apex. The wings of the males are deeply dentate. Yellow rays extend beyond the darker borders of the wings along the veins. The postdiscal band and basal spots are visible on the VHW. Females are darker than the males. The antennae of the Fiery Skippers are distinctly short. This species may be confused with some forms of *Hesperia* and *Polites*.

Distribution and Habitat. The Fiery Skipper ranges from Connecticut to California and south through tropical America to Chile. Although it is common in the south, northward it is only an immigrant. It reaches Indiana, in a few scattered counties, from early August to mid-October. It is uncommon to rare, and absent some years. Look for it in the flower-covered autumn fields, on urban lawns, and along the edges of forests.

Life Cycle. The glossy, pale turquoise egg measures less than 0.75 mm in diameter. Howe (1975) says that the larva is yellow at first, and then changes to yellowish green and has a black head. The half-grown larva is yellowish brown with a prominent dark dorsal line. The mature larva varies from dark gray-brown to dark yellow-brown; it has three dark longitudinal stripes. The chrysalis is usually yellowish brown, but occasionally reddish or greenish. Dorsally, the pupa is mottled with black or brown dashes. The larvae feed on a variety of grasses (Poaceae). In its southern range the larvae of the Fiery Skipper feed on Sugar Cane (*Sacchinarum officinarum*) and Bermuda Grass. This beautiful skipper does not breed in our area.

Genus *Hesperia* Fabricius

There are four species of *Hesperia* found in Indiana. They are medium-sized, mainly tawny skippers with pointed FW and lobed HW. The stigma are prominent, consisting of two rows of silvery scales enclosing a pocket of black or yellow microandroconia (sex cells). The midtibiae are spined; the third tibiae have two pairs of spurs. The VHW spots greatly assist diagnosis of the various species.

26. *Hesperia ottoe* W. H. Edwards. Ottoe Skipper. Plate IV.

Description. The wingspread of this species varies from 1.25 to 1.6 inches (32–41 mm). This is a large prairie species. Males are dull tawny above with indistinct fuscous borders. There is a prominent stigma which contains gray-brown microandroconia. The undersides are pale yellow to buff and are without markings. This species is often confused with the very close *H. pawnee,* which is not found in our area. Female Ottoe Skippers have less fulvous overscaling above and more clearly defined spots.

Distribution and Habitat. It ranges from Montana and Michigan south to Colorado and Texas. It is mainly found in undisturbed prairie areas. Occasionally this rare species may be found in oak and scrub and swampy areas.

The only Indiana specimen of *H. ottoe* was collected by D. Oosting, 6 July 1979, in Jasper County (Anon., 1980). Adults fly from June through July in areas which it inhabits.

Life Cycle. Nielsen (1980) described the early stages of *H. ottoe* found in

PLATE IV

Michigan. The smooth, hemispherical egg is white, gradually turning dull yellowish. The larval head is dark brown. In Michigan its larval foodplant is Fall Witchgrass (*Leptoloma cognatum*). Its life history in our area is unknown.

27. *Hesperia leonardus* Harris. Leonardus Skipper. Plate IV.

Description. The wingspread measures 0.9 to 1.4 inches (22–35 mm). It is easily identified by the dark and reddish cast of its upper surface and by the red HW with its distinct creamy spots. The male stigma is prominent, containing yellow microandroconia. Females are darker and have well-developed VHW spots.

Distribution and Habitat. This species ranges from Ontario to Nova Scotia and southern Maine, south to the Carolinas, Alabama, and Missouri. Irwin and Downey (1973) reported it from several counties in Illinois. I have collected it in a few counties in northern Indiana and in Brown County. Adults may be found locally in late July, August, and September. They are uncommon to rare, and absent in some years. The Leonardus Skipper is a strong flier. Look for it on Ironweed (*Verononia*), as this insect shows a strong preference for the blossoms of this plant among the beautiful array of late summer and autumn wildflowers. This skipper may be found in fields, meadows, scrub oak and pine clearings, and roadsides.

Life Cycle. According to Howe (1975) the early stages of this insect were described by Scudder, Laurent, and Dethier. The egg is about 1.3 mm in diameter and white with a greenish tint; it is finely reticulate. The first larval instar is cream-colored with a dark reddish brown head. The head of the mature caterpillar is black and has two creamy patches and two parallel cream stripes on the face. The pupa is brown and green.

Its foodplants are Panic Grass (*Panicum*), Bent Grass (*Agrostis*), and Tumble Grass (*Eragrostis*). This skipper overwinters as an immature caterpillar and is univoltine in the areas where it breeds.

28. *Hesperia metea* Scudder. Cobweb Skipper. Plate IV.

Description. In this hesperid the adults are brown to olive-ocher, and occasionally dark. Beside the slender and angled stigma of the male FW there are tawny orange patches. The lower surface is blackish with an olive overscaling. The white of the macular band often extends along the veins. Some specimens lack the white spots beneath.

The name "Cobweb Skipper" is pertinent because of the weblike pattern of the veins below. The wingspread of *metea* is about 1 to 1.4 inches (24–35 mm).

Distribution and Habitat. This skipper ranges from Maine to Michigan and south to Florida and Mississippi. Although there are no records from Illinois, John and Wilma Masters (1969) have taken a few specimens each May for a number of years in Perry County.

Howe (1975) says that this skipper appears after the burning of the grass on which the larvae feed. In these conditions it is a transient species; however, it may exist as a permanent resident in some areas.

Look for *metea* in barren areas, rocky sites, clearings, and limestone outcrops. I have never collected it in Indiana.

Life Cycle. The small, white egg measures slightly over 1 mm in diameter. The caterpillar is brown with a greenish-black stripe. The pupa is a drab green and probably overwinters in this stage. The larval foodplant is Bluestem Beard Grass (*Andropogon scoparius*). The adult is one-brooded and has a very short flight period.

29. *Hesperia sassacus* Harris. Indian Skipper. Plate IV

Description. This species has a wingspread of 1 to 1.4 inches (25–35 mm). The male has a slender stigma on the FW, appearing more distinct above and paler below. The FW border is somewhat dentate; the HW border is deeply dentate. The VHW is light tan with a pale band of large connected yellowish spots, which are extended along the veins.

Distribution and Habitat. This species occurs from Maine and southern Ontario westward to Wisconsin, Iowa, and Illinois (Irwin and Downey, 1973) and south to Virginia and Tennessee. In Indiana it appears in late April and may be found in June and July. It is uncommon in northern Indiana counties and apparently absent from the central and southern counties. Look for the Indian Skipper in damp meadows, dry fields and pastures, and acid scrub.

Life Cycle. The egg is broadly hemispherical and scarcely more than 1 mm in diameter. The mature larva is reddish brown mottled with green and light specks. Its larval foodplants are *Panicum, Festuca,* and *Digitaria. H. sassacus* probably hibernates in the pupal stage (Klots, 1964).

Genus *Polites* Scudder

Four species of the genus *Polites* occur in Indiana. They are mostly orange or tawny. The distinctive patterns of the hindwings greatly assist identification. Their antennae are rather short, having a stout club and a somewhat long apiculus. The tibiae are spined. Many of the males have an almost S-shaped stigma.

30. *Polites coras* Cramer. Peck's Skipper. Plate IV.

Description. For years this species was known as *Polites peckius,* hence the common name, Peck's Skipper. However, Pyle (1981), in the *Audubon Field Guide,* uses the common name Yellowpatch Skipper, because of the distinctive yellow patches on the wings. The wingspread measures from 0.75 to 1 inch (19–25 mm). The male above is dark brown, having the tawny orange

patch along the costal margin, usually extending through much of the wing base. Outside the male stigma there is a broad gray-brown patch. Examine the photographs to see the arrangement of the yellowish gold spots on both surfaces of the male and female.

Distribution and Habitat. It occurs from British Columbia east to the Maritime Provinces and south to Oregon, eastern Arizona, Colorado, and Georgia.

Eventually *coras* will probably be found in every county of Indiana. More field collecting should be done in the extreme southeastern counties. It is very common from May through September and occasionally in October. It can be found almost anywhere: open spaces, grassy fields, meadows, marshes, roadsides, flat and hilly areas, freely visiting flowers. It is easy to capture.

Life Cycle. The early stages were described by Scudder and Dethier (Howe, 1975). The pale green egg is about 0.75 mm in diameter and almost spherical. The first-stage caterpillar is whitish, soon becoming greenish, and the head is black. The half-grown larva is maroon mottled with white or gray. Likewise the mature larva is dark maroon, but it is mottled with light brown. The pupa is dull reddish purple. This species hibernates in its third, fourth, or fifth larval stage or as a pupa (Klots, 1964).

In Indiana I have found six pairs *in copula:* 6 June 1970, 10:55 A.M., Tippecanoe County; 10 July 1971, 9:15 A.M., 76° F, North Manchester, Wabash County; 18 August 1971, 3:30 P.M., 90° F, North Manchester; 24 May 1977, 12:55 P.M., 84° F, North Manchester; and two pairs 28 May 1979, 12:20 P.M. and 12:30 P.M., 60° F, Carroll County. As is the case in all skippers, the female was the flight partner.

31. *Polites themistocles* **Latreille. Tawny-edged Skipper. Plate IV.**

Description. This species has a wingspread of 0.75 to 1 inch (19–25 mm) and is dull brown with bright orange in the FW and on the costal area. It can be distinguished from *P. origenes* by the broad, black S-shaped male stigma on the FW. In both sexes the ventral hindwings are usually plain or mustard-colored with some black at the base. On 21 August 1971 I netted a melanic female in North Manchester, Wabash County.

Distribution and Habitat. The "Tawny-edge" ranges from southern Canada throughout most of the United States; however, it is reportedly rare in the Pacific Northwest. It is found throughout Indiana, flying from May to October, in open meadows and grassland.

Life Cycle. The small, pale greenish egg is slightly over 0.75 mm in diameter. The first larval instar is whitish and has a faint dorsal line and a black head. The half-grown larva turns pale brownish yellow, showing a greenish tinge dorsally; it is flecked with dark brown dots. The mature larva is rich purplish brown, yellow-brown, or chocolate. The pupa is whitish to light brown. The larval foodplants are grasses, particularly *Panicum*. The species overwinters in the pupal stage.

In Indiana I have collected four pairs *in copula:* 20 June 1969, 1:25 P.M., Silver Lake, Kosciusko County; 20 June 1971, 1:45 P.M., 85° F, North Manchester, Wabash County; 24 June 1971, 2:00 P.M., 85° F, North Manchester; and 10 June 1982, 2:35 P.M., 73° F, Indianapolis, Marion County. It is univoltine.

32. *Polites origenes origenes* Fabricius. Crossline Skipper. Plate IV.

Description. The wingspread of this species measures 1 to 1.1 inches (25–28 mm). Many specimens closely resemble *P. themistocles.* Generally, *origenes* is larger and darker and the orange in the FW is more restricted; also the stigma is longer and more slender. The faint traces of spots on the VHW of *origenes* are usually absent in *themistocles.* The largest spot of the FW of the female *origenes* is very squarish. I suggest that some of the specimens be identified by specialists.

Distribution and Habitat. *P. o. origenes* occurs in the eastern region from New England to Georgia and west to the Dakotas. It is fairly common in many counties in Indiana from 25 May to September, and rarely early October, but it is never as common as the Tawny-edged Skipper. Look for it in pastures, meadows, and sandy places.

Life Cycle. The pale green egg is about 1 mm in diameter, and it is more reticulated than that of *P. themistocles.* The first larval instar is pallid green with a black head. The half-grown larva is dull olive-green mottled with soiled white. Klots (1964) says that this species hibernates in its fourth (sometimes third) larval instar.

I have found four pairs *in copula:* 10 July 1969, 3:30 P.M., Silver Lake, Kosciusko County; 11 July 1969, 3:10 P.M., Silver Lake; 6 June 1970, 10:55 A.M., Tippecanoe County; and 11:00 A.M., 85° F, Morgan Monroe State Forest. In all cases the female was the flight partner. It is univoltine.

33. *Polites mystic* W. H. Edwards. Long Dash. Plate IV.

Description. The wingspread of this species ranges from 1 to 1.25 inches (25–32 mm). The upper end of the stigma in the FW connects with the subapical dark patch, giving *mystic* its common name. The VHW is somewhat reddish; the light spots form a curved band, but these spots are not as large as in *P. coras* and *P. vibex,* two other Indiana species. Some *mystic* females are very dark and the HW is nearly solid reddish brown, displaying a narrow band of tiny, separated light spots.

Distribution and Habitat. This species occurs from the Maritime Provinces west to Manitoba and south to Virginia and Illinois. Irwin and Downey

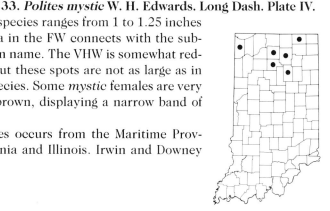

(1973) limit its range to northeastern Illinois, from 22 May through 15 July. In Indiana I have found it in May and June and occasionally in July. I collected the first *mystic* in the state on 6 June 1969 in the tamarack bog at Mongo, LaGrange County, only seven miles from the Michigan border. The Long Dash prefers flowery meadows, bogs, forest paths, stream banks, and roadsides where wildflowers grow.

Life Cycle.   The pale green egg is hemispherical and finely reticulate. The first larval instar is pale greenish yellow and has a black head. The half-grown larva is pale chocolate and mottled with dull white. The mature chocolate-colored larva has some white mottling and a dark dorsal line. The blackish or dark brown pupa has long tawny hairs on the head and abdomen. The foodplants for this species are various grasses (Poaceae), among which is Bluegrass (*Poa*). The species overwinters in the second or third molt.

I have found only one pair *in copula*: 30 May 1977, 4:55 P.M., 80° F, North Manchester, Wabash County. While copulating the pair perched on a blade of marsh grass in an open field.

Genus *Wallengrenia* Berg

34. *Wallengrenia egeremet* Scudder. Northern Broken Dash. Plates IV and V.

Until recently *W. egeremet* was considered a subspecies of *W. otho* (*Wallengrenia otho egeremet*), but now that it is known that the two fly together in the same places without interbreeding, they are separated into two distinct species. In some areas there is considerable overlapping in the ranges of the two species.

Description.   The Northern Broken Dash ranges from Ontario and Quebec south to Florida and Texas. In Indiana adults fly from June through August and occasionally to mid-September. I have found them commonly on Dogbane flowers, associating with the rare Northern Hairstreak (*Euristrymon ontario*). Many nymphalids also seem to prefer Dogbane. Dogbane attracts dozens of species of butterflies (in the Orient Lantana is similarly popular). *W. egeremet* occurs in shrub rows, fields, meadows, and grasslands.

Life Cycle.   The greenish or yellowish egg is less than 1 mm in diameter. The larva is apple-green with darker green mottling; it has a yellow-edged dorsal stripe and a brown head. Since the two subspecies have only recently been separated, a description of the pupa awaits further research.

I have collected one pair *in copula,* which I had reported as *Wallengrenia otho egeremet:* 9 August 1971, 12:15 P.M., 79° F (with high humidity), North Manchester, Wabash County, on Dogbane flowers.

Genus *Pompeius* Evans

35. *Pompeius verna* W. H. Edwards. Little Glassywing. Plate V.

Description. The Little Glassywing has a wingspread of 1 to 1.25 inches (25–32 mm). This skipper is blackish or dark brown with distinctive whitish and squarish hyaline spots on the FW, especially the large, somewhat elongated spot below the end of the cell on the male and the more squarish spot on the female. The pattern of these spots separates *verna* females from those of *Polites, Wallengrenia,* and *Euphyes ruricola,* other similar species occurring in Indiana.

Distribution and Habitat. This species may be found from New England and Michigan westward to Nebraska and south to Texas and Georgia. Until now it has been collected in only fourteen of the counties in Indiana, but a look at the dot map suggests that most likely it will be found in many more counties. Adults fly from June to August, but Masters and Masters (1969) reported two specimens taken in September 1964. Locally *verna* may be fairly common some years but absent others. Look for it in open forests, grassy fields, fence-rows, and cleared areas.

Life Cycle. The small egg (about 0.85 mm in diameter) is at first white, becoming greenish before hatching. The first larva is cream-colored, then greenish with a dark brown head. The half-grown larva is light green showing many tiny spinelike hairs over the body. It has a dark green dorsal line and a subdorsal line on each side. The mature larva is yellowish green to yellowish brown flecked with many minute brown spots. In its last instar the body stripes are dark and the head a deep reddish brown. The only known foodplant is *Tridens flavus*. The hibernation stage for *verna* is unknown.

Genus *Atalopedes* Scudder

36. *Atalopedes campestris* Boisduval. Sachem; Field Skipper. Plate V.

Description. The wingspread of this hesperid measures from 1 to 1.4 inches (25–35 mm). The males and females are tawny orange. The male is readily recognized by the massive stigma in the FW. The underside of the wings are mostly yellow, showing an indistinct band of paler spots on the hindwings. The female is generally orange or dark above with a distinctive hyaline spot under the end of the FW cell. The VHW of the female is olive or dark yellow with a macular band of yellow spots.

Distribution and Habitat. The Sachem ranges from the Atlantic to the Pacific, mostly in the southern half of the United States, but it occurs as a wanderer northward as far as Colorado, Nebraska, Iowa, and New York. Irwin and

PLATE V

Top row

Northern Broken Dash, *Wallengrenia egeremet* UN♂. 9 August 1971, North Manchester, Wabash Co., IN.

W. egeremet UN♀. 10 August 1975, Brown County State Park, Nashville, IN.

Little Glassywing, *Pompeius verna* UP♂. 2 July 1969, North Manchester, Wabash Co., IN.

P. verna UN♂. 30 June 1969, Silver Lake, Kosciusko Co., IN.

Second row

P. verna UP♀. 1 July 1969, Silver Lake, Kosciusko Co., IN.

P. verna UN♀. 2 July 1969, North Manchester, Wabash Co., IN.

Sachem or Field Skipper, *Atalopedes campestris* UP♂. 5 August 1968, North Manchester, Wabash Co., IN.

A. campestris UN♂. 5 August 1968, North Manchester, Wabash Co., IN.

Third row

A. campestris UP♀. 30 August 1969, North Manchester, Wabash Co., IN.

A. campestris UN♀. 4 September 1969, North Manchester, Wabash Co., IN.

Delaware Skipper, *Atrytone logan logan* UP♂. 8 July 1969, Silver Lake, Kosciusko Co., IN.

A. l. logan UN♂. 5 July 1969, North Manchester, Wabash Co., IN.

Fourth row

A. l. logan UP♀. 9 July 1969, Silver Lake, Kosciusko Co., IN.

A. l. logan UN♀. 27 June 1970, North Manchester, Wabash Co., IN.

Byssus Skipper, *Problema byssus* UP♂. 22 July 1973, Griffith, Lake Co., IN. Coll. Irwin Leeuw

P. byssus UP♀. 22 July 1973, Griffith, Lake Co., IN. Coll. Irwin Leeuw

Fifth row

Mulberry Wing Skipper, *Poanes massasoit* UP♂. 4 July 1973, North Manchester, Wabash Co., IN.

P. massasoit UN♂. 4 July 1973, North Manchester, Wabash Co., IN.

P. massasoit UP♀. 25 July 1984, Nasby Fen, Mongo, LaGrange Co., IN.

P. massasoit UN♀. 25 July 1984, Nasby Fen, Mongo, LaGrange Co., IN.

Sixth row

Hobomok Skipper, *Poanes hobomok* UP♂. 8 June 1974, Whitewater Memorial State Park, Union Co., IN.

P. hobomok UN♂. 22 June 1967, Silver Lake, Kosciusko Co., IN.

P. hobomok UP♀. 8 June 1979, Whitewater Memorial State Park, Union Co., IN.

P. hobomok Un♀. 8 June 1979, Whitewater Memorial State Park, Union Co., IN.

Seventh row

Zabulon Skipper, *Poanes zabulon* UP♂. 6 June 1975, Brown County State Park, Nashville, IN.

P. zabulon UN♂. 10 August 1975, Brown County State Park, Nashville, IN.

P. zabulon UP♀. 1 August 1978, Whitewater Memorial State Park, Union Co., IN.

P. zabulon UN♀. 1 August 1978, Whitewater Memorial State Park, Union Co., IN.

Downey (1973) have many records from Illinois, where it is common in August and September. Their 23 May records were probably overwintering adults.

This species is common in a few northern Indiana counties from late July to September. Masters and Masters (1969) found it to be scarce in late summer in Perry County. It may be found in fields and pastures, and even on urban lawns and gardens. It is an immigrant to our state.

Life Cycle. The greenish white egg is less than 1 mm in diameter. The young larva is whitish with a tinge of green and has a black head. The dark olive-green mature larva is profusely covered with minute dark tubercles bearing short black hairs. Its middorsal line is dark green. The chrysalis is blackish brown with white patches on the sides of the thorax.

The foodplants of *campestris* are various grasses (Poaceae), including Bermuda Grass (*Cynodon dactylon*). I have taken one pair *in copula:* 6 August 1971, 3:15 P.M., resting on *Helianthus strumesus,* a sunflower in a marshy field near North Manchester, Wabash County. It is multivoltine in Indiana.

Genus *Atrytone* Scudder

37. *Atrytone logan logan* W. H. Edwards. Delaware Skipper. Plate V.

Description. The wingspread ranges from 1 to 1.4 inches (25–35 mm). This skipper is easily identified by its black veins and discocellular mark on the FW above and by the bright yellow-orange HW beneath. The females have more extensive dark markings than the males, the veins and wing borders being darker. It should be noted that many authorities prefer the name *Atrytone delaware* for this species.

Distribution and Habitat. The Delaware Skipper occurs from Massachusetts to Minnesota and the Dakotas to Florida and Texas. It is probably common throughout Indiana from late June to September. Apparently many counties have not been adequately covered. Look for this skipper on woodland paths and trails, pond margins, bogs, floodplains, and grassy lowlands. When disturbed, it often flies only a short distance and alights on the same path.

Life Cycle. The life history of *A. logan* is not completely known. The bluish white larva has a crescent-shaped black band near the anal plate. The head is black and white. The pupa is greenish white with black tips and has a bristly blunt head. The larval foodplants of this species are Woolly Beard Grass (*Erianthus diverticatus*), Bluestem (*Andropogon*), Switch Grass (*Panicum virgatum*), and probably some other grasses.

I have taken one pair *in copula:* 29 June 1970, 3:30 P.M., 89° F, in a grassy field, Silver Lake, Kosciusko County. It has only one brood in Indiana.

Genus *Problema* Skinner and R. C. Williams

38. *Problema byssus* W. H. Edwards. Byssus Skipper. Plate V.

Description. The Byssus Skipper has a wingspread from 1.25–1.5 inches (32–38 mm). The wings of the male are considerably smaller than those of the female. The absence of a stigma in *P. byssus* separates it from the *Atrytone* group. *Byssus* is a large, brownish skipper with distinct yellowish markings on the upper wing surfaces. The VHW has a faint spotband or patch beyond the end of the cell. Some specimens are very dark, which obscures the lighter markings.

Distribution and Habitat. *P. byssus* is a local species, says Howe (1975), not often encountered in its wide range in the south and midwest. It has been reported from Florida, Georgia, and Alabama north to Illinois, Iowa, and Kansas. Heitzman (Howe, 1975) found it in Texas.

The first Byssus Skippers collected in Indiana were found by Irwin Leeuw near Griffith, Lake County, on 22 July 1973. He generously deposited the specimens with me. It has been reported in only four counties, all in northwestern Indiana. Look for this local and rare species in undisturbed prairie regions in June and July.

Life Cycle. The early stages are described by Heitzman (Howe, 1975). The large egg (about 1.5 mm in diameter) is chalky white, hemispherical with a flattened summit. The first-stage larva is pale green, displaying a tiny white mark dorsally at each intersegmental fold. Its head is dull red-brown. The half-grown larva is pale green or yellowish green and it is covered with small black warts and tiny white hairs; its mottled head is orange-brown or light reddish brown. The mature larva is bluish green with a yellow tint dorsally; its head is mostly reddish brown with a few colored lines and streaks. The pupa is long, slender, and cream-colored, and it is sparsely sprinkled with tiny brown dots. This species overwinters in the fourth larval instar. It is univoltine.

Genus *Poanes* Scudder

39. *Poanes massasoit* Scudder. Mulberry Wing Skipper. Plate V.

Description. The wingspread ranges from about 1 to 1.1 inches (24–28 mm). This is a dark brown skipper with rounded wings. The male may be unmarked or have a few discal orange spots. The FW of the female usually contains a few small whitish spots. The VHW has a conspicuous yellowish discal band of squarish connected spots and a broad yellowish dash through the cell to the apex of this band. In some specimens the VHW is suffused with rusty brown obscuring the yellow spots.

Distribution and Habitat. This skipper ranges from Maryland to New England and westward to Nebraska and South Dakota. Irwin and Downey (1973) mention records for northern Illinois. Price (1970) found it in northwestern Ohio.

I have found it locally common in the bogs of northeastern Indiana in June and July; however, some years it is scarce. The Mulberry Wing flies low among the tall grasses, weaving its way through the stems to another resting place—thus it is easily overlooked. Although it visits many kinds of flowers, it is partial to Swamp Milkweed (*Asclepias incarnata*). In Wabash County it may be found in boggy fields and marshes.

Life Cycle. Laurent (Howe, 1975) describes the eggs as opaque white and nearly round. The young larva is dirty yellow with a pale brown head. The body is covered with long yellow hairs. The second instar larva is similar to the first except that the color is olive green. It is a grass or sedge feeder. According to Shapiro (1965), the larval foodplant is *Carex*.

40. *Poanes hobomok* Harris. Hobomok Skipper. Plate V.

Description. The Hobomok wingspread is from 1 to 1.4 inches (24–35 mm). The male is bright yellowish orange on the upper wings; both wings have a black border. Generally the female is not as brightly colored and the FW base is brown. The underwing surfaces are more yellowish in both sexes. Dimorphic females of the form "*pocahontas*" can be found, especially in the southern counties of Indiana. I have taken several "*pocahontas*" in May in Brown County State Park. The light spots of the FW are blurred in *hobomok;* in *P. zabulon* the spots are sharp and clear-cut.

Distribution and Habitat. It ranges from Minnesota, Ontario, and New Hampshire south to Maryland and west to South Dakota, Nebraska, and Illinois. It is widespread throughout Indiana, flying from May to late August or early September. Apparently *hobomok* is more common in northern Indiana and *zabulon* in the southern counties. I have found *hobomok* mostly frequently in woods, on animal and man-made paths. It also occurs in moist gullies, fencerows, and meadows.

Life Cycle. The life histories of *hobomok* and *zabulon* have often been confused, so little is known with certainty. Klots (1964) states that the third-stage larva is dark green to brown, with many small black tubercles in transverse lines, bearing short black spines. The white head is covered with many white hairs. The caterpillar or chrysalis may overwinter. The larval foodplants are grasses (Poaceae).

Although *hobomok* is a common species, I have found only one pair *in copula:* 28 May 1979, 11:55 A.M., a cool 60° F, mating in the grass between Deer Creek and a nearby woods in Carroll County.

41. *Poanes zabulon* Boisduval and Leconte. Zabulon Skipper. Plate V.

Description. The wingspread of *zabulon* measures from 1 to 1.4 inches (25–35 mm), the same as *hobomok,* but the wings are more triangular. Although both species look much alike (especially the males), the more extensive yellow area on the HW of *zabulon* should be noted. On the VHW there is a row of dark spots which runs from the lower, outer corner of the cell. Even in the dark females these spots can be seen.

Distribution and Habitat. This skipper ranges from Massachusetts west to Iowa, south to Georgia and rarely to Texas. In Indiana it occurs in many counties; however, the records show it to be missing in many of the northwestern and northeastern counties, especially from Steuben to Wayne counties along the Indiana/Ohio border. The Zabulon Skipper flies from May to September. It probably has two broods. I have found it on roadsides, hillsides, along the banks of streams, and in pastures.

Life Cycle. There is very little reliable information on the early stages of the Zabulon Skipper. According to Shapiro (Howe, 1975) its larval foodplants are the grasses *Tridens* and *Eragrostis.*

42. *Poanes viator* W. H. Edwards. Broad-winged Skipper. Plate VI.

Description. *Poanes viator* is a robust brown-winged skipper with a wingspread of 1.25 to 1.75 inches (30–44 mm). The forewings are mostly brown with bright orange spots confined largely to the posterior half of the wing except for a large cell spot; subapical spots are often present. Both sexes have these spots on the FW, but the spots are paler on the females. The male does not have a stigma.

Distribution and Habitat. This local and widely scattered species ranges from Massachusetts and southern Ontario west to Minnesota and Nebraska, and south to Florida, Alabama, Louisiana, and Texas.

Blatchley (1891) reported it as scarce in Putnam and Lake counties. Subsequently, it has been found in Porter, LaGrange, Steuben, and Wabash counties; however, it is rare and local, in scattered colonies. *Viator* flies in July and August. Look for it in marshes where its foodplant, Marsh Millet (*Zizaniopsis miliacea*), grows.

Life Cycle. Nothing is known about its early stages or mating behavior in Indiana. Howe (1975) reports its biology as described by Laurent. Shapiro (Howe, 1975) mentioned Wild Rice (*Zizania*) as a foodplant.

Genus *Euphyes* Scudder

43. *Euphyes dion* W. H. Edwards. Sedge Skipper. Plate VI.

Description. The wingspread measures approximately from 1.25 to 1.6 inches (32–41 mm). In this rather brown skipper, there are restricted areas of

PLATE VI

Top row Broad-winged Skipper, *Poanes viator* UP♂. 10 July 1979, Spring Lake Forest Preserve, Cook Co., IL. Coll. Irwin Leeuw

P. viator UP♀. 18 July 1979, Spring Lake Forest Preserve, Cook Co., IL. Coll. Irwin Leeuw

Sedge Skipper, *Euphyes dion* UP♂. 9 July 1969, Silver Lake, Kosciusko Co., IN.

E. dion UN♂. 30 June 1969, North Manchester, Wabash Co., IN.

Second row *E. dion* UP♀. 9 July 1969, Silver Lake, Kosciusko Co., IN.

E. dion UN♀. 10 July 1969, Silver Lake, Kosciusko Co., IN.

Scarce Swamp Skipper, *Euphyes dukesi* UP♂. 27 June 1970, North Manchester, Wabash Co., IN.

E. dukesi UP♀. 3 July 1963, Wabash Canal, Paulding Co., OH. Coll. Homer F. Price

Third row Black Dash, *Euphyes conspicua conspicua* UP♂. 16 July 1969, North Manchester, Wabash Co., IN.

E. c. conspicua UN♀. 16 July 1969, North Manchester, Wabash Co., IN.

E. c. conspicua UP♂. 10 July 1973, Camp Mack, Milford, Kosciusko Co., IN.

E. c. conspicua UN♀. 21 July 1973, North Manchester, Wabash Co., IN.

Fourth row Two-spotted Skipper, *Euphyes bimacula* UP♂. 20 June 1969, North Manchester, Wabash Co., IN.

E. bimacula UP♀. 21 June 1969, North Manchester, Wabash Co., IN.

Dun Skipper, *Euphyes ruricola metacomet* UP♂. 20 June 1969, Silver Lake, Kosciusko Co., IN. This specimen was mating with the next one.

E. r. metacomet UP♀. 20 June 1969, Silver Lake, Kosciusko Co., IN.

E. r. metacomet UN♂. 16 June 1969, North Manchester, Wabash Co., IN.

Fifth row *E. r. metacomet* UN♀. 16 August 1973, North Manchester, Wabash Co., IN.

Dusted Skipper, *Atrytonopsis hianna* UP♂. 5 June 1982, Newaygo Co., MI. Det. M. C. Nielsen

A. hianna UP♀. 5 June 1982, Newaygo Co., MI. Det. M. C. Nielsen

Pepper-and-Salt Skipper, *Amblyscirtes hegon* UP♂. 13 June 1979, Brown County State Park, Nashville, IN.

Sixth row *A. hegon* UP♀. 15 May 1972, Pennsylvania State Game Lands, Allegheny Co., PA. Det. H. K. Clench

Roadside Skipper, *Amblyscirtes vialis* UP♂. 1 June 1978, Brown County State Park, Nashville, IN.

A. vialis UN♀. 1 June 1978, Brown County State Park, Nashville, IN.

A. vialis UP♂. 23 May 1974, Allegan State Game Area, Allegan Co., MI. Coll. Irwin Leeuw

orange on the upper wing surfaces. But the presence of two longitudinal pale rays on the VHW distinguish it from all other species except *E. dukesi.*

Distribution and Habitat. *E. dion* ranges from the Carolinas north to New York and Ontario, west to Kansas, Nebraska, and Wisconsin.

The type locality has been restricted to Lake County by Miller and Brown (1981). I have collected specimens on 4 July 1973 in a woodland bog, North Manchester, Wabash County; 12 June 1979, in a marshy field, North Manchester; 14 July 1980, in the tamarack bog, Pigeon River Fish and Game Area, LaGrange County; and 30 June 1981, in Leisure, Madison County. David Eiler, a field companion, has also collected *dion* in LaGrange County and on 21 July 1981 in Hancock County. The Sedge Skipper occurs locally and is rare, in bogs and marshy fields.

Life Cycle. The life history of this species is not fully understood. Howe (1975) states that "the egg is light green and finely reticulate. Young larvae are yellowish green with yellowish hairs and a black head and collar." The larval foodplants are the aquatic sedges. It is probably one-brooded.

44. *Euphyes dukesi* Lindsey. Scarce Swamp Skipper. Plate VI.

Description. The wingspread measures 1.25 to 1.5 inches (32–38 mm). This species resembles *dion* in that both have longitudinal pale rays on the HW; however, the FW of *dukesi* are proportionally shorter and broader and never have the subapical light spots near the costal margin. Both species are moderately large with brown backgrounds. The male has no markings except for the stigma and a few dull orange regions in the basal areas of both wings. The FW of the female has two or three orange spots.

Distribution and Habitat. *E. dukesi* has been found in Alabama, Mississippi, Louisiana, Arkansas, North Carolina, Virginia, Michigan, Ohio, Illinois, and Indiana. Homer F. Price, Payne, Ohio, collected one male 24 July 1962 in Steuben County, the first state record. I collected one more 27 June 1970 at North Manchester, Wabash County. These constitute the only known records for Indiana. The adults appear to fly in June and July in Indiana and are found in bogs or shaded wetlands.

Life Cycle. The life history of *dukesi* has not been recorded.

45. *Euphyes conspicua conspicua* W. H. Edwards. Black Dash. Plate VI.

Description. The wingspread of the Black Dash measures from 1 to 1.4 inches (25–35 mm). The male FW is tawny with broad brown borders and a conspicuous stigma. The FW of the female is almost black with a curved band of glassy yellow spots. The HW of both sexes has a distinctive path of light spots, which are tawny orange on the male and yellowish on the female.

Distribution and Habitat. This species ranges from Massachusetts south to

Virginia and west to Ohio, Indiana, Illinois, Michigan, Minnesota, and Nebraska.

I have found the Black Dash to be local but common in marshes and boggy meadows, in June and July, mostly in the northern counties of Indiana. I have seen adults taking nectar from the blossoms of Swamp Milkweed (*Asclepias incarnata*).

Life Cycle. The life history of the Black Dash is largely unknown. Its larval foodplants are probably sedges (*Carex*). I have found one pair *in copula*: 3 July 1970, 1:35 P.M., North Manchester, Wabash County, mating among the sedges of a woodland marsh. It has one brood.

46. *Euphyes bimacula* Grote and Robinson. Two-spotted Skipper. Plate VI.

Description. The wingspread varies from 1.1 to 1.25 inches (28–32 mm). The Two-spotted Skipper is a dark species with rather pointed forewings with restricted tawny areas. There are no pale regions on the HW. The VHW are dull olive to olive-yellow with lighter-colored veins and white fringes on the wing and edge.

Distribution and Habitat. *E. bimacula* is a local species, ranging from Maine to Ontario south to Virginia, Michigan, Iowa, and Nebraska. Look for this rare and local skipper in boggy or marshy meadows. Adults fly from late June to July and are usually found in colonies. Basically, the Two-spotted Skipper is a northern species, preferring cool climates.

Life Cycle. Much of its life history has not been recorded. The egg, according to Laurent (Howe, 1975), is pale green, finely reticulate, and hemispherical. The larvae probably feed on sedges (*Carex*).

I have found one pair *in copula*: 20 June 1969, 1:00 P.M., North Manchester, Wabash County, in a marshy meadow. It is univoltine.

47. *Euphyes ruricola metacomet* Harris. Dun Skipper. Plate VI.

Description. This species has a wingspread of 1 to 1.25 inches (25–32 mm), one wing measuring from 11–14 mm. It was formerly known as *E. vestris metacomet*. The male is dark brown above and unmarked except for the FW stigma. The female differs in that it has a few small translucent spots on the FW. Generally, both sexes are lighter on the underneath surfaces. In a few specimens the head and palpi are orange.

Distribution and Habitat. This species has a broad range from southern Canada to Baja California and northern Mexico. In Indiana I have found it to be common throughout most of our counties, with the adults flying from June to September. This small skipper dashes from plant to plant and to the lower tree branches in our deciduous forests. It also occurs in fields, roadsides, pastures, and hilly places.

Life Cycle. Until recently the early stages remained unknown. Reportedly, the larvae feed on grasses, but its foodplants in Indiana have not been identified. According to Howe (1975), the egg is pale green during oviposition and turns red before hatching. The first larval instar is yellow and covered with short white hairs. The head is shiny brown. The older stage is green with a whitish appearance, having white hairs only on the last segment; its head is orange with creamy vertical stripes. The mature translucent green larva is again an overcast white with numerous wavy white dashes; the head is brownish and blackish with two creamy bands and a velvet spot on the face. Basically, the pupa is whitish green with the thorax yellowish green and the head pale brownish.

I have netted two pairs *in copula:* one on 20 June 1969, 2:00 P.M., Silver Lake, Kosciusko County, in a woods, copulating on a raspberry twig; and another pair on 7 August 1979, 12:40 P.M., 88° F, copulating on a branch of a Butternut tree, just three feet above the ground. The temperature was 72° F, so the climate was just right for this and many other mating species.

Genus *Atrytonopsis* Godman

48. *Atrytonopsis hianna* Scudder. Dusted Skipper. Plate VI.

Description. The wingspread is from 1.25 to 1.5 inches (32–35 or 36 mm). This is a dark brown skipper with several hyaline spots in the FW and without spots in the cell. Its most distinguishing characteristic is the violet to pale gray area in the VHW. The male has no stigma. Occasionally, there may be a double pair of small cell spots in the female.

Distribution and Habitat. The Dusted Skipper occurs through most of the eastern United States from New England to Manitoba, south to Georgia and Arkansas.

Blatchley (1891) reported *hianna* only from Lake and LaGrange counties. Although this species has been reported subsequently from two more counties, I have never collected it in Indiana. This skipper colonizes areas which have been burned over and which contain its reported foodplant, Beard Grass (*Andropogon scoparius*). Adults take nectar from Blackberry, Clover, and Strawberry blossoms. Look for *hianna* in open dry fields, in acid, sandy barrens where scrub oak and pine grow, and in cleared, burned areas.

Life Cycle. According to Pyle (1981), the caterpillar has seven instars. It overwinters in tube tents above the base of the hostplant.

Genus *Amblyscirtes* Scudder

49. *Amblyscirtes hegon* Scudder. Pepper-and-Salt Skipper. Plate VI.

Description. Formerly this species went by the name *samoset,* a junior synonym of *hegon.* The wingspread of this small black skipper ranges from 0.9

to slightly over 1 inch (22–26 mm). The upper blackish wings have a dull greenish cast. The FW spots are faint and whitish, forming a somewhat curved band. The VHW is heavily dusted with greenish gray and has checkered fringes.

Distribution and Habitat. The range extends from southeastern Canada to Georgia and west to Manitoba and Iowa. In Indiana it has been reported from only a few central and southern counties. Marc Minno found the first *A. hegon* in Indiana in Martin County 8 June 1978. I collected my first specimens in Brown County State Park on 13 June 1979, where they were feeding from Dogbane blossoms along Skinner Creek by the edge of a woods. David Eiler has several specimens from in and near Turkey Run State Park, Parke County, collected 16–17 June 1980.

Adults fly from May to August, preferring the edges of forests in hilly areas. They also occur along stream banks and in hayfields, usually flying rather close to the ground.

Life Cycle. The mature larva is pale green with a darker green dorsal line running below the spiracles. The brownish head has reddish eyespots. The chrysalis is straw-colored with a greenish tinge. The larval foodplants are various species of *Sorghum* and Kentucky Bluegrass (*Poa secundum*). I know of no mating records of *hegon* in Indiana, but it probably has only one brood.

50. *Amblyscirtes vialis* W. H. Edwards. Roadside Skipper. Plate VI.

Description. The wingspread is 0.9 to 1.25 inches (22–32 mm). This is a dark brown, almost black skipper with rounded wings. Small white spots near the tip of the FW form a cluster. The underwings are brown with a distinct violet-gray shading on the outer portions of the wings. The fringes are brown and buff.

Distribution and Habitat. *A. vialis* occurs in most states in the United States, except Alaska. Although the Roadside Skipper is common but widely scattered in most areas, it has been recorded in only a few Hoosier counties. It is locally common in the southern half of the state, but rare to absent in the northern counties. Look for it in our state parks and forested areas. Adults, where found, fly from mid-May to early September, resting on the bare ground on woodland trails and paths, along railroads, and wet protected places.

Life Cycle. Among the recorded larval foodplants of this species are Kentucky Bluegrass (*Poa pratensis*), *Agretis, Avena,* and Bermuda Grass (*Cynodon dactylon*). It is probably univoltine in our area.

51. *Amblyscirtes belli* H. A. Freeman. Bell's Roadside Skipper. Plate VII.

Description. The wingspread of this species is 0.9 to 1.25 inches (22–33 mm). *A. belli* is dark brown or blackish with a series of white, somewhat V-shaped spots on the FW. It never has a light spot in the cell of the FW. The lower surface is dark.

PLATE VII

Distribution and Habitat. This species ranges from Texas, Oklahoma, Arkansas, and Missouri east through Mississippi to Georgia and Florida. Basically, *belli* is a southern species. Therefore, it is surprising that Marc Minno found it in Indiana, 31 July 1975, in Perry County (personal correspondence). Look for it in wooded ravines, creek beds, fields, and gardens.

Life Cycle. Heitzman (Howe, 1975) reported the early stages of this species in great detail. The whitish egg is about 1 mm in diameter. At first the larva is white but changes to a translucent green with darker green lines and whitish orange head. The pupa has a rust-colored thorax, creamy-colored head, and yellowish wing cases. Its larval foodplant in Missouri reportedly is *Uniola latifolia,* a grass.

Genus *Lerodea* Scudder

52. *Lerodea eufala* W. H. Edwards. Eufala Skipper. Plate VII.

Description. The wingspread measures from 0.9 to 1.25 inches (22−32 mm). *L. eufala* is usually lighter than *Nastra lherminier,* with which it may be confused. The Eufala Skipper is plain gray-brown with 3 to 5 small hyaline spots on the FW; otherwise, it is without markings. The VHW is brown with a dusting of gray except for the anal fold. Females are larger and lighter than the males. The male lacks the FW stigma.

Distribution and Habitat. The Eufala Skipper ranges widely over most of southern United States from the Central Valley of California to the mid-Atlantic north to Nebraska and east to Virginia.

Although *eufala* is common in much of its range, it is very rare in Indiana. It has been found in five widely scattered counties. I have collected a few specimens in Brown County State Park on 25 May 1976 and 1 June 1978. It appears to be rare and local from late May through June. Possibly it appears again in the fall. Look for it along streams, on hillsides, and in oak openings.

Life Cycle. The egg is about 1 mm in diameter and is pale green. The first larval instar is yellowish with a black head. The half-grown larva is similarly colored, but it has a dark green dorsal line and several whitish lateral lines. The mature larva is vivid green with a dark dorsal stripe. It also has yellowish and whitish lateral stripes. It has a frontal horn.

In our area the larval foodplant of *eufala* is probably alfalfa, though it feeds on various grasses throughout its range.

Genus *Panoquina* Hemming

53. *Panoquina ocola* W. H. Edwards. Long-winged Skipper. Plate VII.

Description. The wingspread is from 1.25 to 1.4 inches (32−35 mm). The FW is slender and pointed. Generally, *ocola* is a variable species, but most

specimens are dark yellowish brown on the upper and under surfaces. Also, the FW yellow spots vary. The VHW is mostly unmarked.

Distribution and Habitat. This species ranges from Florida and Texas north to New York, Ohio, and Indiana. However, Price (1970) mentioned only one record from Ohio: 26 September 1949, in a slough of the St. Joseph's River near Egerton. In Indiana *P. ocola* must be exceedingly rare. Blatchley (1891) states that *ocola* was "recorded by Edwards occurring at Whiting, Lake County, where Worthington has found it in small numbers." On 20 August 1967 I collected one male in North Manchester, Wabash County. There are no records for any other county except Kosciusko. Look for *ocola* along the edges of woods, on flowers, and in damp clearings.

The Long-winged Skipper is a fast and erratic flier, but it is not difficult to net when feeding on nectar from flowers.

Life Cycle. Little is known with certainty of its early stages. Pyle (1981) says that the egg is white and the larva is yellow, becoming bluish green on the first two segments and grayish green on the rest of the body, which is marked with green spots and lines. The pupa is greenish and has a short tongue case.

The larval foodplants of the Long-winged Skipper are grasses (Poaceae), Rice (*Orza sativa*), and Sugar Cane (*Sacchinarum officinarum*). Information about its mating behavior and number of broods is lacking for Indiana.

Part Three

Species Accounts –
The Butterflies

Superfamily Papilionoidea Latreille

The Superfamily Papilionoidea (true butterflies) differs in many ways from the Superfamily Hesperioidea (the skippers). The most noticeable difference is in the antennae. In the true butterflies the antennae are swollen or knobbed at the end; in the skippers, they are usually recurved or hooked. The body proportions of the two groups also vary. In the butterflies the body is more slender in proportion to the wing, while the skippers have relatively broader bodies.

The true butterflies are often brightly colored while the majority of the skippers are dull. The pupa of the butterfly is rarely enclosed in a cocoon, but the pupa of the skipper is usually enclosed in a loose cocoon.

Among the butterflies and skippers most species are diurnal; however, I have found a few to be crepuscular and others rarely attracted to ultraviolet lights. In India, I collected seventeen species at a 400-watt mercury-vapor lamp, only two species being skippers. In recent years the collecting of moths (Heterocera), which are mostly nocturnal, has been revolutionized by using various types of ultraviolet lights and light traps.

There is no universal agreement about the number of families that should be included in this large Superfamily Papilionoidea. Since I am following Miller and Brown (1981), the Harvester (*Feniseca tarquinus*) will be considered in the family Lycaenidae, not in Liphyridae where some experts have placed it.

Of the Superfamily Papilionoidea, the following families are found in Indiana: Papilionidae, Pieridae, Lycaenidae, Riodinidae, Libytheidae, Heliconiidae, Nymphalidae, Apaturidae, Satyridae, and Danaidae.

Family Papilionidae

Swallowtails (Papilionidae) are a worldwide family of medium-sized to large butterflies. Although many species lack the tails on the hindwings, the six species occurring in Indiana all have tails. The front legs are fully developed with an epiphysis on the tibia. There is only one anal vein in the HW.

In the tropics the Swallowtails are the largest and most magnificent of butterflies! What a thrill it was to capture one of the Birdwings (*Troides*) or an Apollo (*Parnassius*) of the high Himalayas! But Indiana collectors and naturalists need not be envious, for the species found in this state are also varied and beautiful.

Subfamily Papilioninae
Tribe Troidini Ford
Genus *Battus* Scopoli

54. *Battus philenor philenor* (Linnaeus). Pipevine Swallowtail. Plates VIII, IX.

Description. The wingspread of this species varies greatly from 2.75 to 4.5 inches (70–114 mm), but size is not a reliable determination of the sex. The upper HW is metallic blue or green; the VHW has bright red-orange spots. The males are brighter than the females. In addition, the male has a pocket of scent scales along the anal margin of the HW. The submarginal whitish spots of the upper FW are larger in the female. Spring forms are much smaller than the summer and fall forms.

Distribution and Habitat. This nominate subspecies ranges from New England and southern Ontario, south to central Florida, and westward to Arizona. In the fall, strays have been found in southern California.

In Indiana it is common from late April to mid-September, and rarely to 13 October, in woodland paths and trails, meadows, fields, gardens, orchards, roadsides, and along streams. Eventually, *B. p. philenor* will most likely be recorded in every county of the state. This species is rather difficult to capture unless it is resting on flowers or fluttering around a decoy impaled on a lower branch.

The Pipevine Swallowtail has a distasteful chemical in its body (evidently derived from its larval foodplants), which keeps rodents, birds, and other predators from eating it. Thus *B. p. philenor* serves as a protective model for several palatable species that closely resemble or mimic the dark colors of the adult *philenor*. Reportedly, these mimics include the dark female *Pterourus g. glaucus,* female *P. t. troilus,* female *Papilio polyxenes asterius*—all swallowtails, and also *Basilarchia arthemis astyanax* (both sexes), and the female *Speyeria diana.* On 20 July 1977 I collected the model and all of the mimics listed above except *S. diana* at Camp Mack, Milford, Kosciusko County. I have never collected *S. diana* in Indiana. It is exceedingly rare in the state; however, I have a few specimens from Virginia.

Life Cycle. The spherical, rust-colored eggs are laid in clusters. The dark purplish brown larva has three paired rows of tentacles, which are longest on the head. The pupa is pale brown or lavender to greenish yellow.

Its larval foodplants are Dutchman's Pipe (*Aristolochia macrophylla*), Virginia Snake-root (*A. serpentaria*), Wild Ginger (*Asarum*), and Knotweed (*Polygonum*). This species overwinters as a pupa or adult.

I found one pair *in copula* 23 April 1976, 2:50 P.M., 70° F, Silver Lake, Kosciusko County. The mating pair settled on a branch of a Hawthorn tree. The female was the active flight partner. It has two broods in Indiana.

Tribe Leptocirini W. F. Kirby
Genus *Eurytides* Hübner

55. *Eurytides marcellus* Cramer. Zebra Swallowtail. Plates X, XI.

Description. The wingspread varies from 2.4 to 3.5 inches (60–89 mm), depending on seasonal differences and sex. Spring specimens of *E. marcellus* are small with short wings and short tails, and the dark areas are more restricted. Later spring specimens are called "*telamonides*" and are larger with longer wings and wider dark markings and show more white on the tips of the tails. The summer form is referred to as "*lecontei*" and is much larger, with longer wings and tails, and restricted light and red markings. The summer forms are the darkest and may be found until mid-October in Indiana. The photographs show that the Zebra Swallowtail is one of our most distinctive and beautiful butterflies.

Distribution and Habitat. This species ranges from the Lake States and southern Ontario east to New England and south along the Atlantic to central Florida and the Gulf states.

In Indiana the Zebra Swallowtail is widely scattered throughout the state; however, the northwestern counties probably need to be researched more extensively. It is fairly common (most years) from April to October. Adults were still flying on 13 October 1968 in a woods, Silver Lake, Kosciusko County. Look for *marcellus* on woodland trails and flyways, in meadows bordering forested areas, along waterways, and in hayfields. It is a strong flier and is easily damaged by a vigorous swing of the net. When *marcellus* is resting on flowers, put the net down carefully from a position directly above it. A decoy Zebra placed on a wet patch will soon attract others.

Life Cycle. The green egg hatches into a smooth, pea-green larva with yellow and black cross-bands, widest and darkest in the thoracic region. The pupa is short and stubby. The larval foodplant is the Pawpaw (*Asimina triloba*). This species overwinters in the pupal stage.

I have found two pairs *in copula*: 16 June 1968, 9:00 P.M. and 19 May 1978, 1:45 P.M., 82° F, both in a woods near Silver Lake, Kosciusko County. The flight partner of the first pair could not be determined because the pair took refuge in a dense raspberry patch. In the second pair the female was the flight partner. The Zebra Swallowtail has two broods in Indiana, possibly three.

PLATE VIII

Pipevine Swallowtail, *Battus philenor philenor* UP♂. 1 August 1969, Silver Lake, Kosciusko Co., IN.
B. p. philenor UN♂. 1 August 1973, Silver Lake, Kosciusko Co., IN.

PLATE IX

Pipevine Swallowtail, *Battus philenor philenor* UP♀, summer form. 23 August 1979, North Manchester, Wabash Co., IN.
B. p. philenor UN♀, spring form. 22 May 1978, Silver Lake, Kosciusko Co., IN.

PLATE X

Zebra Swallowtail, *Eurytides marcellus* UP♂, summer form. 27 July 1973, Silver Lake, Kosciusko Co., IN.

E. marcellus UN♀, summer form. 26 June 1977, Silver Lake, Kosciusko Co., IN.

PLATE XI

Zebra Swallowtail, *Eurytides marcellus* UP♂, spring form. 13 May 1978, Silver Lake, Kosciusko Co., IN. This specimen was mating with the next one.
E. marcellus UP♀, spring form. 13 May 1978, Silver Lake, Kosciusko Co., IN.

Tribe Papilionini Latreille

Genus *Papilio* Linnaeus

56. *Papilio polyxenes asterius* Stoll. Eastern Black Swallowtail. Plates XII, XIII.

Description. The wingspread is 2.6 to 3.5 inches (67–89 mm). This Swallowtail is bluish black above with more blue on the HW, especially in the female. The band of yellow spots is more prominent in the male, but the spots are narrower in the female. The bright orange eyespot, with its black-centered pupil in the HW, is distinctive. The female mimics *Battus philenor*.

Distribution and Habitat. This species ranges from southern Canada to Florida, westward to the Rockies, through New Mexico to Arizona and southward to Mexico.

The Eastern Black Swallowtail is common throughout Indiana from late April to 22 October (rarely). It frequents gardens, meadows, open fields, edges of streams and lakes; however, it seldom flies in the woods. When feeding on nectar, it is easily captured.

Life Cycle. The egg is yellow. The young larva is brownish black with a white saddle, resembling a bird dropping. The mature larva is leafy green with each segment crossed by a black band dotted with tiny, round yellow spots. The overwintering pupa is brown or leafy green.

The larval foodplants are mostly species of the Parsley family (Umbelliferae): Carrot, Parsley, Caraway, Celery, Dill, Wild Carrot (*Daucus*), and others. Thus, it sometimes becomes a destructive pest in our gardens.

One record of *P. p. asterius in copula* was reported to me by my daughter, Linda Fisher, who has a minor in college biology. A pair was captured while breeding on 5 July 1978, 3:30 P.M., Daleville, Delaware County. Unfortunately, the active flight partner was not determined. In Indiana this species has two or more broods. The first-brood individuals are smaller, with larger yellow spots than those of the dry-season brood.

Genus *Heraclides* Hübner

57. *Heraclides cresphontes* (Cramer). Giant Swallowtail. Plates XIV, XV.

Description. Howe (1975) and many others still place this magnificent butterfly in the genus *Papilio*. The wingspread measures 3.4 to 5.5 inches (86–140 mm), making it the largest butterfly in our area. The pictures clearly distinguish the uniquely patterned *cresphontes* from the other swallowtails. The yellow markings are more extensive on the underwing surfaces than on the upper wings.

Distribution and Habitat. The Giant Swallowtail ranges in the eastern

United States from the Canadian border to Mexico and westward along the southern border to Arizona.

In Indiana it is fairly common some years in the northern half of the state, especially in August; however, adults fly from April 30 to late August. Masters and Masters (1969) refer to the Perry County specimens as *H. cresphontes pennsylvanicus* Chermock & Chermock, but the subspecific differences are probably of minor significance. Records of *cresphontes* are greatly needed from many of our southern counties.

The Giant Swallowtail, or "Orange Dog," prefers citrus groves or paths and trails through the woods. Great success in catching these strong fliers can be achieved by impaling the first specimen on a thorn or twig within easy reach of the net. Look for them in clover/alfalfa fields, along forest edges, roadsides and glades. Apparently *cresphontes* is not as rare and sporadic in our area as in many areas of its range.

Life Cycle. The mature larva is olive or dark brown with creamy white or buff markings and a broad saddle around the middle of the body. The scent horns (osmateria) are orange and diffuse a very strong odor.

In Indiana its favorite larval foodplants are the various forms of cultivated citrus, especially the cultivated orange tree found in greenhouses. In our woodlands the larva feeds on Prickly Ash (*Zanthoxylum americanum*) (September in Kosciusko County) and Hoptree leaves (*Ptelea*). If you raise the larvae, remember that they require a constant supply of fresh leaves. The pupa is mottled with grayish brown. In its northern range *cresphontes* has two broods.

Genus *Pterourus* Scopoli

58. *Pterourus glaucus glaucus* (Linnaeus). Tiger Swallowtail. Plates XVI, XVII, XVIII, XIX.

Description. The wingspread of the Tiger Swallowtail measures from 3.1 to 5.5 inches (79–140 mm), averaging smaller than *H. cresphontes*. In Indiana dimorphic females (black and yellow) are found, but surprisingly most of the females in the state are black. Usually in its northern range most of the females are yellow.

Distribution and Habitat. This species occurs from central Alaska and Canada to the Atlantic and southeast of the Rocky Mountains to the Gulf. Thus, the nominate *glaucus* is found throughout most of the United States east of the Rockies.

The Tiger Swallowtail is common throughout Indiana from early April to mid-October. Adults fly in town and country, frequenting woodlands, gardens, fields, rivers, streams, roadsides, hilly and open areas. The black *glaucus* female form mimics the distasteful Pipevine Swallowtail. Adult males (always yellow) are often seen flying high in the treetops. I have watched them dart down at the more secretive black females when they appear near the forest

PLATE XII

Eastern Black Swallowtail, *Papilio polyxenes asterius* UP♂. 10 July 1969, Silver
Lake, Kosciusko Co., IN.
P. p. asterius UN♂. 21 August 1973, Delphi, Carroll Co., IN.

PLATE XIII

Eastern Black Swallowtail, *Papilio polyxenes asterius* UP♀. 1 August 1973, Silver
  Lake, Kosciusko Co., IN.
P. p. asterius UN♀. 2 August 1969, Mongo, LaGrange Co., IN.

PLATE XIV

Giant Swallowtail, *Heraclides cresphontes* UP♂. 27 July 1978, Silver Lake, Kosciusko
   Co., IN.
H. cresphontes UN♂. 1 August 1973, Silver Lake, Kosciusko Co., IN.

PLATE XV

Giant Swallowtail, *Heraclides cresphontes* UP♀. 27 July 1978, Silver Lake, Kosciusko Co., IN.
H. cresphontes UN♀. 5 August 1978, North Manchester, Wabash Co., IN.

PLATE XVI

Tiger Swallowtail, *Pterourus glaucus glaucus* UP♂. 21 July 1969, Peru, Miami Co.,
  IN.
P. g. glaucus UN♂. 21 August 1984, Brown County State Park, Nashville, IN.

PLATE XVII

Tiger Swallowtail, *Pterourus glaucus glaucus* UP♀, black form. 15 May 1982, Mongo, LaGrange Co., IN.

P. g. glaucus UN♀, black form. 7 August 1973, North Manchester, Wabash Co., IN.

PLATE XVIII

Tiger Swallowtail, *Pterourus glaucus glaucus* UP♀, yellow form. 9 August 1981, Camp Mack, Milford, Kosciusko Co., IN.

P. g. glaucus UN♀, yellow form. 25 July 1984, Mongo, LaGrange Co., IN.

PLATE XIX

Tiger Swallowtail, *Pterourus glaucus glaucus* UP♂, partially melanic. 21 August 1984, Brown County State Park, Nashville, IN.

floor. Adults feed on nectar from a wide variety of flowers, domestic and wild. On cold mornings, when the wings are pumping to control body temperature (thermoregulation), adults are easily caught. On cold evenings the adults open their wings toward the setting sun.

Life Cycle. The yellowish green egg is globular and large for a butterfly. The young larva is brown and white, resembling bird droppings. The mature larva is green and swollen in front; it has large false eyespots of orange and black. The sticklike pupa is mottled green or brown. This species overwinters in its pupal stage.

The larval foodplants of the Tiger Swallowtail include a great variety of plants, mostly broadleaf trees and shrubs: Cherry (*Prunus*), Birch (*Betula*), Mountain Ash (*Sorbus*), Poplar (*Populus*), Willow (*Salix*), Apple (*Malus*), Tulip Tree (*Liriodendron*), Maple (*Acer*), Basswood (*Tilia*), and *Magnolia*.

I have collected only one pair *in copula*: 8 August 1981, 5:00 P.M., 70° F, following a rain, Lake Waubee, Kosciusko County. The mating pair was resting on a wet patch of ground. When I touched the black female with my finger, it took off carrying the limp, yellow male which had its wings closed. The active flight partner is not always so easily determined. This species probably has two broods in Indiana.

59. *Pterourus troilus troilus* (Linnaeus). Spicebush Swallowtail. Plates XX, XXI, XXII.

Description. The wingspread measures from 3.5 to 4.5 inches (89–114 mm). Both the male and the female are brownish black above with creamy white or yellowish spots around the outer margin of the FW. The clouded green areas in the HW of the male distinguish it from the female, where the comparable area is blue and somewhat more extensive. In both sexes the VHW has two rows of bright, curved red-orange spots. The Eastern Black Swallowtail and the Pipevine Swallowtail lack the dorsal orange spot on the costa of the HW.

Distribution and Habitat. The Spicebush Swallowtail ranges from southern Canada south to Florida and west to eastern Texas and eastern Kansas. It generally occurs east of the Mississippi River.

P. t. troilus has been reported throughout Indiana. Adults fly from late April to 13 October (late), where it is common in woodlands, pine barrens, fields, orchards, gardens, edges of forests, along streams and rivers, and wherever flowers grow. I have found them in huge mud-puddle associations, especially on the Skinner Creek trails in Brown County. Sassafras grows in large clumps in the Brown County State Park, attracting hundreds of individuals.

Life Cycle. The pale green egg hatches into a dark green larva with two eyespots on the metathorax and two less prominent spots back of the hump. The smooth chrysalis is grayish brown and somewhat swollen near the wing cases. It overwinters in the pupal stage.

The larval foodplants or hostplants of *troilus* include Spicebush (*Benzoin*), Sassafras, Magnolia, and Prickly Ash (*Zanthoxylum americanum*).

I have collected only one pair of this common butterfly *in copula:* 17 August 1971, 1:15 P.M., 76° F, Silver Lake, Kosciusko County, mating in a woodland raspberry patch. After chasing the disturbed pair for nearly 100 yards through the woods with its heavy underbrush, the author determined that the female was the active flight partner; however, sex determination in such crowded quarters was difficult. It has two broods in Indiana.

Family Pieridae Duponchel

The Pieridae includes the Whites, Sulphurs, Marbles, and Orangetips. World-wide this large family contains approximately 1000 species; however, only 50 to 60 species have been found in North America. Presently, Indiana has 14 species. A majority of the pierids are some shade of white, yellow, or yellowish green; only a few species have orange wing tips, or greenish yellow marbling. Seasonal forms abound, varying greatly in size and color. Life history details will be presented under each species found in Indiana. Howe (1975) gives the distinguishing characteristics of this family.

Subfamily Pierinae Duponchel
?♠

Tribe Pierini Duponchel
?♠

Genus *Pontia* Fabricius

60. *Pontia protodice* Boisduval and Leconte. Checkered White. Plate XXIII.

Description. Some experts prefer the genus *Pieris* over *Pontia* for this species. The wingspread of *protodice* measures from 1.25 to 1.75 inches (32–45 mm). Generally, this pierid is white with charcoal or brown markings, but the females are more heavily marked than the males. Spring-form males are darker than the summer males, which are nearly immaculate white except for the black spot in the FW cell. Numerous gradations of color occur. The color pattern of the dorsal side is repeated on the ventral side, with more dark scales along the veins of the HW.

Distribution and Habitat. *P. protodice* occurs more commonly in the southern half of the United States from California to Florida, and less commonly northward to New York, Michigan, North Dakota, Montana, and Oregon. Rarely, it may be found in southern Alberta and southern Manitoba. Along with other collectors, I found it to be common in Mexico.

In Indiana the Checkered White is not as common as the introduced Eu-

PLATE XX

Spicebush Swallowtail, *Pterourus troilus troilus* UP♂. 14 August 1975, Silver Lake, Kosciusko Co., IN.
P. t. troilus UN♂. 2 August 1969, Mongo, LaGrange Co., IN.

PLATE XXI

Spicebush Swallowtail, *Pterourus troilus troilus* UP♀. 14 August 1976, Silver Lake, Kosciusko Co., IN.
P. t. troilus UN♀. 15 May 1982, Mongo, LaGrange Co., IN.

PLATE XXII

Spicebush Swallowtail, *Pterourus troilus troilus* UP♂, aberrant wing shape. 5 August 1977, Brown County State Park, Nashville, IN.

Pipevine Swallowtail, *Battus philenor philenor* UP♂, aberrant wing shape. 31 August 1978, Silver Lake, Kosciusko Co., IN.

PLATE XXIII

Top row

Checkered White, *Pontia protodice* UP♂. 4 July 1978, Mongo, LaGrange Co., IN.
P. protodice UN♂. 24 August 1971, Mongo, LaGrange Co., IN.
P. protodice UP♂, "dwarf." 24 August 1971, Mongo, LaGrange Co., IN.

Second row

P. protodice UP♀. 24 August 1971, Mongo, LaGrange Co., IN.
P. protodice UN♀. 18 August 1977, Silver Lake, Kosciusko Co., IN.
P. protodice UP♀, "dwarf." 24 August 1971, Mongo, LaGrange Co., IN.

Third row

Veined White or Mustard White, *Artogeia napi oleracea* UP♂, heavily veined spring form. 14 April 1978, Mongo Tamarack Bog, LaGrange Co., IN.
A. n. oleracea UN♂, spring form. 29 April 1978, Mongo Tamarack Bog, LaGrange Co., IN.
A. n. oleracea UN♀, spring form. 29 April 1978, Mongo Tamarack Bog, LaGrange Co., IN.

Fourth row

A. n. oleracea UP♀, with faint spots. 10 May 1978, Mongo Tamarack Bog, LaGrange Co., IN.
A. n. oleracea UP♂, summer form. 24 June 1982, Mongo Tamarack Bog, LaGrange Co., IN.
A. n. oleracea UN♂, summer form. 8 August 1984, Mongo Tamarack Bog, LaGrange Co., IN.

Fifth row

A. n. oleracea UP♂, with faint spots on upper wing. 23 June 1977, Mongo Tamarack Bog, LaGrange Co., IN.
Cabbage White, *Artogeia rapae* UP♂. 17 June 1969, Silver Lake, Kosciusko Co., IN.
A. rapae UN♂. 20 September 1984, North Manchester, Wabash Co., IN.

ropean Cabbage White. Competition between these two species may have restricted the populations of *protodice*. Adults fly from early spring (April) to October; however, the summer forms are sometimes scarce or absent. The Checkered White seems to prefer dry fields, vacant lots, railroad yards, weedy plots, and waste places.

Life Cycle. The spindle-shaped egg is yellow. The mature larva is bluish green, speckled with black, striped with purplish green, and covered with downy hairs. The pupa is bluish gray with black specks. The larva feeds on most species of Cruciferae (Cabbage and Mustard family). Because many of these plants grow in our gardens, it would become a pest were it more abundant.

I have found one pair *in copula:* 24 August 1971, 11:15 A.M., 65° F, Mongo, LaGrange County. The male, as in all pierids, was the active flight partner. When the female rejects the approaches of the male, she does so by raising her abdomen to an almost perpendicular angle over her own thorax and then vigorously vibrates her abdomen. In some cases the female simply flies high into the air when being pursued by a determined male or males, until both sexes give up and flutter to the ground, usually far apart. *Protodice* has three broods in the northern part of its broader range.

Genus *Artogeia* Verity

61. *Artogeia napi oleracea* Harris. Veined White; Mustard White. Plate XXIII.

Description. Some writers still prefer to place this species in the genus *Pieris*. The wingspread measures 1.5 to 1.6 inches (32–41 mm). Not only is this species geographically variable, but the generations vary from one brood to another. The Veined White is a chalky white butterfly, usually without black markings on the upper wing surfaces except for brownish black dustings and traces of black on the apical border. The VHW and the apex of the FW are yellowish white. In the spring form the veins are more prominent and greener than in the summer and fall forms. The latter-season forms are often unmarked except for dustings of black and yellow, especially on the VHW.

I have collected a few specimens in the Mongo Tamarack bog which have a faint spot in cell M_3 of the FW. The spot or spots in *Artogeia rapae* are larger and always present. (There may be some cross mating between *napi* and *rapae*.)

Distribution and Habitat. This species occurs in the Canadian Zone of northern United States and Canada, west to the Pacific. Blatchley (1891) reported *Pieris napi oleracea-aestiva* Harris from Kosciusko County, the specimens being collected by A. B. Ulrey in the summer of 1890.

The first specimens I found in Indiana were collected on 12 July 1971 in the Mongo Tamarack bog, LaGrange County. Since that date I have collected a few specimens there every year, including the various seasonal forms. In the bog, it is not uncommon from 29 April to 9 September. David Eiler (personal communication) found *A. napi oleracea* in the Cedar Lake bog, LaGrange County, on 26 July 1980. *Artogeia napi oleracea* formerly occurred in northern Illinois, but it is now apparently extirpated in the state (Irwin & Downey, 1973, Illinois Natural History Survey).

The Veined White usually prefers bogs, where it can be seen slowly flying up and down the streams choked with watercress (Cruciferae). Jewelweed (*Impatiens*), shrubby cinquefoil (*Dasiphora fruticosa*), the dangerous poison sumac (*Rhus vernix*), and narrow-leaved and broad-leaved cattail (*Typha*) grow near the somewhat hidden streams. Only rarely will the Veined Whites leave the bog and only occasionally will the European Cabbage Whites visit flowers in the bog. Thus, the purity of both species may be assured. A similar species, *Artogeia virginiensis*, occurs in Michigan, but its habitat and flight patterns are distinctly different. *A. virginiensis* flies only in April and May.

Life Cycle. The pale egg is vase-shaped. The mature larva is greenish with a middorsal stripe and a yellow lateral stripe on each side of the abdomen.

I have found five pairs *in copula,* all in the Mongo Tamarack bog, LaGrange County, and all near Watercress (*Nasturtium officinale*). The first pair was found 23 July 1975 at 12:35 P.M., 90° F. On 29 April 1978, 11:00 A.M., 70° F, the heavily veined spring form was observed *in copula* on a leaf of a Marsh Marigold (*Caltha palustris*) close to its larval foodplant, *Nasturtium officinale*. Two more pairs were found 11 July 1978 at 2:25 P.M., the temperature reading 73° F for both pairs. The fifth pair was found 8 August 1978, 10:45 A.M., 70° F. In every case the male was the active flight partner. *A. napi oleracea* has three broods in Indiana. It usually occurs in small or medium-sized colonies in our northern bogs.

Besides the Watercress, other host plants are *Dentaria, Barbarea, Arabis, Thlaspi arvense,* and perhaps other Cruciferae.

62. *Artogeia rapae* (Linnaeus). Cabbage White. Plates XXIII, XXIV.

Description. *A. rapae* has a wingspread of 1.25 to 1.9 inches (32–48 mm). The male has only one submarginal spot on the FW while the female has two spots. All Whites of similar size that might be confused with the Cabbage White have been described earlier in this work.

Distribution and Habitat. The Cabbage White was accidentally introduced from Europe into Quebec and then spread throughout most of North America. It occurs in all life zones from Lower Austral to Canadian; however, it may be scarce or absent in desert or semidesert regions unless those dry areas have been irrigated. It has spread to the Hawaiian Islands and other Pacific islands.

The Cabbage White is the only Indiana butterfly that I have found in all 92

PLATE XXIV

Top row   Cabbage White, *Artogeia rapae* UP♀. 20 September 1984, North Manchester, Wabash Co., IN.

A. rapae UN♀. 20 September 1984, North Manchester, Wabash Co., IN.

A. rapae UP♀, lower ocelli on upper wing diffused. 20 October 1983, Silver Lake, Kosciusko Co., IN.

Second row   *A. rapae* UP♀, "dwarf." 10 September 1969, North Manchester, Wabash Co., IN.

Olympia Marblewing, *Euchloe olympia* UP♂. 26 May 1979, Lyman, SD.

E. olympia UN♀. 26 May 1979, Lyman, SD.

Third row   Falcate Orangetip, *Falcapica midea* UP♂. 11 April 1976, Rochelle, Madison Co., VA.

F. midea UN♂. 11 April 1976, Rochelle, Madison Co., VA.

Common Sulphur, *Colias philodice philodice* UP♂, small. 20 August 1967, North Manchester, Wabash Co., IN.

Fourth row   *C. p. philodice* UP♂. 30 August 1969, Silver Lake, Kosciusko Co., IN.

C. p. philodice UN♂. 20 September 1984, North Manchester, Wabash Co., IN.

C. p. philodice UP♀. 27 June 1969, Silver Lake, Kosciusko Co., IN.

Fifth row   *C. p. philodice* UN♀. 27 June 1969, Silver Lake, Kosciusko Co., IN.

C. p. philodice UP♀, "*alba*." 7 September 1968, Silver Lake, Kosciusko Co., IN.

C. p. philodice UN♀, "*alba*." 4 June 1970, North Manchester, Wabash Co., IN.

counties. Adults are very common throughout the state from late March to early November. Look for it everywhere in town, country, and city.

Life Cycle. Its life history has been described in many books and agricultural pamphlets. The larvae feed on all of the cruciferous crops in our area, making this species a very serious pest.

Between 1970 and 1982 I have collected 406 pairs of the Cabbage White *in copula*. Only a very brief summary of the most relevant data will be presented.

Mating occurs from early morning until late in the evening (from 9:30 A.M. to 6:30 P.M.). A few probably remain *in copula* throughout the night. Pierids, like most other butterflies, generally mate on warm, humid days, periods free from strong winds but not necessarily free from gentle rain followed by periods of sunshine. In general, mating occurs from 11:00 A.M. until 4:00 P.M. Temperatures at which mating has been observed vary from a low of 64° F (rare) to a high of 98° F; however, the mid-70s to mid-80s account for the vast majority of observations. The Cabbage White may be found copulating almost anywhere, even while flying across a major highway. Alfalfa fields, clover fields, and gardens where cabbages and other Cruciferae (larval foodplants) grow, supplied the greatest number of breeding pairs.

Although many entomologists report only three broods, my data show that in 1969 there were five broods in northeastern Indiana: (1) 23 April to 6 May; (2) 16 June to 1 July; (3) 12 July to 4 August; (4) 19 August to 5 September; and (5) 14 September to 22 September. This fact should not go unnoticed, for this serious European pest has been found breeding in a dozen or more counties. The Cabbage White has three to five broods each year.

Numerous observations show that a female that is unprepared for copulation will raise her abdomen nearly upright above the opened wings and vibrate both abdomen and antennae, a proven rejection method. A mating pair may be bombarded by five or more males, but the author has never seen the copulating pair separated by the additional male activity.

Subfamily Anthocharinae Tuft

ఇ

Tribe Anthocharini Tuft

ఇ

Genus *Euchloe* Hübner

63. *Euchloe olympia* (W. H. Edwards). Olympia Marblewing. Plate XXIV.

Description. The wingspread measures 1.5 to 1.75 inches (38–44 mm). Members of this Holarctic genus lack the orange tips found in some of the tropical species. A similar species, *Falcapica midea,* has orange wing tips and is found in southern Indiana. In *E. olympia* the VHW is marbled with green,

forming three rather distinct bands, and the dorsal FW has light gray markings on the apex.

Distribution and Habitat. It ranges from West Virginia and Pennsylvania to Minnesota and Colorado south to Texas. There are authentic records for Indiana, Illinois, and Michigan.

In Indiana *olympia* is local and rare, reported mostly from the northwestern counties. Adult Olympia are warier than the other pierids, flying rapidly away from their pursuers. Howe and others mention the hilltopping behavior of this species. Males fly back and forth, "patroling" a particular area of the open hillside. I observed this phenomenon among many species in the West Himalayas.

Adult Olympia have a brief flight period, mid-April to mid-May. Sidney Badger (personal communication) found it in Lake and Pulaski counties. When an adult is resting, with its wings nearly closed, on yellow mustard flowers, the camouflage is almost perfect.

Life Cycle. The mature larva is bright green with lateral and dorsal lines of slate blue and a subdorsal yellowish line on each side of the body. The chrysalis is rosy purple at first, then fades to grayish brown. The larvae feed on the buds and flowers of several kinds of Cruciferae, especially on Hedge Mustard (*Sisymbrium officinale*) and Rock Cress (*Arabis lyrata*). Olympia overwinters in the pupal stage. The species is univoltine (one brood).

Genus *Falcapica* Klots

64. *Falcapica midea midea* (Hübner). Falcate Orangetip. Plate XXIV.

Description. This nominate subspecies has a wingspread of 1.4 to 1.5 inches (35–38 mm). Formerly, *midea* was placed in the genus *Anthocharis*. Hoosiers can be proud that this beautiful butterfly was selected to appear on a 13-cent U.S. postage stamp with first-day sales in Indianapolis on 6 June 1977. The hooked, or "falcate," apex of the FW is characteristic. Both sexes are basically white, but only the male has the orange patch on the apex of the FW. The VHW is finely mottled with yellow and brown.

Distribution and Habitat. It occurs from Massachusetts and Connecticut, south to Georgia, and west to Illinois and Texas. Apparently it is not uncommon in the southern counties of Indiana bordering on the Ohio River. Otherwise it is scarce or absent.

Adults fly from late April to mid-May, the flight period seldom lasting over two weeks. Their flight is rather low, erratic, and slow. Look for this orangetip in deciduous forests and mixed open Pine-Oak or Oak-Hickory woodlands, as well as along streams and rocky sites. Hilltopping behavior has also been observed in this species.

Life Cycle. The small elongated ovum is greenish yellow. The mature larva is moss green and finely striped with a multitude of colors. The dorsal stripe is orange and the lateral stripe is white and somewhat wide. The slender, long pupa has a spinelike process on its head.

The larval foodplants of the Falcate Orange consist of various kinds of Cruciferae: *Arabis, Cardamine, Barbarea, Capsella bursa-pastoris* (Shepherd's Purse), and *Sisymbrium officinale*. Larvae feed only on the flowers, buds, and tender seed pods.

In its northern range it has only one brood. It overwinters in the pupal stage.

Subfamily Coliadinae Swainson
Ꮚ
Tribe Coliadini Swainson
Ꮚ
Genus *Colias* Fabricius

65. *Colias philodice philodice* Godart. Common Sulphur. Plates XXIV, XXV.

Description. The wingspread of this yellow sulphur measures 1.4 to 2 inches (35–51 mm). Both sexes are greenish yellow in the spring and fall, and mostly yellow in midsummer. The males always have a blackish border without spots, and the females have yellow or white spots in the border areas. Both sexes, and the albino female form, have the dark spot in the FW cell and the orange spot in the lower wing cell, the spots varying in intensity. Putative hybrids from *philodice* x *eurytheme* often have over half of the wing covered with orange patches.

Distribution and Habitat. The Common Sulphur ranges over most of North America northward into the Hudsonian Zone; however, it is rare or absent in peninsular Florida and western California. It avoids deserts and heavily forested areas.

It occurs throughout Indiana, particularly in clover fields, parks, pastures, and gardens. *Philodice* is a very common species, adults occurring from late March to mid-November. In 1969 I collected very large specimens in Delphi, Carroll County. Large mud-puddle associations occur; frequently the butterflies all face in the same direction, with their wings nearly or completely closed.

Life Cycle. The eggs are yellowish green and laid singly on the leaves of various legumes, especially clovers (*Trifolium*). The mature larva is yellowish green with a darker middorsal line and an irregular whitish lateral line. The green pupa loses its color as the imago within develops. The larval foodplants consist of numerous legumes (Leguminoseae), both native and introduced species.

From 1968 through 1982 I have collected or observed 118 pairs *in copula*. As in *A. rapae*, the information is overwhelming and difficult to analyze. Only a few pairs were mating before 11:00 A.M., the vast majority mating between noon and 4:00 P.M. A few, however, were mating as late as 6:35 P.M. The coldest mating temperature was 60° F, but most activity occurred during the higher 70s and the 80s. Courting activity normally begins when the temperature reaches 68° F. Mating reaches a peak in August and September; however, mating occurs from mid-June until early October. In Indiana this species is bivoltine.

Colias philodice and the next species, *Colias eurytheme*, occasionally hybridize, but from 1964 to 1982 only two pairs have been found crossbreeding, even though both species fly together in the same hayfields. It should be noted that *philodice* does best on clovers (*Trifolium*) while *eurytheme* is more successful on alfalfa (*Medicago sativa*). On 5 September 1969 a female *C. eurytheme* was found mating with a male *C. philodice*, 1:05 P.M., Silver Lake, Kosciusko County. The other pair was collected 24 August 1977, 1:25 P.M., 64° F, at Silver Lake, with the male again being *philodice*. Although some hybridization takes place between these two species, it is best for the present to treat them as two separate species.

Only one male of *C. eurytheme* was found breeding with an "*alba*" form female. This is quite a contrast to *C. philodice*, where 40 percent of the mating females were "*alba*" forms. It is hard to explain genetically why such a high percentage of *philodice* males mated with "*alba*" females. This matter needs more research. The rejection method of this species is the same as used by other pierids. The male is always the active flight partner.

66. *Colias eurytheme* Boisduval. Orange Sulphur; Alfalfa Butterfly. Plate XXV.

Description. *C. eurytheme* has a wingspread of 1.6 to 2.4 inches (41–60 mm). Both sexes are much alike, being bright orange on the dorsal wing surfaces, with black borders, except for the yellow spots found in the borders of the females. The FW cell spot is black and the HW cell spot reddish orange. The underwing surfaces are orange or greenish yellow with prominent spots. As in the former species, the Orange Sulphur shows great seasonal variation in size and color. Some variants may be hybrids (*eurytheme* x *philodice*). Melanic and aberrant individuals are known. Spring specimens have much median yellow.

Distribution and Habitat. The species ranges from the Maritime Provinces west to the Pacific, south to subtropical Florida, and in the coastal Northwest.

It is common throughout Indiana from May to November. Although it prefers alfalfa fields, it can be found in gardens and open places. In 1969 I collected very large *eurytheme* in Delphi, Carroll County.

Life Cycle. The long, pitcher-shaped white egg is laid on either side of a leaf. The larva is grassy green with a lateral pink stripe just below a white stripe; the body is covered with tiny white hairs. The greenish pupa shows dashes of yellow and black. It overwinters in the pupal stage.

PLATE XXV

Larvae are injurious to legumes, sometimes becoming a serious pest to alfalfa crops.

I have found 23 pairs of *Colias eurytheme in copula,* mostly in alfalfa fields, from 1968 through 1982. Pairs were found mating between 11:55 A.M. and 4:35 P.M., with the temperatures usually in the 70s and 80s. However, one pair was mating at a cold 64° F. The male is always the active flight partner. *C. eurytheme* apparently copulate later in the day than *C. philodice.* The Orange Sulphur has at least two broods.

Genus *Zerene* Hübner

67. *Zerene cesonia* (Stoll). Dogface Butterfly. Plate XXVI.

Description. The wingspread usually measures 1.9 to 2.5 inches (48–64 mm). The wing surfaces, above and below, are mostly yellow in both sexes. The FW is somewhat curved and pointed. The black markings in the upper FW, along with the black "eye" spot in the cell, suggest a dog's face or head. Late cold-weather individuals often have a rosy scaling, especially on the VHW and the tips of the FW (form "*rosa*"). White females have been reported. This species is quite variable.

Distribution and Habitat. It ranges from southern California to Florida, irregularly north through the midwest to Canada and northeast, south to Argentina. Do not confuse our midwestern species with the California Dogface Butterfly, *Z. eurydice,* which appeared on a 13-cent U.S. postage stamp in 1977.

Blatchley (1891) reported *Colias caesonia* (name used then) from our western border counties: Vanderburgh, Lake, and Vigo. In October 1877 three or four specimens were taken near ponds in the Wabash River bottom, Vigo County, but Blatchley says that it has not been seen since. No doubt his records were correct, for he stated that the larvae feed upon clover and False Indigo (*Amorpha fruticosa*). Lee D. Miller found it to be very common in Warrick County in the summer of 1957 (personal communication). Masters and Masters (1969) state that *Colias (Zerene) cesonia cesonia* can be found each year in Perry County in September and October, though the numbers are quite variable. According to Irwin and Downey (1973), the first author took two fresh males at Cornell, Livingston County, Illinois, on 16 August 1966, where it is uncommon to rare. The majority of Illinois records occur in late summer and autumn; however, an early date was 5 April and the late date was 15 October. Immigrant species wander far from their breeding grounds, especially when populations become overcrowded. In Mexico the Dogface Butterfly was abundant (by dozens and sometimes hundreds) on roadside flowers (1973 collecting trip).

Life Cycle. The mature caterpillar is green with a light lateral line. The body is cross-banded with yellow and black. Even the larvae have many individual variants. The main larval foodplants are False Indigo (*Amorpha californica*), Lead Plant (*A. fruticosa*), and clovers (*Trifolium*). The Dogface Butterfly hibernates as a pupa and/or an adult.

Genus *Phoebis* Hübner

68. *Phoebis sennae eubule* (Linnaeus). Cloudless Giant Sulphur. Plate XXVI.

Description. The wingspread of this species ranges from about 2.5 to 2.75 inches (63–70 mm). The males are yellow or lemon yellow above and unmarked. Beneath there are a few faint, scattered pinkish spots. Females are fringed with marginal black spots; a distinct eyespot occurs in the FW cell. White forms are also known.

Distribution and Habitat. This subspecies occurs in the southeastern United States from the Subtropical to the Upper Austral Zone; also in states adjacent to the Mexican border, straying northward to Colorado, Nebraska, and New York. In Indiana it has been recorded in 14 counties, mostly in the western and southern counties. Blatchley (1891) reported *eubule* only from Vanderburgh County, where a Mr. Evans took one to six specimens almost every season, in open woods, during July and August.

On 31 May 1978 I collected one male, which was flying very fast and only a few feet above the ground, in an open, woody area in the Brown County State Park, not far from Skinner Creek. I've taken a few there in July and August, probably migrants. In any case Cloudless Sulphurs are sporadic and migratory in our state wherever found. Migratory hordes may be a possibility.

Life Cycle. The pitcher-shaped egg is white at first, soon turning pale orange. The mature larva is yellow or greenish, striped laterally, with black dots across the back. The larva constructs a tent made by pulling the leaf of one of its foodplants together. By day it hides in this tent made of leaf and silk.

Its larval foodplants are Partridge Pea (*Chamaecrista cinerea*), sennas (*Cassia*), and clovers (Fabaceae). Two broods occur in the northern part of its range.

69. *Phoebis philea* (Johanssen). Orange-barred Giant Sulphur. Plate XXVI.

Description. This beautiful pierid is truly a giant; it has a wingspread of 2.75 to 3.25 inches (70–83 mm). Its yellow and orange patterns distinguish *philea* from all other butterflies.

Distribution and Habitat. This species occurs over much of the New World Tropics, south Florida, and south Texas. Infrequently it strays northward to Nebraska, New York, Indiana, and Kansas.

Blatchley (1891) recorded a single specimen from Jefferson County, collected by Mr. C. C. Hubbard. The only other record is by Cooper (1938) who

PLATE XXVI

Top row Dogface Butterfly, *Zerene cesonia* UP♂. 29 July 1973, Puebla State (southern mountains, 5,000 ft), Mexico.
Z. cesonia UN♂. 29 July 1973, Puebla State (southern mountains, 5,000 ft), Mexico.
Z. cesonia UP♀. 28 July 1973, Mitla, Oaxaca State, Mexico.

Second row Cloudless Giant Sulphur, *Phoebis sennae eubule* UP♂. 31 May 1978, Brown County State Park, Nashville, IN.
P. sennae UN♂. 28 July 1973, Mitla, Oaxaca State, Mexico.

Third row *P. sennae* UP♀. 28 July 1973, Mitla, Oaxaca State, Mexico.
Orange-barred Giant Sulphur, *Phoebis philea* UP♂. 31 January 1968, Usumacinta River at border, Mexico.

Fourth row *P. philea* UN♂. 31 January 1968, Usumacinta River at border, Mexico.
Mexican Yellow or Yellow Sulphur, *Eurema mexicana* UP♂. 28 July 1973, Yagul, Mexico.

raised an imago from a larva found in Shelby County. Klots (1951) includes Indiana in its range. From 20–22 July 1973 I collected a few in Tajin, Mexico. Unless *philea* is visiting flowers, its fast flight makes capture very difficult. Look for *philea* in gardens, parks, and roadsides where flowers grow.

Life Cycle. The pale ovum is spindle-shaped. The larva is yellowish green, darker dorsally, tapering at each end. It has fine, black granulations bearing black spines. The pupa is bowed and variable in color. Its larval food-plants are sennas (*Cassia*). *Philea* is bivoltine.

Genus *Eurema* Hübner

70. *Eurema mexicana* (Boisduval). Mexican Yellow; Yellow Sulphur. Plate XXVI.

Description. It has a wingspread of 1.4 to 1.9 inches (35–48 mm). Both sexes have deeply indented black FW margins which are shaped to form a "dog's head." The wings are creamy white to pale yellow above. The male is deeper yellow on the upper margins of the DHW and DFW; the VHW is bright yellow to yellowish green with varying degrees of rust-colored dusting. The male has the black margin continuing on his short tails.

Distribution and Habitat. This little Sulphur is a Central American species, which ranges far northward into the Mississippi Valley. Strays wander to Wyoming, North Dakota, Minnesota, Ontario, and Michigan.

Irwin and Downey (1973) reported two old records from Indiana: 16 October 1904 and 7 October 1917 from Hessville, Lake County. Migrations of *E. mexicana* have been recorded in Illinois. Its appearance in our area must be sporadic and irregular. I have never seen it in Indiana, but I found it to be very common (dozens and hundreds) in Vera Cruz, Mexico, on 22 July 1973. Wherever wildflowers were in bloom along the highways, one stop could result in a tremendous catch.

Life Cycle. The life history of *mexicana* is not known in detail. Its larval foodplant is Senna (*Cassia*).

Genus *Pyrisitia* Butler

71. *Pyrisitia lisa lisa* (Boisduval and Leconte). Little Yellow. Plate XXVII.

Description. Many entomologists place *lisa* in the genus *Eurema*. The wingspread measures 1 to 1.5 inches (25–38 mm). This common and widespread little Sulphur needs very little description. In both sexes the wing surfaces are mostly yellow with black FW tips. The black wing margins are reduced on the DHW of the female. Sometimes the females are white with black markings.

Distribution and Habitat. *Lisa* occurs on mainland America and in the West Indies from south America northward to Vermont, Quebec, Ontario, Michigan, Iowa, North Dakota, and Colorado. It is common from Virginia and Kansas southward to Florida and Texas.

The Little Sulphur is usually common throughout Indiana from late May through September, rare in October; however, some years it may be absent or uncommon.

Mud-puddle associations are not uncommon. Look for *lisa* along roadsides, in clover and alfalfa fields, in open areas near trees. This species is highly migratory, occasionally being observed in huge flocks. The Midwest is frequently refilled with fresh immigrants.

Life Cycle. The egg is very small. Mature larvae are green and downy, with one or two white lateral stripes. Its larval foodplants consist of many legumes, *Cassia, Chamaecrista fasciculata, Trifolium* (clovers), and *Amphicarpa* (Hog Peanut).

Genus *Abaeis* Hübner

72. *Abaeis nicippe* (Cramer). Sleepy Orange. Plate XXVII.

Description. Howe (1975) uses the name *Eurema (Abaeis) nicippe* for this species. Its wingspread measures 1.4 to 1.9 inches (35–48 mm). The upper wing surfaces of both sexes are orange except for the black borders, which are more extensive in the male, especially noticeable on the DHW. The VHW of the female is more brownish and mottled. In the male the FW discal spot is more prominent and the DHW blackish border is toothed, a feature lacking in the female.

Distribution and Habitat. The Sleepy Orange is widespread and common in the South and Southwest; uncommon northward east of the Rocky Mountains. It occurs from the Subtropical to the Upper Austral Zone in the East and the Lower Sonoran Zone in the West (Howe, 1975).

In Indiana it is irregular and uncommon in the northern half of the state from July to November. In late summer it is more common in our southern counties. The common name, "Sleepy," is a misnomer, for its flight, when disturbed, is very rapid. Look for *nicippe* in open woodlands, margins of ponds and waterways, wet meadows, and valleys.

Life Cycle. The ovum is narrow and long. The mature greenish larva is slender, pubescent, with lateral stripes of white, yellow, and black. The pupa is ashy green to brownish black. The larvae feed on Senna (*Cassia*), clovers (*Trifolium*), and other legumes. Klots (1964) speaks of three broods; I have no breeding records for Indiana.

PLATE XXVII

Top row   Little Yellow, *Pyrisitia lisa lisa* UP♂. 13 September 1983, North Manchester, Wabash Co., IN.
P. l. lisa UN♂. 4 July 1977, Brown County State Park, Nashville, IN.
P. l. lisa UP♀. 25 September 1973, Fort Wayne, Allen Co., IN.
P. l. lisa UN♀. 6 July 1968, Silver Lake, Kosciusko Co., IN.

Second row   *P. l. lisa* UP♀, albinistic. 14 July 1968, North Manchester, Wabash Co., IN.
P. l. lisa UN♂. 20 August 1975, North Manchester, Wabash Co., IN.
P. l. lisa UP♂. 5 August 1977, Brown County State Park, Nashville, IN.
P. l. lisa UP♀, albinistic. 5 August 1977, Brown County State Park, Nashville, IN.

Third row   Sleepy Orange, *Abaeis nicippe* UP♂. 21 July 1981, Whitewater Memorial State Park, Union Co., IN.
A. Nicippe UN♀. 14 August 1968, Tri-County Fish and Game Area, North Webster, Kosciusko Co., IN.
Dwarf Yellow or Dainty Sulfur, *Nathalis iole* UP♂. 24 August 1968, Camp Mack, Milford, Kosciusko Co., IN.
N. iole UN♂. 5 July 1974, Fort Wayne, Allen Co., IN.

Fourth row   *N. iole* UN♀. 5 August 1975, North Manchester, Wabash Co., IN.
Harvester, *Feniseca tarquinius tarquinius* UP♂. 23 May 1977, Salamonie River State Forest, Wabash Co., IN.
F. t. tarquinius UN♂. 1 September 1973, Mongo, LaGrange Co., IN.
F. t. tarquinius UP♀. 2 August 1983, Laketon, Wabash Co., IN.

Fifth row   American Copper, *Lycaena phlaeas americana* UP♂. 30 August 1969, North Manchester, Wabash Co., IN.
L. p. americana UN♂. 30 August 1969, Burlington, Howard Co., IN.
L. p. americana UP♀. 30 August 1969, North Manchester, Wabash Co., IN.
L. p. americana UN♀. 24 August 1969, Elkhart, Elkhart Co., IN.

Sixth row   Bronze Copper, *Hyllolycaena hyllus* UP♂. 23 July 1969, North Manchester, Wabash Co., IN.
H. hyllus UN♂. 12 June 1969, North Manchester, Wabash Co., IN.
H. hyllus UP♀. 10 August 1973, North Manchester, Wabash Co., IN.
H. hyllus UN♀. 22 July 1969, Silver Lake, Kosciusko Co., IN.

Genus *Nathalis* Boisduval

73. *Nathalis iole* **Boisduval. Dwarf Yellow; Dainty Sulphur. Plate XXVII.**

Description. The wingspread of this tiny Sulphur measures 0.75 to 1.1 inches (19–28 mm). *Iole* is the smallest pierid in North America. Both sexes have yellow wing surfaces with the apical areas blackish. Black borders occur dorsally on the lower FW margin and the upper margin of the HW. Blackish areas are more extensive in the female. The male has a distinct sex patch on the DHW near the base of the costa. The HW of the female is more orange-colored.

Distribution and Habitat. This species ranges from Florida, Georgia, Tennessee, and Texas north to Indiana, Illinois, Michigan, Minnesota, and Nebraska, also west to the Pacific.

In Indiana *iole* is locally common in many counties from July to the end of November. Some years this migratory butterfly fails to invade our state. It inhabits hayfields, roadsides, railroads, and almost any dry place where there are flowers. Look for white males, occurring rarely in local populations.

Life Cycle. The variable larvae are usually dark green and covered with stiff hairs. It has a broad purplish stripe dorsally, and a double yellow and black stripe laterally. The green pupa lacks the drawnout head horn found on most pierids.

The larvae feed on *Bidens pilosa, Thelosperma trifida, Stellaria media* (common Chickweed), and probably other plants.

Family Lycaenidae Leach

The hairstreaks, blues, and coppers comprise the main members of this large and diverse family. Recently, Eliot (1973) shifted the Harvester (*Feniseca tarquinius*) from the family Liphyridae to the family Lycaenidae. In *The Butterfly Book* by J. W. Holland (1940) the Harvester was included with the lycaenids. However, Howe (1975) in *The Butterflies of North America*—a work expected to replace the older classic—places *F. tarquinius* in a separate family, Liphyridae. There are sound arguments on both sides, and the debate among the experts may not be resolved for some time.

Including the Harvester, there are presently 29 members of the family Lycaenidae in Indiana.

Subfamily Miletinae Corbet
*

Tribe Spalgini Toxopeus
*

Genus *Feniseca* Grote

74. *Feniseca tarquinius tarquinius* (Fabricius). Harvester. Plate XXVII.

Description. The wingspread measures 1.1 to 1.3 inches (28–32 mm). It is unlike any of the other lycaenids found in our area. The dorsal wing surfaces are orange-brown to orange-yellow with blackish brown borders and splotches. The ventral wing surfaces are paler and the markings fainter.

Distribution and Habitat. The Harvester occurs in the Maritime Provinces west to Ontario, south to Florida, the Gulf States, and Central Texas.

Indiana records are widely scattered throughout the state (only 12 counties). Blatchley (1891) reported it only in Jefferson County, where it was rare, but stated that it should occur all over the state. In Wabash, Kosciusko, and La-Grange counties it is present some years, uncommon or even absent other years. Adults fly from mid-May to mid-September. Blatchley rightly called this species "The Wanderer."

Look for the Harvester in damp places: boat-launching sites, wooded river banks, and wet forest trails.

Life Cycle. The Harvester is the only butterfly in North America whose larvae feed on aphids; thus it is our only carnivorous species. Two genera of woolly aphids, *Schizoneura* and *Pemphigus*, which are found mostly on Alder (*Alnus*), Beech (*Fagus*), Ash (*Fraxinus*), Witch Hazel (*Hamamelis*), Wild Currant (*Ribes*), and Hawthorn (*Crataegus*), comprise the main food source for this larva. After feeding for a while, the mature Harvester larva becomes greenish brown. The greenish brown pupa, which is very irregular in shape, curiously resembles a "monkey's head" or an "ace of clubs." It hibernates in the pupal stage and perhaps also as an adult. In our area it is bivoltine.

Subfamily Lycaeninae Leach
*

Genus *Lycaena* Fabricius

75. *Lycaena phlaeas americana* Harris. American Copper. Plate XXVII.

Description. Its wingspread is 0.9 to 1.1 inches (22–28 mm). The dorsal wing surfaces are the color of bright copper or brass, the males being more highly colored. Spring populations are brighter and have smaller spots than later broods. The ventral surfaces are somewhat dull. Females are larger than males.

Distribution and Habitat. *L. p. americana* occurs in the Upper Austral, Transition, and lower Canadian Zones through most of the northeastern U.S. southward to Georgia, North Carolina, Kentucky, and Arkansas, and west to parts of Kansas.

The American Copper is very common in northern and central Indiana from May 15 to September 15; in our most southern counties it is uncommon, rare, or absent. It occurs in fields, yards, waste places, and margins of ponds and lakes. When "nectaring" (feeding) it is easily captured. Sidney Badger (personal communication) found the form "*fasciata*" in Howard County. The "*fasciata*" form was also quite abundant in Warrick County in April 1956 (Lee D. Miller, personal communication). Other aberrations may be found. The pugnacious Copper attacks much larger animals, even the large swallowtails.

Life Cycle. The green egg is distinctly ribbed. The mature larva is either green with rose markings or dull rose with yellow markings on its side. Its larval foodplants are Sheep Sorrel (*Rumex acetosella*), Garden Sorrel (*Rumex acetosa*), and Yellow Dock (*Rumex crispus*). It hibernates in the pupal stage.

I have found four pairs *in copula*: 21 September 1968, 8:45 A.M., 50° F (an extremely low temperature for mating, indicating that the pair had remained attached through the night), North Manchester, Wabash County; 30 August 1969, 10:30 A.M. and 7 September 1969, both in North Manchester; and 29 May 1972, 9:05 A.M., Mongo, LaGrange County. It is curious that no pairs of this species were found mating in the afternoons. The female is the active flight partner. In Indiana, the American Copper has at least two broods.

Genus *Hyllolycaena* Miller and Brown

76. *Hyllolycaena hyllus* (Cramer). Bronze Copper. Plate XXVII.

Description. For many years this species was known as *Lycaena thoe*, but this name was changed by Miller and Brown in 1979 (Bulletin 51, Allyn Museum). This is the largest of our "coppery" Coppers, with wingspread reaching 1.25–1.4 inches (32–35 mm). The upper surface of the male is dark coppery brown, that of the female bright orange to yellowish. Ventrally, both sexes have the FW bright orange with black spots and gray margins. The DHW and VHW orange bands are distinctive.

Distribution and Habitat. The Bronze Copper is found in Pennsylvania, Ohio, Illinois, Indiana, and Kansas. In Indiana it is fairly common in central and northern counties from early June to late October. It is uncommon or absent in many southern counties.

Primarily, *hyllus* is associated with the Blue Flag, *Iris versicolor*, which grows in wet meadows, bogs, and woodland swamps. It perches on grasses and sedges, seldom flying unless disturbed.

Life Cycle. The bright yellowish green larva is "slug-shaped" (resembling the common garden slug) and has a darker stripe along its back. The larval foodplants of the Bronze Copper are Knotweed (*Polygonum*) and Yellow Dock (*Rumex crispus*). *Hyllus* overwinters as an egg.

I have found three pairs *in copula*: 10 September 1969, 12:15 P.M., 62° F; 9 July 1970, 2:15 P.M., 80° F; and 10 June 1973, 5:35 P.M., 85° F, all in North Manchester, Wabash County, and all breeding among the Blue Flag (*Iris versicolor*) in marshy fields. In our area it has a June brood and a July-August brood (bivoltine).

Genus *Epidemia* Scudder

77. *Epidemia epixanthe* (Boisduval and Leconte). Bog Copper. Plate XXVIII.

Description. All three species of *Epidemia* found in Indiana (Bog Copper, Dorcas Copper, and the Purplish Copper) are similar and easily confused. In the latter two species, the males are larger and have purplish reflections, the orange zigzags are more distinct, and the ventral wing surfaces are darker tan or brown. In the Bog Copper, the ventral surface of the wings in both sexes is much paler (yellow to whitish) with some black spots, heavier on the FW; near the border of the VHW there is a submarginal row of tiny red spots.

Distribution and Habitat. Klots (1964) gives the range of the Bog Copper from Newfoundland, Maritime Provinces, Quebec, and Ontario, south to Pennsylvania, New Jersey, northern Indiana, Michigan, Minnesota, also (?) Iowa, Nebraska, and Kansas.

Although recent records for Indiana may be questionable, I believe Blatchley's (1891) report to be correct. He confined it to Lake County, where it was rare. He added that it probably occurs throughout the northern half of the state, is single-brooded, and emerges in June and July in the vicinity of cranberry bogs and peat meadows. It is closely restricted to acid bogs.

If *Epidemia epixanthe* remains on the Indiana butterfly list, it probably will prove to be *E. e. michiganensis*. Jim Aldrich, environmental specialist of the Indiana Department of Natural Resources, and David M. Wright, Lansdale, Pennsylvania, compiled an up-to-date cranberry map for Indiana. In the summer of 1982 Dr. Wright visited most of the extant cranberry habitats in Indiana, but found no *epixanthe*. However, the absence of a particular species for a year or even longer does not provide conclusive evidence that the species was never there or will never return. Wright (personal communication) feels that the Pinhook Bog, LaPorte County, is the most promising place to find the Bog Copper in Indiana, but even conditions in this bog were not quite right. A discussion of the highly speculative arguments about where this butterfly may show up in future collections is beyond the scope of this book. But it is not

PLATE XXVIII

Top row   Bog Copper, *Epidemia epixanthe michiganensis* UP♂. 1 August 1960, Ostego Co., MI. Det. M. C. Nielsen

E. e. michiganensis UN♀. 14 July 1978, Ostego Co., MI. Det. M. C. Nielsen

Dorcas Copper, *Epidemia dorcas dorcas* UP♂. 25 July 1984, Nasby Fen, Mongo, LaGrange Co., IN.

E. d. dorcas UN♂. 25 July 1984, Nasby Fen, Mongo, LaGrange Co., IN.

E. d. dorcas UP♀. 13 July 1974, Mongo Tamarack Bog, LaGrange Co., IN.

Second row   *E. d. dorcas* UN♀. 20 July 1979, Mongo Tamarack Bog, LaGrange Co., IN.

Purplish Copper, *Epidemia helloides* UP♂. 20 July 1978, Camp Mack, Milford, Kosciusko Co., IN.

E. helloides UP♂. 16 July 1978, Camp Mack, Milford, Kosciusko Co., IN.

E. helloides UN♂. 16 July 1978, Camp Mack, Milford, Kosciusko Co., IN.

Third row   *E. helloides* UP♀. 16 July 1978, Camp Mack, Milford, Kosciusko Co., IN.

Great Purple Hairstreak, *Altides halesus halesus* UP♂. 15 June 1973, Woodland Hills, Los Angeles, CA. Det. F. Sidney Badger

A. halesus UP♀. 15 March 1978, Woodland Hills, Los Angeles, CA. Det. F. Sidney Badger

Coral Hairstreak, *Harkenclenus titus titus* UP♂. 4 July 1971, North Manchester, Wabash Co., IN.

Fourth row   *H. t. titus* UN♂. 4 July 1978, Mongo, LaGrange Co., IN.

H. t. titus UP♀. 4 July 1971, North Manchester, Wabash Co., IN.

H. t. titus UN♀. 25 June 1970, North Manchester, Wabash Co., IN.

H. t. titus UN♀. 27 June 1970, North Manchester, Wabash Co., IN.

Fifth row   Acadian Hairstreak, *Satyrium acadica acadica* UP♂. 23 June 1977, Mongo, LaGrange Co., IN.

S. a. acadica UN♂. 23 June 1977, Mongo, LaGrange Co., IN.

S. a. acadica UP♀. 9 July 1973, North Manchester, Wabash Co., IN.

S. a. acadica UN♀. 4 July 1973, North Manchester, Wabash Co., IN.

Sixth row   *S. a. acadica* UN♀. 23 June 1977, Mongo, LaGrange Co., IN.

Edwards' Hairstreak, *Satyrium edwardsii* UP♂. 3 July 1975, Illinois Beach State Park, Lake Co., IL. Det. Irwin Leeuw

S. edwardsii UN♂. 29 July 1980, Pigeon River Fish and Game Area, Mongo, LaGrange Co., IN.

S. edwardsii UP♀. 3 July 1975, Illinois Beach State Park, Lake Co., IL. Det. Irwin Leeuw

difficult for me personally to anticipate that it may show up some day in the Binkley Bog of Steuben County, in the Cedar Lake bogs of LaGrange County, or even perhaps in other bogs where one or both species of cranberry grow (*Vaccinium macrocarpon* and *V. oxycoccus*).

Life Cycle. The early stages of *epixanthe* are not completely known. According to Klots (1964) the eggs are laid on the lower surfaces near the tips of the shoots of the foodplant, Wild Cranberry (*Vaccinium macrocarpon*). The Bog Copper hibernates in the egg stage and can withstand flooding. Wright (1983) has just published a very full life history.

78. *Epidemia dorcas dorcas* (W. Kirby). Dorcas Copper. Plate XXVIII.

Description. The wingspread is 1 to 1.2 inches (25–30 mm). The male is dark copper-brown above with bright deep purple reflections. The female is mostly dark brown with the orange or buff markings largely restricted to the outer third of the wings. Below, both sexes are dull yellowish to pinkish brown. The thin, submarginal reddish line does not always appear.

Since there are no distinguishable differences in the genitalia of *dorcas* and *helloides*, some experts consider them to be a single species, perhaps representing geographic forms or environmental forms. Although the two species closely resemble each other, in Indiana *dorcas* is smaller and darker brown above. The ranges of the two species overlap in southern Ontario, Michigan, northwestern Ohio, and Indiana. More research is greatly needed.

Distribution and Habitat. *Dorcas* occurs in the Canadian and Transitional zones from Labrador and Newfoundland to Alaska, southward to Saskatchewan, northern Minnesota, Michigan, northwestern Ohio, Indiana, and Maine and New Hampshire.

In recent years, *dorcas* has been found in limited numbers in the Mongo tamarack bog, LaGrange County. On 20 July 1979 David Eiler and I found a colony of hundreds in this area, which is the state's largest tamarack bog. They were resting on *Potentilla fruticosa* (Shrubby Cinquefoil). Eiler had no trouble photographing them, for the Dorcas Copper is very calm and not as "nervous" as many other butterflies, including the very similar *E. helloides*. The slower, fluttering flight and short distance traveled by *dorcas* were in sharp contrast to the more erratic and longer flight of *helloides*.

David Eiler (personal communication) found a few *dorcas* around some small patches of Shrubby Cinquefoil in a small prairielike area, not in a wet area. This finding is unusual, because *dorcas* inhabiting the Mongo bog are almost exclusively confined to the wet bog. Eiler also found *dorcas* in a fen that had twice been burned a few years earlier.

Life Cycle. Although most sources report the early stages as largely unknown, a rarely cited early paper by William W. Newcomb (1911) presents much useful information (reprint of this paper courtesy David Wright). According to Newcomb, the eggs are laid on the fresh shoots of *Potentilla fruticosa* and are the overwintering stage. In Michigan eggs are laid during the later part of July and early August. The caterpillars emerge about mid-April. The pupae develop between 15–20 June, and the adult butterflies appear from late June to early July. There is one brood. The Michigan data are likely representative of the *dorcas* found in Indiana. Howe (1975) refers briefly to Newcomb's findings.

79. *Epidemia helloides* (Boisduval). Purplish Copper. Plate XXVIII.

Description. The wingspread measures 1.15 to 1.30 inches (29–34 mm). The male dorsally is purplish to orange-brown. The FW of the female is orange with larger dark spots and has a narrow black border. The species varies greatly. Not all specimens of *helloides* can be separated from *dorcas*, especially in the western states. However, in Indiana, the differences in size and flight behavior are distinct.

Distribution and Habitat. It ranges from southern British Columbia eastward to Quebec, Michigan, northern Illinois, and Indiana and southward to Iowa, western Kansas, northern New Mexico, southern Utah and northern Baja California.

In Indiana adults occur from 5 June to 19 October (being more common in July and August) in our northern counties. It is more widespread than *dorcas*. Look for it in marshy fields, borders of ponds and lakes, and other moist places.

Life Cycle. The egg is whitish. The grass-green larva bears many spines covered with colorless hairs. The mature larva has yellow longitudinal stripes on its back and sides and a number of lateral oblique yellowish lines. The pupa is marked with gray and brown.

The larval foodplants are docks (*Rumex*), Knotweed (*Polygonum*), and Baby's Breath (*Galium*). The number of broods has not been determined in our state.

Subfamily Theclinae Swainson
ã
Tribe Eumaeini Doubleday
ã
Genus *Atlides* Hübner

80. *Atlides halesus halesus* (Cramer). Great Purple Hairstreak. Plate XXVIII.

Description. This beautiful hairstreak has a wingspread of 1.25 to 1.5 inches (32–38 mm). The dorsal wing surfaces of the male are a brilliant iridescent blue with blackish margins and stigma. It has one or two HW tails and a few blue marks by the HW margin. The female is similar but duller and the blue

is more restricted to the wing bases. The abdomen ventrally is coral-red and the wings below are purplish gray except for the red at the base of the wings and the metallic blue and green spots.

Distribution and Habitat. It ranges from Florida, north to New Jersey and Illinois and west to California. According to Blatchley (1891), Worthington found it in small numbers in Lake County, Indiana. Ehrlich and Ehrlich (1961) say that strays have been taken in northern Indiana.

This species seldom wanders far from the parasitic Mistletoe (*Phoradendron*) which grows on oak, walnut, cottonwood, juniper, and sycamore trees. Its erratic flight makes it difficult to catch except when perched on flowers. I have never found it in Indiana, but I have taken it in Fresno, California, on 27 June 1973. The presence of Mistletoe in Perry County makes this a likely area.

Life Cycle. The egg is laid on Mistletoe. The larva is green and slightly pubescent; it has darker green bands on its sides, a middorsal stripe, and also a yellowish lateral stripe above the base of the legs. Its primary foodplant is Mistletoe (*Phoradendron flavescens*). The mottled dull black and brown pupa overwinters. Reportedly, it has two broods.

Genus *Harkenclenus* dos Passos

81. *Harkenclenus titus titus* (Fabricius). Coral Hairstreak. Plate XXVIII.

Description. The wingspread ranges from 1.0 to 1.25 inches (25–32 mm). This species is our only common hairstreak lacking tails on the HW. The underside is distinctive with the submarginal band of coral-red spots on the secondaries, appearing on the primaries of some specimens. The wings are grayish brown above without markings except for the scent pad on the male. Sometimes the female has a few orange-red spots near the angle of the HW, and the male may have a single spot.

Distribution and Habitat. *Harkenclenus t. titus* is the northern subspecies found in Indiana; however, Masters and Masters (1969) found the subspecies as *Chrysophanus* (=*Harkenclenus*) *titus mopsus* in Perry County in late June. *Mopsus* is larger and somewhat lighter with the VHW discal spots prominently larger and ringed with white (Ferris and Brown, 1980).

Harkenclenus t. titus occurs in the southern Canadian provinces and over most of the United States except for the Gulf Coast and the extreme Southwest. *Mopsus* occurs from the District of Columbia south to Georgia and west to Kansas.

The nominate subspecies is widely distributed throughout Indiana. Its flight period is usually from late June through July, rarely in August. It prefers the flowers of the Butterfly Weed (*Asclepias tuberosa*), Spreading Dogbane (*Apocynum androsaemifolium*), sweet clovers, and goldenrods. Look for it in meadows, roadsides, and along bodies of water. Frequently it may be found near wild cherry clumps. Although a rapid flier, it is easily captured on flowers.

Life Cycle. According to Howe (1975), the eggs are laid on the twigs of wild plum and wild cherry (*Prunus* spp.) and hatch the following spring. The mature larvae are greenish with pinkish coloration in the middle of the back. It has one brood.

Genus *Satyrium* Scudder

82. *Satyrium acadica acadica* (W. H. Edwards). Acadian Hairstreak. Plate XXVIII.

Description. The wingspread of this species ranges from 1.1 to 1.25 inches (28–32 mm). Dorsally, the wings are grayish brown with an orange patch on the HW near the tail. Ventrally, the wings are a uniform steel gray with bands of black dots bordered with white markings on both the FW and HW; on the VHW a bluish area is separated by a black dot and the thin tail.

Distribution and Habitat. The nominate species occurs from southeastern Canada southward to New Jersey and Michigan. In Indiana it is uncommon to locally common in our northern counties from June through July. Otherwise, it has been recorded only in Union, Franklin, Scott, and Jefferson counties, indicating that it is rare in the southern half of the state.

Adults are fond of Swamp Milkweed and Dogbane flowers, especially in damp fields and meadows where willows (*Salix*) are nearby. Some years colonies of *acadica* are quite large.

Life Cycle. The Acadian Hairstreak overwinters in the egg stage. The grass-green larva has two yellowish longitudinal lines. Its larval foodplant is *Salix*. In Indiana, I have found only one pair *in copula*: 10 June 1977, 10:45 A.M., 60° F, settled in a patch of sedge grass off Lake Waubee, Milford, Kosciusko County. Both Dogbane and Willow were nearby. Normally it should have one brood in July.

83. *Satyrium edwardsii* (Grote and Robinson). Edwards' Hairstreak. Plates XXVIII, XXIX.

Description. The wingspread measures 1.0 to 1.25 inches (25–32 mm). This species can be confused with the Acadian Hairstreak and the Banded Hairstreak; however, their habitats differ considerably. Dorsally and ventrally the Edwards' Hairstreak is light gray-brown. The VFW and VHW bands consist of rows of discontinuous small, dark brown oval spots fringed with white. The submarginal orange spots on the VHW are not as extensive as they are in *acadica*.

Distribution and Habitat. *Edwardsii* ranges from the Maritime Provinces west to Manitoba and south to Georgia and Texas.

In Indiana it occurs in a few scattered counties (mostly northern), being un-

PLATE XXIX

Top row	Edwards' Hairstreak, *Satyrium edwardsii* UN♀. 4 July 1978, Elgin, Kane Co., IL. Det. Irwin Leeuw
	Banded Hairstreak, *Satyrium calanus falacer* UP♂. 3 July 1978, North Manchester, Wabash Co., IN.
	S. c. falacer UN♂. 3 July 1978, Silver Lake, Kosciusko Co., IN.
	S. c. falacer UP♀. 4 July 1978, Mongo, LaGrange Co., IN.
Second row	*S. c. falacer* UN♀. 4 July 1978, Mongo, LaGrange Co., IN.
	Hickory Hairstreak, *Satyrium caryaevorum* UP♂. 14 July 1969, North Manchester, Wabash Co., IN.
	S. caryaevorum UN♂. 25 June 1969, North Manchester, Wabash Co., IN.
	S. caryaevorum UP♀. 25 June 1969, Silver Lake, Kosciusko Co., IN.
Third row	*S. caryaevorum* UN♀. 9 July 1969, Silver Lake, Kosciusko Co., IN.
	S. caryaevorum UN♂. 22 June 1978, Silver Lake, Kosciusko Co., IN. Det. F. H. Rindge
	Striped Hairstreak, *Satyrium liparops strigosum* UP♂. 11 July 1973, North Manchester, Wabash Co., IN.
	S. l. strigosum UN♂. 5 July 1971, North Manchester, Wabash Co., IN.
Fourth row	*S. l. strigosum* UP♀. 4 July 1978, Pigeon River Fish and Game Area, Mongo, LaGrange Co., IN.
	S. l. strigosum UN♀. 6 June 1969, North Manchester, Wabash Co., IN.
	Red-banded Hairstreak, *Calycopis cecrops* UP♂. 16 August 1982, Strahl Creek, Brown County State Park, Nashville, IN.
	C. cecrops UN♀. 18 August 1982, Strahl Creek, Brown County State Park, Nashville, IN.
Fifth row	Olive Hairstreak, *Mitoura gryneus gryneus* UP♂. 21 July 1981, Whitewater Memorial State Park, Union Co., IN.
	M. g. gryneus UN♂. 21 July 1981, Whitewater Memorial State Park, Union Co., IN.
	M. g. gryneus UP♀. 21 July 1981, Whitewater Memorial State Park, Union Co., IN.
	M. g. gryneus UN♀. 21 July 1981, Whitewater Memorial State Park, Union Co., IN.
Sixth row	Hoary Elfin, *Incisalia polios* UP♂. 26 April 1974, Illinois Beach State Park, Lake Co., IL. Coll. Irwin Leeuw
	I. polios UN♂. 16 April 1976, Illinois Beach State Park, Lake Co., IL. Coll. Irwin Leeuw
	I. polios UP♂. 26 April 1974, Illinois Beach State Park, Lake Co., IL. Coll. Irwin Leeuw
	I. polios UP♀. 17 April 1976, Illinois Beach State Park, Lake Co., IL. Coll. Irwin Leeuw

common in June and July. Adults prefer Scrub Oak thickets and the edges of woods, where they usually perch on twigs and leaves, and occasionally on woodland flowers. Both *acadica* and *calanus* have more host plants than does *edwardsii*. The swift-flying Edwards' Hairstreak is sometimes difficult to net.

Life Cycle. The eggs are laid under the next year's buds or on rough twigs, where they overwinter. The brownish caterpillar is covered with numerous blackish warts that contain brown hairs. Its foodplant is Scrub Oak (*Quercus ilicifolia*) and other oaks. M. C. Nielsen, of Lansing, Michigan (personal communication), found *S. edwardsii* larvae (many full-grown) in ant nests at the base of small Black Oaks.

84. *Satyrium calanus falacer* (Godart). Banded Hairstreak. Plate XXIX.

Description. The wingspread of this species measures 1.0 to 1.25 inches (25–32 mm). It cannot always be distinguished from *edwardsii* and from *caryaevorum*; however, there are genitalic differences. In *edwardsii*, the ventral transverse lines, especially on the HW, are broken into separate, narrow, white-edged oval spots. In *caryaevorum* these transverse lines are more irregular, the segments offset inwardly. In *falacer* the ventral transverse lines are smooth and continuous. Our subspecies, *S. c. falacer*, lacks the orange spot on the upper HW found in the nominate subspecies.

Distribution and Habitat. The Banded Hairstreak ranges from southern Canada west to Manitoba, south to Georgia, the Gulf States, and Texas. It is common and widespread in Indiana from late June to mid-July. Former Indiana records under the name *S. calanus* (Florida Hairstreak) probably belong to the subspecies *S. calanus falacer*. Look for this butterfly in deciduous forests, roadsides, and in our state parks. On 3 July 1979 I collected an adult *falacer* at 10:20 P.M. in an open woods near Silver Lake, Kosciusko County, while collecting moths with a "black light" placed on a white sheet over the hood of the car.

Life Cycle. The dimorphic larva is either grass-green or brown; the body has longitudinal lines of lighter and darker shades. Its larval foodplants are Hickory (*Carya*), Oaks (*Quercus*), and Butternut (*Juglans cinera*). The Banded Hairstreak hibernates in the egg stage. It has one brood.

85. *Satyrium caryaevorum* (McDunnough). Hickory Hairstreak. Plate XXIX.

Description. The wingspread of *caryaevorum* ranges from 1.0 to 1.25 inches (25–32 mm). Above it is brownish with a slate-colored cast. Below it is a more sooty gray to slate with a distinctly bluish cast. The VFW transverse band has white markings on both the inner and outer edges. It has a blue area near the tail and between the small orange spots.

Distribution and Habitat. The Hickory Hairstreak ranges from Vermont

and Connecticut west through southern Canada to Minnesota and Iowa, and south to Kentucky, Ohio, and western Pennsylvania.

In Indiana it is found mostly in our northern counties; it is absent from the extreme southern counties, with a few scattered records elsewhere. *Caryaevorum* is usually uncommon to common in June and July; however, on 12 July 1978, it was abundant at Silver Lake, Kosciusko County. David Hess was collecting with me at that time. Hundreds perched on the Hickory tree leaves and on sumac and other shrubs along the edge of a woods by a meadow. Look for this species in deciduous woods, roadsides, and borders of fields. It visits flowers, especially Milkweed (*Asclepias*) and Dogbane (*Apocynum*).

I collected my first mating pair of *S. caryaevorum* on 22 June 1968 on a Hickory tree leaf in a Silver Lake woods, Kosciusko County. Dr. Frederick H. Rindge prepared a slide of the male genitalia of the above and confirmed my tentative identification.

Life Cycle. The early stages are imperfectly known. The grass-green larva has a dark green band on the back and greenish side markings. The chrysalis is pubescent and mottled brown.

The larval foodplants consist of Hickory (*Carya*) and perhaps ashes (*Fraxinus*). Likely it hibernates in the egg stage. It has one brood.

I have found one pair *in copula*: 26 June 1978, 3:50 P.M., 83° F, on dogbane near the edge of a woods, North Manchester, Wabash County. Like other lycaenids, the female was the flight partner.

86. *Satyrium liparops strigosum* (Harris). Striped Hairstreak. Plate XXIX.

Description. The wingspread measures 1.0 to 1.4 inches (25–35 mm). The Striped Hairstreak has distinct, widely spaced, broken, and offset lines on the underside. It is brownish above and buff-brown below. There are lines and orange areas near the tail, fewer and smaller above than below.

Distribution and Habitat. *S. l. strigosum*, the commonest subspecies in the United States, ranges from northern Georgia northward to New England and southern Canada and westward to Mississippi, eastern Kansas, and Wisconsin.

In Indiana the records are scattered throughout the state north of Brown County. Adults fly in June through July and occasionally in August (10 August 1973, Silver Lake, Kosciusko County). It is usually local and uncommon. Look for it in deciduous forests, along hedgerows and hawthorn thickets, and in shrubby areas. Although this species occasionally alights on flowers, it more commonly perches on leaves. In July 1978 the Striped Hairstreak was common in Kosciusko and LaGrange counties.

Life Cycle. According to Howe (1975), the larva is bright green and marked laterally with oblique yellowish green lines. Its larval foodplants are

Quercus (oak), *Salix* (willow), *Malus* (apple), *Prunus* (plum), *Crataegus* (hawthorn), *Vaccinium* (blueberries), *Rubus* (blackberry), members of the rose family (Rosaceae), and perhaps others.

The chrysalis is mottled. This species overwinters in the egg stage. It is univoltine.

Genus *Calycopis* Scudder

87. *Calycopis cecrops* (Fabricius). Red-banded Hairstreak. Plate XXIX.

Description. The wingspread measures 0.75–1.0 inch (19–25 mm). This species is easily identified by examining the ventral patterns of red, black, and white on the forewings and hindwings. The lines are irregular, especially on the VHW; the innermost line is flame-red and broad. The angle of the HW and the two tails are diagnostic.

Distribution and Habitat. Klots (1951) gives the range as Florida, the Gulf States, and Texas north to New York (Long Island), Indiana, Missouri, and Michigan.

In Indiana it has been found in only a few southern counties. I first found *cecrops* in the Brown County State Park on 25 and 26 May 1976 near Strahl Lake. On 19 August 1981 I collected fifteen specimens (mostly worn) on Sumac in the same park. Normally it is rare or absent. Masters and Masters (1969) found it scarce in late May and July in Perry County. Blatchley (1891) found a single specimen in Monroe County, 17 August 1890. In recent years this hairstreak appears to be increasing. Look for it near lakes and ponds and on woodland trails.

Life Cycle. Pyle (1981) states that the dimpled, pearly white egg is laid in leaf litter. The caterpillar is at first pale yellow, then darkens with age. It has a thick, brown hairy coat with a blue-green back stripe. The chrysalis is chestnut-brown and mottled with black. The Dwarf Sumac (*Rhus capallina*) and *Croton* (and possibly *Myrica*) are the larval foodplants. *Cecrops* probably has two broods in Indiana.

Genus *Mitoura* Scudder

88. *Mitoura gryneus gryneus* (Hübner). Olive Hairstreak. Plate XXIX.

Description. The wingspread measures 0.9 to 1.0 inch (22–25 mm). The male is dark brown above with variable amounts of orange-brown or golden-brown; it has a small stigma. In the female, the orange is more extensive. Ventrally, both sexes are bright green with a prominent white postmedian line inwardly edged with reddish brown. In *M. hesseli*, a similar species, the HW area just outside the postmedian line has dark brown patches occurring in M₁ and

M_3 which are not present in *gryneus*. Spring forms of *gryneus* have more orange on the upper wings than do the summer forms.

Distribution and Habitat. This subspecies ranges from southern New England to Georgia and west to western Ontario, eastern Nebraska, eastern Kansas, and northeastern Texas (Howe, 1975). Blatchley (1891) lists the Olive Hairstreak as rare in Lake County, a Worthington record. I found it in the Whitewater Memorial State Park, Union County, on 21 and 22 July 1981, associated with Red Cedar trees (*Juniperus virginiana*) and perched on nearby low flowers. Its flight is swift and darting, making it difficult to follow when flushed; however, it often returns to the same area. Milkweed flowers (Asclepiadaceae) attract many adults. Look for them by roadsides, rocky ravines, and places where Red Cedars grow. Frequently, the Olive Hairstreak appears in colonies. Habitat destruction through urbanization has restricted its range. It is uncommon to rare locally in April and May and in July and August.

Life Cycle. The egg is pale green. The mature caterpillar is greenish with a yellowish tint and has pale green diagonal lines high on the sides. The pupa is dark brown. It hibernates as a chrysalis. It has two broods each season, according to Blatchley, which appear in May and again in August.

Genus *Incisalia* Scudder

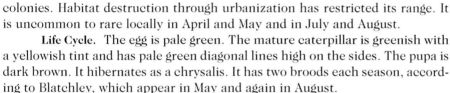

89. *Incisalia polios* Cook and Watson. Hoary Elfin. Plate XXIX.

Description. The Hoary Elfin has a wingspread of 0.75 to 1.0 inch (19–25 mm). The hindwings lack the prominent tails of many of the Hairstreaks. The outer margin of the HW is not deeply scalloped, but a short tail projection appears at the end of the cubital. The VFW has a distinct terminal gray band and the VHW outer area is bright and extensive; otherwise the species is dusky, grayish brown above. The stigma appears in the FW discal cell of the male.

Distribution and Habitat. *Polios* ranges from the mountains of Virginia northward and westward to Michigan and the Mackenzie River and eastern Alaska and southward through the Rocky Mountains to northern New Mexico (Howe, 1975). Montgomery (1931) added *polios* to the Indiana state list, and I disagree with Masters and Masters (1969), who say that this species needs confirmation to stay on our state list. Although I have never found it in Indiana, it has been reported from Lake and St. Joseph counties.

Reportedly, *polios* occurs in dry, open, barren, and rocky places, appearing early in the spring.

Life Cycle. The immature larva is rosy to yellow, turning green when older. Its larval foodplant is Bearberry (*Arctostaphylos uva-ursi*). It has one brood. It overwinters in the pupal stage.

90. *Incisalia irus irus* (Godart). Frosted Elfin. Plate XXX.

Description. This Elfin has a wingspread of 0.9 to 1.25 inches (22–32 mm). Both *irus* and *henrici* have short tails at the end of vein Cu₂ on the HW. The male *irus* has a scent patch on the upperside of the FW. The VHW is usually ruddy brown. The male is grayish brown above; the female is more reddish.

Distribution and Habitat. The nominate *irus* ranges from southern New England southward to South Carolina and westward to Michigan and northwestern Illinois. Irwin and Downey (1973) say that they have records from Lake County, Indiana. Ehrlich and Ehrlich (1961) list *irus* for northwestern Indiana. I have specimens in my collection from Ohio but none from Indiana. It was reported in May from Pulaski County (Anonymous, 1972). Adults occur in April and May, flying along roadsides, in pine barrens, and open brushy fields near wooded areas. Apparently the Frosted Elfin is local and rare in our state.

Life Cycle. According to Howe (1975) the larvae of *irus* feed on the flowers and fruit of Wild Lupine (*Lupinus perennis*) and Wild Indigo (*Baptisia tinctoria*). The first plant is common in the Hoosier Prairie Preserve, Lake County, and the second plant is not uncommon in Kosciusko County. Thus, the Frosted Elfin should be carefully searched for in these and additional counties. The larva is yellowish green. The chrysalis is enclosed in a loose cocoon of woven leaf fragments. It overwinters in this stage.

91. *Incisalia henrici turneri* Clench. Henry's Elfin. Plate XXX.

Description. The wingspread measures 0.9 to 1.1 inches (22–28 mm). The FW of the male lacks a scent pad and the VHW is without the basal hoary patch found in the Hoary Elfin. This subspecies has short tails. It is orange-brown above and more yellowish beneath than the nominate subspecies.

Distribution and Habitat. This Elfin ranges from Quebec, Ontario, Michigan, and Nebraska south to central Florida, Texas, and Missouri. In Indiana it is uncommon in a few scattered counties, mostly in the southern portion of the state. As Masters and Masters (1969) have suggested, the nominate subspecies should occur in northern Indiana, but there are no records for it. Although Howe (1975) states that the midwestern subspecies (*turneri*) ranges from south central Kansas to northern Texas, I have found it in late April, 31 May, and 1 June, 1978, in the Brown County State Park, Nashville, Indiana. It prefers shady, swampy, deciduous forests and wet trails. It visits Blueberry, Huckleberry, and Redbud flowers.

Life Cycle. The larva is reddish to brownish green with lighter oblique side dashes. Its larval foodplants consist of the flowers and fruits of *Vaccinium, Cercis canadensis, Gaylussacia,* and *Prunus*. It overwinters in the pupal stage. It is univoltine.

92. *Incisalia niphon clarki* Freeman. Eastern Pine Elfin. Plate XXX.

Description. The wingspread ranges from 0.75 to 1.25 inches (19–32 mm). This northern subspecies, *clarki*, is more common than the nominate form. *Clarki* is smaller, paler on both surfaces, and the markings on the VHW are not as crisp and contrasting as in the southern subspecies.

Distribution and Habitat. Although the range of the subspecies *clarki* is New Jersey and Pennsylvania northward to Nova Scotia and westward to southern Manitoba, it was first found in Indiana by Marc Minno (personal communication) on 10 April 1976 in the Spring Mill State Park, Lawrence County. He reported it to me as *Callophrys niphon*. In addition to the Lawrence County record, Minno also found one female in Monroe County on 27 May 1978. These are the only state records.

Look for this Elfin in Pine and pine-oak woods, especially where the trees border fields. It also occurs along roadsides and glades.

Life Cycle. The green larva is longitudinally striped with whitish lines (Howe, 1975). It is well camouflaged among the pine needles on which it feeds, chiefly *Pinus virginiana* and *P. rigida*, and perhaps other hard pines. The brown chrysalis overwinters. It has one brood.

Genus *Euristrymon* Clench

93. *Euristrymon ontario ontario* (Edwards). Northern Hairstreak. Plate XXX.

Description. The wingspread ranges from 1.0 to 1.25 inches (25–32 mm). Dorsally, the wings are grayish brown with a trace of orange near the tails. This species resembles *E. favonius*, but *ontario* has less extensive orange on the VHW, and the postmedian and subterminal lines are farther apart. The diagnostic characteristic of *ontario* is the irregular, white "W" on the VHW. The two tails and the black crescents capped with orange crescents (sometimes limited to one or two in cells M_3 and Cu_1) and the bluish patch in cell Cu_2 clearly identify this butterfly.

Distribution and Habitat. *Ontario* ranges from southern Canada and Massachusetts south and west through Ohio, Georgia to Texas, New Mexico, and Arizona.

I collected the first Northern Hairstreak in Indiana on 20 June 1967 at North Manchester, Wabash County, when it was taking nectar from the flowers of Spreading Dogbane (*Apocynum androsaemifolium*). It also favors Common Milkweed (*Asclepias syriaca*) and Swamp Milkweed (*A. incarnata*). It is easily captured on flowers.

The Northern Hairstreak is uncommon to rare from mid-June through July, and may even be absent some years. It occurs mainly in our northern counties,

PLATE XXX

Top row   Frosted Elfin, *Incisalia irus irus* UP♂. 5 May 1962, Montcalm Co., MI. Det. M. C. Nielsen

I. i. irus UP♀. 22 May 1971, Allegan Co., MI. Det. M. C. Nielsen

Henry's Elfin, *Incisalia henrici turneri* UP♂. 31 May 1978, Brown County State Park, Nashville, IN.

I. h. turneri UP♀. 31 May 1978, Brown County State Park, Nashville, IN.

Second row   *I. h. turneri* UN♀. 1 June 1978, Brown County State Park, Nashville, IN.

Eastern Pine Elfin, *Incisalia niphon clarki* UP♂. 10 April 1976, Spring Mill State Park, Lawrence Co., IN. Det. Marc Minno

I. n. clarki UN♂. Mack Lake National Forest, Oscoda Co., MI. Coll. David Eiler

Northern Hairstreak, *Euristrymon ontario ontario* UP♂. 28 June 1978, Silver Lake, Kosciusko Co., IN.

Third row   *E. o. ontario* UN♂. 21 June 1971, North Manchester, Wabash Co., IN.

E. o. ontario UP♀. 28 June 1978, Silver Lake, Kosciusko Co., IN.

White M Hairstreak, *Parrhasium m-album* UP♂. Pontiac, IL. Coll. R. R. Irwin

P. m-album UN♂. 24 June 1923, Lakeland, FL. Coll. R. R. Irwin

Fourth row   *P. m-album* UP♀. 1 May 1957, Indianapolis, Marion Co., IN. Coll. David S. White

Gray Hairstreak, *Strymon melinus humuli* UP♂. 30 July 1969, Silver Lake, Kosciusko Co., IN.

S. m. humuli UN♂. 29 July 1969, North Manchester, Wabash Co., IN.

S. m. humuli UN♀. 7 June 1980, Mounds State Park, Brookville, Franklin Co., IN.

Fifth row   *S. m. humuli* UN♂. 31 August 1980, Huntingburg, DuBois Co., IN.

S. m. humuli UN♂. 29 August 1980, near Hovey Lake State Recreation Area, Posey Co., IN.

Marine Blue, *Leptotes marina* UP♂. 19 July 1978, Indiana Dunes, Porter Co., IN. Det. Marc Minno

Reakirt's Blue, *Hemiargus isola* UP♂. 24 July 1973, Puebla State, (southern mountains, 5,000 ft.), Mexico.

Sixth row   *H. isola* UN♀. 24 July 1973, Puebla State, (southern mountains, 5,000 ft.), Mexico.

Eastern Tailed Blue, *Everes comyntas comyntas* UP♂. 1 June 1968, North Manchester, Wabash Co., IN.

E. c. comyntas UN♂. 27 August 1969, North Manchester, Wabash Co., IN. This specimen was mating with the next one.

E. c. comyntas UP♀. 27 August 1969, North Manchester, Wabash Co., IN.

but I have taken a few in Brown and Monroe counties. The species may be found in open woods and along fences, especially where Dogbane thrives.

Life Cycle. The early stages are not well known. In our area, Hawthorn (*Crataegus*) and various oaks (*Quercus*) constitute the larval foodplants for this insect.

Genus *Parrhasius* Hübner

94. *Parrhasius m-album* (Boisduval and Leconte). White M Hairstreak. Plate XXX.

Description. The wingspread of this unusual Hairstreak measures 1.1 to 1.25 inches (28–32 mm). Formerly this species went by the name *Panthiades m-album* or *Strymon m-album*. The white M (or W) formed by the postmedian line on the VHW distinguish this species.

Distribution and Habitat. This species occurs in the southeastern United States north to New Jersey, Pennsylvania, Ohio, and Kansas. In Indiana strays have been found in only five counties. Blatchley (1891) found it rare in Jefferson and Decatur counties. This species is essentially southern and nowhere abundant. Its flight is fast and erratic. It can be caught on Dogbane flowers which edge deciduous woods, in forest clearings, and woodland trails. Adults fly from late May through August.

Life Cycle. The pubescent, light yellowish green larva has a black head, a middorsal stripe, and seven green lateral stripes. The brown chrysalis overwinters probably in debris below oak trees. Various oaks (*Quercus*) constitute the only certain larval foodplants. The number of broods, if any, has not been determined for Indiana; however, in its northern range it reportedly has two broods.

Genus *Strymon* Hübner

95. *Strymon melinus humuli* (Harris). Gray Hairstreak. Plate XXX.

Description. The wingspread is 1.0 to 1.25 inches (25–32 mm). It is easily identified by its blue-gray color, light underside, and the prominent orange spot at the anal region of the HW, which shows dorsally and ventrally. *S. m. humuli* is smaller, darker above and beneath, more brownish ventrally, and has smaller orange-red markings on the HW than in the nominate subspecies. Also, in *humuli* the postmedian lines beneath are straighter.

Distribution and Habitat. It ranges from southern Canada south through Florida and Texas into Central America. *Humuli* is usually common and widely distributed throughout Indiana from April to October. Look for it in woodland marshes, open deciduous woods, roadsides, parks, vacant lots, meadows, and other open places. Although its flight is swift, it is easily captured on flowers.

Life Cycle. The egg is pale green. The variable larva is usually grass-green to translucent green, with white diagonal side stripes. Its larval food-plants are Knotweed (*Polygonum*), Mallow (*Mallow*), Hops (*Humulus*), St. Johnswort (*Hypericum*), cultivated beans (*Phaseolus*), Hawthorn (*Crataegus*), and others. The larvae bore in the seeds and fruits of these plants. The chrysalis is brown and is the overwintering stage. It has two broods in our area.

Subfamily Polyommatinae Swainson
ॐ
Tribe Lampidini Tutt
ॐ
Genus *Leptotes* Scudder

96. *Leptotes marina* (Reakirt). Marine Blue. Plate XXX.

Description. The wingspread measures 0.6 to 1.0 inch (16–25 mm). Dorsally, the male is a uniform light purple to lavender blue. The female is dull violet above with a broad brown border and brownish suffusion to the bases of both the FW and HW. The VHW is covered with brown bars and spots, without a broad white area toward the basal inner angle.

Distribution and Habitat. It ranges from southern Texas to central California. During the summer it may be found as an immigrant in Illinois and Nebraska. I collected a few in Vera Cruz, Mexico, in July 1973. Irwin and Downey (1973) reported that *marina* is only a rare casual in Illinois.

Marc Minno (personal communication) found the first *Leptotes marina* in Indiana (the state record) on 19 July 1978 in the Indiana Dunes, Porter County. In our area, this species should be found by canals, streams, and other waterways, but only as a very rare immigrant.

Life Cycle. According to Pyle (1981), the egg is green and ridged with white. The larvae are variable from pure green to rich brown. The pupa has short hairs and is dark yellow with paler wing cases. The larval foodplants are Alfalfa (*Medicago sativa*), Sweet Pea (*Lathyrus odoratus*), False Indigo (*Amorpha*), and others.

Genus *Hemiargus* Hübner

97. *Hemiargus isola* (Reakirt). Reakirt's Blue. Plate XXX.

Description. The wingspread is 0.75 to 1.1 inches (19–28 mm). Dorsally, the male is lilac-blue. The female is dusky with a bluish interior. The VHW has a prominent postmedian band of large, black, almost circular spots ringed with white.

Distribution and Habitat. Its range includes Minnesota, southern Michi-

gan, western Ohio, Louisiana, and Mississippi, westward to British Columbia and California, and southward to Costa Rica.

The Reakirt's Blue was found in Newton County, Indiana, on 24 June 1972 by Conway and Seaborg (Anonymous, 1972), a state record. In the north and east of its broader range, *isola* is sporadic, local, and rare. I have never collected it in Indiana, but I did collect some in Puebla State, Mexico, on 24 July 1973 at an altitude of 5,000 feet. Look for it on roadside flowers, gardens, fields, and open areas where legumes and flowers abound. This largely tropical species, when present, occurs in the spring and may persist until late autumn, partially depending on the weather and other conditions.

Life Cycle. Its life history has not been described. The larva feeds on the flowers and fruits of legumes, including Mesquite (*Prosopis*), ornamental Acacia (*Albizzia*), and Indigo (*Indigofera*).

<h2 style="text-align:center">Tribe Everini Tutt</h2>

ﴥ

<h2 style="text-align:center">Genus Everes Hübner</h2>

98. *Everes comyntas comyntas* (Godart). Eastern Tailed Blue. Plate XXX.

Description. The wingspread ranges from 0.75 to 1.0 inch (19–25 mm). *Comyntas* is the only member of this tribe in Indiana which has tailed hindwings. In Indiana and elsewhere adults have several seasonal variations. Early spring males are usually pale with narrow black markings; summer-brood males are darker with wide margins. Early spring females have more extensive blue scaling, while summer females are dark brown to slaty gray above and without the blue scaling.

Distribution and Habitat. This nominate subspecies is widely distributed east of the 110th meridian, and its range extends from Montreal, Quebec, southward to Florida. The Eastern Tailed Blue, with its various forms, occurs throughout Indiana and has been recorded in nearly every county. Adults fly from April to October, appearing almost everywhere, along roadsides, in meadows, orchards, farmlots, edges of woods and fencerows, and in city parks and lawns. It is easily captured.

Life Cycle. The eggs are laid in flower buds and stems. The variable larva is dark green and pubescent with faint brown and lighter lateral stripes. Look for the eggs and larvae on White Clover (*Trifolium repens*), Red Clover (*T. pratensis*), and *Lespedeza stipulaceae*. *Comyntas* hibernates as a mature larva.

I have found twenty-one pairs *in copula*. The earliest mating pair was observed on 1 June and the latest on 7 October. Mating occurred every month from June to early October. In all but two cases, copulation took place in the afternoon from 12:40 P.M. to 6:20 P.M., with temperatures ranging from 68° F to

95° F. Both pairs which mated in the morning were observed after 11:20 A.M., when the temperatures were already 70° F or above. The most favorable conditions for mating of this species seem to be temperatures in the 70s and 80s, high humidity and even light rain interrupted by sunshine, little or no wind, and, of course, females ready for breeding. In every pair, as in all lycaenids, the female *comyntas* was the flight partner. It has multiple broods.

Tribe Celastrini Tutt

❧

Genus *Celastrina* Tutt

99. *Celastrina ladon ladon* (Cramer). Spring Azure. Plate XXXI.

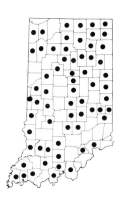

Description. Many authors prefer the name *C. argiolus pseudargiolus* for our subspecies, but I am following Clench and Miller (1980). The wingspread of the Spring Azure, or Common Blue, measures 0.75 to 1.25 inches (19–32 mm). The spring brood is a deep silvery violet-blue, and the female has a coal-black FW border. The summer brood is not as highly colored, being violet-blue above with the basal half of the FW and most of the HW showing washes of white; the female is still black-bordered and whiter than the male.

Klots (1964) gives a fine description of this group with its many geographical and seasonal variations. Paul Opler, who is preparing a county atlas of eastern United States butterflies, is calling the summer brood *Celastrina neglecta major*, a separate species (personal communication). Differences among the experts may prevail for some time.

Distribution and Habitat. This herald of spring ranges from Alaska east to Canada and south throughout the entire United States to Mexico and Panama.

In Indiana it is abundant in our northern counties and probably common throughout the state. Adults fly from April to September. The Spring Azure may be found in open deciduous woods, fields, roadsides, woodland trails, and brushy areas from sea level to the hills.

Life Cycle. The pale green eggs are laid in flowers and buds. The larvae are highly variable, usually cream-colored or greenish. Those found in the eastern United States are whitish, rose-tinted with a faint, dusky dorsal stripe and very faint lateral oblique greenish stripes. According to Howe (1975), the caterpillars are attended by ants. The pupa is plump, ovoid, and brownish. The larval foodplants include Flowering Dogwood (*Cornus florida*), Black Snakeroot (*Cimicifuga racemosa*), Meadowsweet (*Spiraea salicifolia*), Sumac (*Rhus*), Blueberry (*Vaccinium corymbosum*), and other plants. They have survived on Nasturtium, Clover, Willow, and Milkweed. This species hibernates in the pupa stage.

In Indiana I have taken two pairs *in copula*: 23 June 1969, 2:30 P.M., North

PLATE XXXI

Top row

Spring Azure, *Celastrina ladon ladon* UP♂. 23 June 1969, North Manchester, Wabash Co., IN. This specimen was mating with the next one.
C. l. ladon UP♀. 23 June 1969, North Manchester, Wabash Co., IN.
C. l. ladon UN♂. 10 August 1975, Brown County State Park, Nashville, IN.
C. l. ladon UN♀. 10 August 1975, Brown County State Park, Nashville, IN.

Second row

C. l. ladon UP♂. 9 July 1973, North Manchester, Wabash Co., IN.
C. l. ladon UP♀. 13 July 1973, North Manchester, Wabash Co., IN.
Sooty Azure, *Celastrina ebenina* UP♂. 2 May 1976, near Red River, Manifee Co., KY.
C. ebenina UP♀. 28 April 1954, Frank, Pendleton Co., WV.

Third row

Silvery Blue, *Glaucopsyche lygamus couperi* UP♂. 4 April 1981, South City Park, Griffith, Lake Co., IN. Coll. Irwin Leeuw
G. l. couperi UN♂. 16 May 1979, South City Park, Griffith, Lake Co., IN. Coll. Irwin Leeuw
G. l. couperi UP♀. 16 April 1981, South City Park, Griffith, Lake Co. IN. Coll. Irwin Leeuw
G. l. couperi UN♀. 21 May 1977, South City Park, Griffith, Lake Co., IN. Coll. Irwin Leeuw

Fourth row

Karner Blue, *Lycaeides melissa samuelis* UP♂. 11 June 1980, Hoosier Prairie Preserve, Griffith, Lake Co., IN.
L. m. samuelis UP♀. 11 June 1980, Hoosier Prairie Preserve, Lake Co., IN.
Northern Metalmark, *Calephelis borealis* UP♂. 2 July 1971, Silver Lake, Kosciusko Co., IN.
C. borealis UN♂. 2 July 1971, Silver Lake, Kosciusko Co., IN.

Fifth row

C. borealis UN♀. 8 July 1970, Silver Lake, Kosciusko Co., IN.
Swamp Metalmark, *Calephelis muticum* UP♂. 31 July 1979, North Manchester, Wabash Co., IN.
C. muticum UN♂. 30 July 1979, North Manchester, Wabash Co., IN.
C. muticum UN♂. 12 July 1971, Mongo Tamarack Bog, LaGrange Co., IN.

Sixth row

C. muticum UN♂. 22 July 1984, Nasby Fen, Mongo, LaGrange Co., IN.
C. muticum UN♂. 12 July 1971, Mongo Tamarack Bog, LaGrange Co., IN.

Manchester, Wabash County; and 11 April 1981, 10:50 A.M., 64° F, Wabash County. The latter pair was perched on a raspberry stem about 2.5 feet above the ground. The humidity was high. The female was the flight partner. This nominate subspecies has three broods in Indiana.

100. *Celastrina ebenina* Clench. Sooty Azure. Plate XXXI.

Description. The wingspread of this dark species varies from 0.75 to 1.25 inches (19–32 mm). This recently named species has been fully described and documented by Harry K. Clench (1972). The male is blackish brown with some blue scaling on the wing bases. The female is a lustrous, pale bluish gray, black-bordered, with extensive whitish suffusion. Ventrally, both sexes are pale ash to bluish white. The VHW is irregularly dotted with black; the marginal spots are large along the entire border.

Distribution and Habitat. It ranges from Illinois and western Pennsylvania south to Missouri and North Carolina. Marc Minno found the first Indiana specimens in Monroe County on 29 April 1978 (personal communication). *Ebenina* prefers moist deciduous forests and shaded northern slopes where Goat's Beard grows.

Life Cycle. Pyle (1981), the most complete source of information on this relatively new species, reports that the ribbed egg is greenish. The mature larva is a uniform whitish blue-green and faintly yellow tiger-striped. Its larval foodplant is Goat's Beard (*Aruncus dioicus*). The brownish flecked, black pupa is the overwintering form. It has one brood in April and early May. I have collected *ebenia*, but had confused it with dark-colored specimens of *C. ladon*, known then as *Lycaena pseudargiolus* var. "*nigra*" (Holland, 1940).

Tribe Scolitantidini Tutt

Genus *Glaucopsyche* Scudder

101. *Glaucopsyche lygamus couperi* Grote. Silvery Blue. Plate XXXI.

Description. The wingspread measures 1.0 to 1.25 inches (25–32 mm). Dorsally, the male is silvery blue with narrow black wing margins. The female is similar but the wing margins are broader and more diffused. In both sexes the ventral wings are dusted with gray scales. The second spot from the costal on the VHW is set inward more than the first and third, appearing as a crooked row of black dots ringed with white. The dots on the ventral lower wings are small.

Distribution and Habitat. The Silvery Blue ranges from New Brunswick and Quebec west to Manitoba, British Columbia, and California, including Illinois, Minnesota, Wisconsin, and Michigan.

In Indiana *couperi* is uncommon to rare in a few scattered counties from mid-April through July. Records are from northern and northeastern border counties. Recently, records for the Silvery Blue are coming mostly from Lake County. Erwin Leeuw sent me a fine series which he had collected from 10–21 May 1979, in the South City Park, Griffith, Lake County. The heavy pedestrian and vehicular travel (even snowmobiles) in this city park is endangering the remaining colonies. Since 1976 this species has been found annually in Lake County.

The Silver Blue never lingers into the summer. Look for it in our state and city parks, especially near lakes, streams, and other waterways.

Life Cycle. The early stages of *G. lygamus* have been well described; however, the color of the mature larva varies with the different subspecies. According to Howe (1975), the mature larvae are slug-shaped and variably colored—pale green, pale coffee to purplish. Many larvae have a darker dorsal stripe, frequently reddish brown with a purplish tinge. The larva has oblique whitish dashes and a lateral line that becomes purplish ventrally. The pupa is formed in debris and is attached with a silken girdle. The eggs are laid on various host plants, mostly members of the legume family (Fabaceae): Lupine (*Lupinus*), Vetch (*Vicia*), Locoweed (*Astragalus*), Wild Pea (*Lathyrus*), and others. *Lupinus perennis* is common in the open woods of the Hoosier Prairie Preserve, Lake County, which perhaps explains the presence of the Silvery Blue in this county. Many butterfly species reside near their larval foodplants.

The Silvery Blue overwinters in the pupal stage. It has one brood.

Tribe Polyommatini Swainson
Genus *Lycaeides* Hübner

102. *Lycaeides melissa samuelis* Nabokov. Karner Blue. Plate XXXI.

Description. The wingspread of this subspecies measures 0.9 to 1.25 inches (22–32 mm). Dorsally, the male is silvery blue or dark blue with narrow black margins; females are grayish brown with irregular bands of orange inside the narrow black border on the upper wings. Ventrally, both sexes are slaty gray with the orange bands showing more regularity (less suffusion) and black spots circled with white.

Distribution and Habitat. Our subspecies occurs in the Great Lakes area and the northeast, and in scattered colonies from the Mississippi River eastward and northward. Howe (1975) states that its type locality is Karner (formerly Center), New York.

Indiana records come mostly from the northern tier of counties, especially from Lake County, where Lupine grows undisturbed. With two permits in hand—one from the Indiana Department of Natural Resources and the other from the Nature Preserves Division—David Eiler and I optimistically entered the Hoosier Prairie Preserve in Schererville, Lake County, on 11 June 1980. Soon I had found one male Karner Blue. Eiler looked for Lupine (*Lupinus perennis*), which was soon found growing in patches throughout the preserve. He immediately set up his photography equipment, taking pictures of the wild Lupine flowers and the Karner Blues (males and females) perched on them. Dozens of these beautiful orange-bordered blues were found on the scattered patches of Lupine found throughout the more open wooded areas. Occasionally one was found perched on low vegetation on the open "trails."

Jack Munsee, Marc Minno, Ervin Leeuw, and perhaps others have recently located the Karner Blue in Lake County. *Lupinus* grows in several Indiana counties, so this butterfly should be found in more counties than are recorded on the map.

Life Cycle. The pale green egg has whitish ridges. The pea-green larva is covered with short brown hairs; it has a yellowish tinge and faint oblique stripes on the sides. Its body wall is very translucent. The larvae are attended by ants.

The Karner Blue, in Indiana, feeds mostly on Wild Lupine (*Lupinus perennis*). However, the list of foodplants is long: Alfalfa (*Medicago sativa*), Locoweed (*Astragalus*), *Ascispon americanus*, and others. Adults are abundant in the alfalfa fields of the west but usually represent a different subspecies of *L. melissa*. With such a variety of foodplants and numerous recent records of its presence in Indiana, I do not consider the Karner Blue an endangered species. However, the Indiana Department of Natural Resources is correct in its policy of preserving the natural habitats of this beautiful little butterfly.

This subspecies overwinters in the egg stage and, perhaps, as a young caterpillar. It probably has two broods, April–May and mid-June and July.

Family Riodinidae Grote
ৈ
Subfamily Riodininae Grote
ৈ
Genus *Calephelis* Grote and Robinson

103. *Calephelis borealis* (Grote and Robinson). **Northern Metalmark. Plate XXXI.**
Description. The wingspread measures from 1.0 to 1.25 inches (25–32 mm). This species is very similar to the Swamp Metalmark (*C. muticum*), the only other species in the family found in Indiana. Until 1937 the differences between the two species were overlooked. *Borealis* can usually be distinguished by the blackish shade across the upperside of both wings. The metallic marks are more crescent-shaped and connected, and the outer transverse line marks

are heavier and more prominent than in *muticum*. There are distinct genitalic differences. The Northern Metalmark is found in open woods; the Swamp Metalmark is found in bogs and swamps.

Distribution and Habitat. *C. borealis* occurs in southern New York, northern New Jersey, along the Allegheny and Appalachian mountains to central West Virginia, westward to Pennsylvania and southern Ohio, northern Kentucky, and Indiana.

In Indiana the county records are widely scattered. *Borealis* occurs in dry, hilly meadows and open woods where its foodplant grows. Sidney Badger found this species locally abundant in Howard County (personal communication). From 8–13 July 1969, it was common in a woods near Silver Lake, Kosciusko County. It occurred there each year until 1973; then it suddenly disappeared.

Life Cycle. The early stages were described by dos Passos in 1936 (Howe, 1975). The egg is flattened with large polygonal cells. The stout larva is whitish green with black spots on the back. It is covered with plumelike hairs. Its only larval foodplant is Ragwort (*Senecio obovatus*). Before reaching maturity the larva normally passes through eight instars, usually hibernating during the fifth or sixth instar. Pupation occurs under the leaf litter, where it overwinters.

104. *Calephelis muticum* McAlpine. Swamp Metalmark. Plate XXXI.

Description. The wingspread of *C. muticum* is 0.9 to 1.1 inches (22–28 mm). This species is smaller, brighter reddish above, and has less checkered fringes than *borealis*. A similar species, the Little Metalmark (*C. virginiensis*), is still smaller and more rust-colored above with the wings more rounded. In *muticum* the wings are angular. The upper surfaces are uniformly deep mahogany with fine, blacker scalloping. The Swamp Metalmark lacks the wide, central darkened bands; instead, the bands are formed of silvery green metallic markings.

Distribution and Habitat. The range of *C. muticum* is from Ohio, southern Michigan, Illinois and Missouri.

From 1969 to 1975 the Swamp Metalmark was fairly common in Indiana's largest Tamarack bog, located in the Pigeon River State Fish and Game Area at Mongo, LaGrange County. Collecting in the bog can be somewhat dangerous, not only because of the ever-present poison sumac, but also because of the spongy soil, which makes the collector feel as if he were walking on a spring coil mattress. Adult butterflies occurred in July, rarely in mid-August. Its flight is weak; it moves only a short distance.

On 30 July 1979 I was very surprised to find two *muticum* in a wet meadow near North Manchester in Wabash County. This represents a southward extension of the range. Its larval foodplant, Swamp Thistle (*Cirsium muticum*), was soon discovered near the place where the first specimen was collected. On 17

August 1979 a third specimen was found in the same area. In recent years the Swamp Metalmark has been difficult to find. On 21 July 1983 two specimens were collected in the Sawmill Fen in LaGrange County by David Eiler (personal communication).

Life Cycle. The sculptured egg is laid on the underside of young Swamp Thistle leaves. The pale green larva has plumelike hairs and a few or no black spots along the back. *Muticum* overwinters as a partially grown caterpillar. The pupa is surrounded with fuzzy hair and is supported by a silken girdle. It has only one brood.

Family Libytheidae Boisduval

Genus *Libytheana* Michener

105. *Libytheana bachmanii bachmanii* (Kirtland). Snout Butterfly. Plate XXXII.

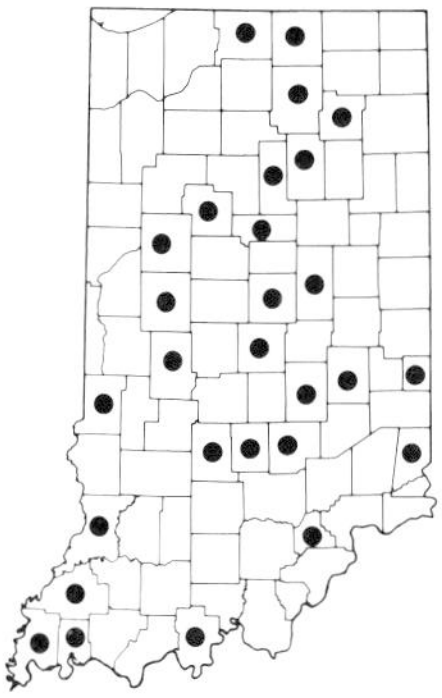

Description. The wingspread measures 1.6 to 1.9 inches (41–48 mm). The long, beaklike palpi clearly distinguish this species. In the Old World members of this genus are called Beaks instead of Snout Butterflies. The photographs make identification easy. Early spring specimens are ventrally dark with little mottling. Summer and autumn forms are light beneath with more extensive mottling.

Distribution and Habitat. The Snout Butterfly occurs over the entire eastern area north to the Canadian Zone. *L. b. bachmanii* occurs in Ohio, Illinois, and Indiana. Apparently this nominate subspecies occurs throughout Indiana from April to early November in favorable years. My earliest record was 6 April 1979 at North Manchester, Wabash County. The rather limp adult was found on the west side of a big barn, where it was protected from the weather. Normally, it is more common in July and August. Look for the Snout Butterfly along roadsides, in woods, fields, and open country. It visits flowers, cultivated and wild. Muddy streams and sandy lake margins attract them; they can be found, sometimes by the dozens, basking in the sunshine. In the spring look for them on Dogwood flowers.

Life Cycle. The egg is pale green and the larva dark green with yellow stripes. The head is small, but the two thoracic segments are enlarged, forming a hump with a pair of yellow-based black tubercles. Its larval foodplant is Hackberry (*Celtis occidentalis*). It has three or four broods and hibernates in the pupal stage.

Family Heliconiidae Swainson

🍃

Subfamily Heliconiinae Swainson

🍃

Genus *Agraulis* Boisduval and Leconte

106. *Agraulis vanillae* (Linnaeus). Gulf Fritillary. Plate XXXII.

Description. Its wingspread is from 2.0 to 2.5 inches (55–65 mm). The upper wings are bright orange-brown with dark brown and black markings. The VFW deepens to crimson basally; the VHW has distinct, elongate spots of brilliant metallic silver. Females are darker and the dark markings are heavier.

Distribution and Habitat. The Gulf Fritillary is a resident throughout the southern United States into Mexico. It migrates northward into the Great Basin, the Rockies, Midwest, Great Lakes, and mid-Atlantic states.

W. S. Blatchley (1891) reported this handsome heliconian from Vanderburgh County in Indiana. He placed it in the family Nymphalidae and subfamily Nymphalinae. Some authorities still agree with this classification. I agree with Alexander Klots, Miller, Brown, and others that the Gulf Fritillary belongs in the family Heliconiidae. Irwin and Downey (1973) assign the Illinois specimens to the subspecies *A. v. nigrior* Michener, following Klots (1951, rev. 1964). They reported that McNeese saw several *vanillae* at Centerville, St. Clair County, Illinois, and collected a newly emerged male on 2 September 1966, which was deposited with the Illinois Natural History Society.

I found *A. vanillae* to be common in Mexico in July 1973, less common in Venice, Florida, in February 1983. It occupies forest edges, roadside flowers, and even city gardens. Authentic recent records are needed for Indiana.

Life Cycle. The oblong egg is yellow and ribbed. The mature larva (about 38 mm) is dark brown with rusty stripes and rows of branching black spines. Its larval foodplant is Passion Flower (*Passiflora incarnata*). However, Blatchley states that those found in Indiana doubtless feed on the allied plant, *Passiflora lutea*. The warty pupa is mottled with brown. In Florida, adults appear in February and March, but dates for Indiana are lacking. The immigrant *vanillae* cannot withstand our cold winters, but look for it in late fall.

Family Nymphalidae Swainson

The family Nymphalidae comprises the largest family of true butterflies. They are called "Brush-footed Butterflies" because the fore legs of both sexes are reduced to useless stumps. The structural features of the highly diversified nymphalids are so great that no satisfactory arrangement of nomenclature exists (there are the "splitters" and the "lumpers," so the confusion persists).

PLATE XXXII

Top row
Snout Butterfly, *Libytheana bachmanii bachmanii* UP♂. 25 July 1978, Camp Mack, Milford, Kosciusko Co., IN.
L. b. bachmanii UN♂. 25 July 1978, Camp Mack, Milford, Kosciusko Co., IN.
L. b. bachmanii UP♀. 26 July 1978, Camp Mack, Milford, Kosciusko Co., IN.

Second row
L. b. bachmanii UN♀. 28 July 1973, North Manchester, Wabash Co., IN.
Gulf Fritillary, *Agraulis vanillae nigrior* UP♀. 10 February 1983, Venice, FL.

Third row
A. v. nigrior UN♂. 10 February 1983, Venice, FL.
Variegated Fritillary, *Euptoieta claudia* UP♂. 15 July 1983, Whitewater Memorial State Park, Union Co., IN.
E. claudia UN♂. 18 August 1984, Mongo, LaGrange Co., IN.

Fourth row
E. claudia UP♀. 3 August 1983, Mongo, LaGrange Co., IN.
E. claudia UN♀. 27 August 1970, Silver Lake, Kosciusko Co., IN.

The majority of the nymphalids are medium to large butterflies. The palpi are robust and hairy. Although the venation varies greatly, the cell is open on one or both wings with few exceptions (may be closed by a very weak vein). Nymphalids have five radial branches on the FW and only one anal vein, never bifurcate. The HW has two anal veins and one well-developed humeral vein. In Indiana there are twenty-nine species, belonging to four subfamilies and twelve genera.

Subfamily Argynninae Blanchard

Genus *Euptoieta* Doubleday

107. *Euptoieta claudia* (Cramer). Variegated Fritillary. Plate XXXII.

Description. *E. claudia* has a wingspread of 1.75 to 2.25 inches (44–57 mm). Dorsally, the wings are shades of brown, yellow, and black—truly variegated—with prominent zigzag markings in the basal half of the wing. It is unlike any of the closely related *Speyeria* which follow.

Distribution and Habitat. This species occurs as a resident in much of the south. Migrants range northward to Minnesota, Manitoba, Wyoming, and other states in the summer.

There are scattered county records throughout Indiana. Usually it is an uncommon migrant, adults appearing in late June until mid-October. *Claudia* flies low to the ground, but its fast and darting flight makes it difficult to catch. Look for adults in open meadows, along fences, the edge of woods, and clearings. It cannot be found in densely wooded areas. It is more common in the summer and fall.

Life Cycle. The cream-colored egg is laid on a variety of host plants. The mature larva is orange-red with a black lateral stripe enclosing white spots with six rows of black spines (Howe 1975). Its larval foodplants include violets and pansies (*Viola*), Passion Flower (*Passiflora*), Stonecrop (*Sedum*), May Apple (*Podophyllum*), Purslane (*Portulaca*), Moonseed (*Menispermum*), and Plantain (*Plantago*). The bluish green chrysalis is ornamented with black, yellow, and orange marks and gold bumps. This species is multivoltine in the south, but only a migrant northward. Our winters are too cold for the adults to survive.

Genus *Speyeria* Scudder

The members of this Nearctic genus are difficult to identify; occasionally the differences between species and subspecies are slight. The limits of variation within a species must be determined, and few workers have become truly competent in this genus. One of the experts on this group is L. Paul Grey, who identified many specimens for the writer.

108. *Speyeria diana* (Cramer). Diana. Plates XXXIII, XXXIV.

Description. The Diana has a wingspread of 3.0 to 3.9 inches (76–98 mm). This species exhibits sexual dimorphism, as the plates show. The male is much smaller than the female. The dark *diana* female probably mimics *Battus philenor*. Unlike other fritillaries, *diana* is without the silver spots on the discal area of the VHW.

Distribution and Habitat. Diana occurs in the mountains and piedmont of West Virginia south to Georgia and west to southern Ohio, Indiana, Missouri, and Arkansas. According to Blatchley (1891), S. G. Evans collected *diana* in the vicinity of Evansville, Indiana, for ten or twelve years from June to mid-August. He found them in upland meadows and along the borders of woods. Masters and Masters (1969) found one male on 15 July 1962 just north of Troy in Perry County.

In recent years the range of this beautiful butterfly has declined, probably as the result of cutting trees (habitat destruction). Through these many years of collecting, I have never found it in Indiana.

Life Cycle. The larvae are black and spiny, feeding on violets (*Viola*). The pupa is mottled with light brown and red. Like other members of this genus, it has only one brood.

109. *Speyeria cybele cybele* (Fabricius). Great Spangled Fritillary. Plate XXXV.

Description. The wingspread is 3.2 to 3.9 inches (82–98 mm). This species is our largest and most common fritillary. The VHW has many silver spots in the discal area. The ground color of *cybele* is less reddish. In the central area of the FW, the male has heavy black scales, lacking in the female. The VHW has a wide light area on the submarginal band and lacks the submarginal dark spot below the cell on the upper FW. Its colors are brighter than in the other subspecies.

Distribution and Habitat. The nominate subspecies ranges from New England south to Georgia and west to the Great Plains except for the northern Middle West and Manitoba. It has been found in nearly every county in Indiana, occurring from mid-May to October. It is common in deciduous woods, especially where woods border wet meadows. It gets nectar from many flowers, both wild and cultivated, and shows a preference for Milkweeds (Asclepiadaceae).

Life Cycle. The early stages of the *cybele* complex have been described by Scudder, Klots, and others (Howe, 1975). The pale brown egg hatches into a black larva with branching spines that are orange at the base. The chrysalis is mottled. The larval foodplants of the Great Spangled Fritillary are various species of violets (*Viola*).

In Indiana I have found eleven pairs *in copula*. Nine pairs were found mating in June, from the 22nd to the 26th, while only two pairs were observed in July (9 July 1969 and 1 July 1980). Six pairs were found on 22 June 1977, 70° F,

PLATE XXXIII

Diana, *Speyeria diana* UP♂. 4 July 1969, Poverty Hollow, Montgomery Co., VA.
S. diana UP♀. 14 August 1969, Poverty Hollow, Montgomery Co., VA.

PLATE XXXIV

Diana, *Speyeria diana* UN♂. 20 August 1969, Poverty Hollow, Montgomery Co., VA.
S. diana UN♀. 20 August 1969, Poverty Hollow, Montgomery Co., VA.

PLATE XXXV

between 2:15 and 3:25 P.M., at Silver Lake, Kosciusko County, where the edge of the woods joined a grassy field. Copulation for these eleven cases occurred at temperatures ranging from 70° F to 84° F. In every case, the female was the flight partner. Although the adults have a long flight period (mid-May through October), the nominate subspecies has only one brood.

On 12 July 1978 I observed a male *cybele* pursue a female. The female seemed to reject the pursuer by positioning herself on the underside of a blade of grass with the male directly above on the upper surface. She remained motionless with her wings closed, as the helpless male fluttered his wings and moved his antennae up and down. He soon left her and pursued another female and was again rejected in the same manner.

110. *Speyeria aphrodite aphrodite* (Fabricius). Aphrodite. Plate XXXV.

Description. The Aphrodite is considerably smaller than the Great Spangled Fritillary, with a wingspread of 2.0 to 2.9 inches (51–73 mm). Adult *S. a. aphrodite* is bright fulvous above and is distinguished by the dark cinnamon-brown disc which normally only partially invades the outer band. The nominate *aphrodite* is very similar to *S. a. alcestis*. In *aphrodite* the FW veins of the male are narrowly lined with black; in *alcestis* the veins are heavily suffused with black scales. *Aphrodite* has a small black spot in the basal area between Cu_2 and 2A on the primaries above; this spot is missing in *alcestis*. In Mongo, LaGrange County, both *aphrodite* and *alcestis* occasionally appear together, though the latter subspecies is more common.

Distribution and Habitat. The nominate subspecies occurs from New York south to North Carolina and Tennessee and west through northern Ohio and other Midwestern states to Nebraska.

In Indiana it occurs in the northern counties. Adults fly from late June to September. Usually Aphrodite is less common than the Great Spangled Fritillary. In Mongo I usually find Aphrodites nectaring on Butterfly Weed (*Asclepias tuberosa*) and other milkweed flowers. In 1968 a few *aphrodite* were found in Wabash and Kosciusko counties, but have been absent in these two counties ever since.

Life Cycle. The Aphrodite larva feeds on the violets (*Viola* spp.) which grow in our area. The caterpillar is blackish brown with black bands and orange-sided spines. The brownish black chrysalis has yellow wing cases and gray abdomen. After hatching, the caterpillar overwinters.

111. *Speyeria aphrodite alcestis* (Edwards). Ruddy Silverspot. Plate XXXVI.

Description. The wingspread is 2.1 to 3.0 inches (55–75 mm); it is only slightly larger, on the average, than the nominate *aphrodite*. The VHW of *alcestis* is uniformly reddish cinnamon-brown, without any band of buff on the

outer margin. A specimen collected 12 July 1971 on milkweed flowers in Mongo, LaGrange County, was identified and verified as *S. a. alcestis* by Paul Grey.

Distribution and Habitat. Blatchley (1891) reported *alcestis* in only two counties: Lake, where Worthington reported it as common; and Monroe, where a single specimen was collected in a meadow 1 July 1886. The Monroe County record probably should be questioned. Recent records are from the far northern counties. Some years it is common from 25 June to late August.

Life Cycle. The egg is greenish and conoidal, with many vertical ribs. The larval head is black, with yellow behind. The velvety-black larva is ornamented with black spines which are yellow at the basal ends. The larval foodplants are violets.

112. *Speyeria idalia* (Drury). Regal Fritillary. Plates XXXVI, XXXVII.

Description. The wingspread measures 2.6 to 3.6 inches (66–92 mm). The Regal Fritillary, with its velvety, blue-black HW, cannot be mistaken for any other member of this genus. The marginal row of spots on the upper HW of the male is fulvous; in the female they are creamy white like the submarginal row.

Distribution and Habitat. This species ranges from southern New England westward to southern North Dakota, southward to northern Virginia, Georgia, northeastern Oklahoma, and eastern Colorado. Harris, in his *Butterflies of Georgia* (1972), pictures a male *S. idalia* from Porter County, Indiana. Blatchley (1891) reported it in Monroe, Vanderburgh, Fayette, and Lake counties. Usually the Regal Fritillary is uncommon to rare in widely scattered counties. Some years it is absent.

Idalia is basically a prairie species; thus it is more common in late summer along railroad tracks and virgin grasslands. It may appear occasionally in wet meadows in woodland areas. Its natural grassland, prairie habitat is rapidly disappearing. Thus in recent years this species has become scarce.

Life Cycle. According to Howe (1975), the black mature larva has six rows of flashy spines surmounted by black bristles. The spines on the two dorsal rows are white and tipped with black. The larval foodplant is Bird's Foot Violet (*Viola pedata*) and probably other species of *Viola*. The caterpillars feed under the cover of darkness. Like other *Speyeria*, *idalia* has only one brood.

113. *Speyeria atlantis* (Edwards). Atlantis Fritillary. Plate XXXVII.

Description. The wingspread of *atlantis* measures 1.75 to 2.6 inches (44–67 mm). The taxonomy of the *atlantis* group is very difficult and the exact subspecies which occurs rarely in Indiana has not been determined. In *atlantis* the outer marginal border of the upper FW is more solidly black than in *aphrodite* and does not consist primarily of a fulvous line between the two black lines. Dorsally, the ground color is darker; ventrally, the color is purplish

PLATE XXXVI

Top row   Ruddy Silverspot, *Speyeria aphrodite alcestis* UP♂. 28 June 1968, Pigeon River State Fish and Game Area, Mongo, LaGrange Co., IN.

S. a. alcestis UN♂. 24 June 1982, Pigeon River State Fish and Game Area, Mongo, LaGrange Co., IN.

Second row   *S. a. alcestis* UP♀. 12 August 1970, Pigeon River State Fish and Game Area, Mongo, LaGrange Co., IN. Det. Paul Grey

S. a. alcestis UN♀. 12 August 1970, Pigeon River State Fish and Game Area, Mongo, LaGrange Co., IN.

Third row   Regal Fritillary, *Speyeria idalia* UP♂. 15 August 1934, North Manchester, Wabash Co., IN.

S. idalia UN♀. 6 July 1969, North Manchester, Wabash Co., IN.

PLATE XXXVII

Top row — Regal Fritillary, *Speyeria idalia* UP♀. 28 August 1983, Green Co., MI. Det. Irwin Leeuw

S. idalia UN♀. 28 August 1983, Green Co., MI. Det. Irwin Leeuw

Second row — Atlantis Fritillary, *Speyeria atlantis* UP♂. 17 July 1959, Mackinac Co., MI. Det M. C. Nielsen

S. atlantis UP♀. 17 July 1959, Mackinac Co., MI. Det. M. C. Nielsen

Third row — Silver-bordered Fritillary, *Clossiana selene* UP♂. 6 June 1969, Pigeon River State Fish and Game Area, Mongo, LaGrange Co., IN.

C. selene UN♂. 6 June 1969, Pigeon River State Fish and Game Area, Mongo, La-Grange Co., IN.

C. selene UP♀. 13 August 1973, Pigeon River State Fish and Game Area, Mongo, LaGrange Co., IN.

Fourth row — *C. selene* UN♀. 14 August 1973, Pigeon River State Fish and Game Area, Mongo, LaGrange Co., IN.

C. selene UP♂. 11 July 1975, North Manchester, Wabash Co., IN.

C. selene UN♀. 24 July 1983, North Manchester, Wabash Co., IN.

brown, not reddish brown as in *aphrodite*. The silver spots in *atlantis* are slightly more extensive.

Distribution and Habitat. *Speyeria atlantis* ranges from the Maritime Provinces south in the mountains to Virginia, west to Michigan, Minnesota, Alberta, Oregon, California, and south through the Rockies.

Blatchley (1891) recorded *atlantis* (he called it the Mountain Silverspot) in two widely separated counties, Lake and Vanderburgh, the latter record by Evans. *Atlantis* is seldom seen in open country, but occurs in narrow mountain passes and grass fields which skirt the forests. It is attracted by decaying animals. It has been recorded in only five Indiana counties, mostly in the northern border of the state.

Life Cycle. The honey-yellow eggs are laid on *Viola*. The mature larva is purplish or blackish with light brown or gray stripes and orange spines. The pupa is brown, specked with black and mottled with light brown. This species overwinters as tiny larvae. It has one brood.

Genus *Clossiana* Reuss

114. *Clossiana selene* (Denis and Schiffermüller). Silver-bordered Fritillary. Plate XXXVII.

Description. The wingspread measures from 1.4 to 2.0 inches (35–51 mm). In general, *selene* is tawny orange to ocherous above and has black lines and dashes as a broken black rim. Dorsally, the FW is orange. The VHW has four rows of metallic silver spots including a row on the margin. The central cell spot is elongated and silvery. The submarginal dots are dark.

This group of Lesser Fritillaries has recently been changed from the genus *Boloria* to *Clossiana*, but the confusion does not end there. Along with many others, I had accepted the subspecies *C. s. myrina* (Cramer) as the one found in Indiana. However, Kohler (1977) reported that "specimens from central Ohio, northern Indiana, and northern Illinois (except the extreme northeast corner), and Iowa previously considered to be *myrina* have been found to be *nebraskensis*." The specimens in my collection seem to represent integrates chiefly between *myrina* and *nebraskensis;* of course, both subspecies may occur in Indiana. The technical differences in the subspecies may be read in several standard publications, such as Ehrlich and Ehrlich (1961), Klots (1964), and Howe (1975). A number of the described subspecies have doubtful status.

Distribution and Habitat. The map does not differentiate the subspecies (one or more) which occur in Indiana. *Selene* ranges from Labrador, Quebec, and Newfoundland west to Alberta and south to the coastal plains of Maryland, North Carolina, and northern Illinois. Irwin and Downey (1973) record their Silver-bordered Fritillary as *Boloria selene myrina* (Cramer), as did Shull and Badger (1971) in their annotated list of Indiana butterflies. In any case, *selene* collected in Indiana are found in the northern counties from mid-May (early) or June to September. Look for them in moist meadows and bogs where willows (*Salix*) and other wild shrubs grow. Every year I have found them in the tamarack bog at Mongo, LaGrange County. On 4 June 1978 I was surprised to find *selene* in a swampy field near North Manchester in Wabash County. A few have been found there each year since then.

Life Cycle. The larva is greenish brown mottled with green. The upper and lateral spines on the prothorax are much longer than the others. Violets (*Viola*) supply the larvae with food. The Silver-bordered Fritillary hibernates as a newly hatched or half-grown larva. It is multivoltine.

115. *Clossiana bellona bellona* (Fabricius). Meadow Fritillary. Plate XXXVIII.

Description. The wingspread measures 1.25 to 1.9 inches (32–48 mm). Some recent literature has treated this butterfly under the species name *toddi* (Holland). However, Howe (1975), Ferris and Brown (1980), and Miller and Brown (1980) use the species name *bellona*. The status of several subspecies is still not clear. In Indiana there apparently is a cline between the nominate *bellona* and *C. b. toddi*. The name *ammiralis* Hemming is a synonym of *bellona*. Thus the subspecies name *C. b. ammiralis* used by Shull and Badger (1972) has been suppressed. The Indiana specimens, which I have examined, have the outer margin of the FW not evenly curved but angled at vein M_2. The VHW has a purplish tone, varying greatly with the seasons and, as such, is not a definitive characteristic for subspecific determination.

Distribution and Habitat. The Meadow Fritillary occurs from the Canadian and Transition zones of eastern North America and the lower elevations of the Rocky Mountains south to Colorado. It is found throughout the state of Indiana, more commonly in the northern counties. Adults fly from late April (earliest date: 26 April 1969, Wabash County) until mid-October (latest date: 13 October 1968, Kosciusko County). The species is more common in May through September. It frequents wet fields, pastures, hayfields, ditches by roadsides, and edges of streams and lakes.

Life Cycle. The egg is greenish yellow. The purplish black larva is mottled with yellow and black and has branching, brown spines. Violets (*Viola*) provide the larvae with food. The Meadow Fritillary overwinters as a half-grown larva. The pupa is yellowish brown.

In Indiana I have found two pairs *in copula*. One pair, which was observed 30 September 1975, 3:45 P.M., 72° F, at North Manchester, Wabash County, had settled in a grassy field for hours. I have watched this common species engage in courtship activities, but have not yet figured out the rejection method used by the females. The other pair was copulating 19 July 1980, 9:50 A.M., 83° F, Liberty, Union County. In both cases, the female was the active flight partner. It has two broods.

PLATE XXXVIII

Top row Meadow Fritillary, *Clossiana bellona bellona* UP♂. 21 August 1973, Delphi, Carroll Co., IN.
C. b. bellona UN♂. 12 August 1973, North Manchester, Wabash Co., IN.
C. b. bellona UP♀. 28 July 1983, North Manchester, Wabash Co., IN.

Second row *C. b. bellona* UN♀. 21 August 1973, Delphi, Carroll Co., IN.
Gorgone Checkerspot, *Charidryas gorgone carlota* UP♀. 20 August 1977, Lawrence, Douglas Co., KS. Coll. David Eiler
C. g. carlota UN♀. 20 August 1977, Lawrence, Douglas Co., KS. Coll. David Eiler

Third row Silvery Checkerspot, *Charidryas nycteis nycteis* UP♂. 7 August 1973, Silver Lake, Kosciusko Co., IN.
C. n. nycteis UP♀. 23 August 1969, Silver Lake, Kosciusko Co., IN.
C. n. nycteis UN♀. 7 August 1973, Silver Lake, Kosciusko Co., IN.

Fourth row Harris' Checkerspot, *Charidryas harrisii* UP♂. 14 June 1974, Montcalm Co., MI. Det. M. C. Nielsen
C. harrisii UP♀. 1 July 1967, Oscoda, MI. Det. M. C. Nielsen
Pearly Crescentspot or Pearl Crescent, *Phyciodes tharos tharos* UP♂. 12 July 1969, Burlington, Carroll Co., IN.

Fifth row *P. t. tharos* UP♂. 26 August 1969, North Manchester, Wabash Co., IN. This specimen was mating with the next one.
P. t. tharos UP♀. 26 August 1969, North Manchester, Wabash Co., IN.
P. t. tharos UN♂. 12 July 1969, Burlington, Carroll Co., IN.
P. t. tharos UP♀. 2 July 1973, North Manchester, Wabash Co., IN.

Sixth row *P. t. tharos* UN♀. 2 August 1973, North Manchester, Wabash Co., IN.
Tawny Crescentspot, *Phyciodes batesii* UP♂. 13 June 1975, Montcalm Co., MI. Det. M. C. Nielsen
Baltimore, *Euphydryas phaeton phaeton* UP♂. 12 July 1973, North Manchester, Wabash Co., IN.

Subfamily Melitaeinae Grote

Tribe Melitaeini Grote

Genus *Charidryas* Scudder

116. *Charidryas gorgone carlota* (Reakirt). Gorgone Checkerspot. Plate XXXVIII.

Description. *Gorgone* has a wingspread of 1.1 to 1.4 inches (28–35 mm). Dorsally it has orange and black in equal bands and a row of black on the HW. Ventrally, the FW is orange with black bands and a whitish tip. Distinctly characteristic of the subspecies *carlota* are the arrowheadlike outer lines and lunules on the VHW.

Distribution and Habitat. This species occurs from the eastern slopes of the Rocky Mountains eastward to the Carolinas and Georgia, and from southern Manitoba to Mexico (Howe). Irwin and Downey (1973) record the subspecies *carlota* in Perry County in a fallow field near a stream, the first state record. As they suggest, *carlota* should be more widespread in Indiana than records indicate. It has thus far been reported from only four counties.

The Gorgone Checkerspot (sometimes called Gorgone Crescentspot) takes nectar from Goldenrod flowers. It may be found in meadows, grassy roadsides, and in pine and open hardwood forests. It should occur from May through July; it is uncommon or rare.

Life Cycle. The eggs are cream-colored, ribbed, and laid in clusters. The yellowish larva has three longitudinal black stripes, and the barbed spines are black. Its larval foodplants are Sunflowers (*Helianthus*), Ragweed (*Ambrosia trifida*), and other Compositae. The pupa is mottled and gray to cream-colored. The larvae feed together and overwinter when half-grown. It has one brood in our area.

117. *Charidryas nycteis nycteis* (Doubleday and Hewitson). Silvery Checkerspot. Plate XXXVIII.

Description. The wingspread measures 1.4 to 1.75 inches (35–48 mm). This nominate subspecies has a wide orange-brown to fulvous band across both wings dorsally, with wide blackish marginal borders. On the basal area of the VFW and VHW the pattern is somewhat paler than in the other subspecies; nevertheless, the silvery sheen is present on the VHW of this form as well as the others.

Distribution and Habitat. The Silvery Checkerspot ranges from southern Canada, the Maritime Provinces west to Manitoba, south to New Jersey, North Carolina, Ohio, Indiana, Missouri, and Kansas.

This nominate subspecies probably occurs throughout Indiana; however, records for the southwestern counties are needed. It is fairly common to very common from 17 May (earliest date noted) to mid-October. Look for it in open deciduous woods, roadsides, meadows and borders of streams, ponds, and other waterways. It is easily captured on flowers or when perched on the tips of shrubs.

Life Cycle. The egg is ridged on the upper third, pitted on the middle third, and smooth on the lower third; it is pale green (Howe, 1975). The mature larva is velvety black with a dull orange middorsal stripe and has purplish streaks on the sides between the stigmata. The entire body is whitish speckled. The pearly-gray pupa is marked with blackish brown. It hibernates as a partially grown larva. Sunflowers (*Helianthus*) and Asters (*Aster*) provide the larvae with food.

I have collected three pairs *in copula*: 17 June 1971, 3:05 P.M., 85° F, Silver Lake, Kosciusko County; 23 June 1977, 3:40 P.M., 82° F, Milford, Kosciusko County; and 28 June 1978, 3:30 P.M., 88° F, Silver Lake, Kosciusko County. The first pair mated in a raspberry patch surrounded by trees. The last pair perched on dogbane. The female was the active flight partner. It has one brood.

118. *Charidryas harrisii* (Scudder). Harris' Checkerspot. Plate XXXVIII.

Description. Formerly this species was known as *Chlosyne harrisii* or *Chlosyne* (*Charidryas*) *harrisii* (Scudder). The wingspread is 1.25 to 1.75 inches (32–44 mm). Dorsally, the wings are light orange with brownish black markings. The VHW has prominent whitish, black-edged basal and median spots and a submarginal row of crescents.

Distribution and Habitat. This species ranges from the Maritime Provinces west to Manitoba and south to New Jersey, Pennsylvania, northern Ohio, Indiana, Michigan, Wisconsin, and Illinois. Irwin and Downey (1971) report 1931 and 1960 records from Illinois. It may be overlooked because of its resemblance to the Silvery Checkerspot. Klots (1951) included Indiana in its range.

In the 1930s *C. harrisii* was not uncommon but sporadic in June and July in Wabash and Kosciusko counties. Unfortunately, specimens I collected then were inadvertently destroyed during our stay in India. The Harris' Checkerspot has been reported from three counties, most frequently from the tamarack bog, Mongo, LaGrange County. This species inhabits bogs, wet meadows, marshes, and other wet places where the Blue Flag (*Iris versicolor*) grows. Destruction of the wetlands is partially responsible for its decrease.

Life Cycle. Scudder and others have detailed the early stages (see Howe, 1975). Hundreds of eggs are laid in clusters on Aster (*Aster umbellatus*) and occasionally on Crownbeard (*Verbesina helianthoides*). The larvae colonize in a silken web, where they overwinter as half-grown caterpillars. The mature larva is orange with black lines and black, branching spines. The white chrysalis has black-tipped tubercles on the back. It has one brood in June and July.

Genus *Phyciodes* Hübner

119. *Phyciodes tharos tharos* (Drury). Pearly Crescentspot; Pearl Crescent. Plate XXXVIII.

Description. The wingspread of the nominate subspecies measures 1.0 to 1.5 inches (25–38 mm). Ehrlich and Ehrlich (1961) give the best detailed key for this genus. *Tharos* can be separated from the other members of the genus by the extensive, relatively unmarked orange-brown basal and limbal areas on the VFW. There is a noticeable difference in the seasonal forms. The summer form, called "*morpheus*," has the VHW almost entirely yellow or cream, while the cool-weather form (early spring and late autumn), called "*marcia*," has the underwing surface variously marked with light gray to brown scales. Our nominate subspecies blends with other subspecies. Work is in progress elsewhere that may further define other subspecies or even new species from this quite variable complex.

Distribution and Habitat. *Tharos* ranges north into Canada, west to the Rocky Mountains, and south to the Gulf States and Florida.

The Pearl Crescent occurs throughout the state of Indiana from April (early) or May to October, being common or abundant in most counties. It is a fast flier, active and pugnacious, frequently pursuing other butterflies near its perch. *Tharos* visits most flowers (cultivated and wild). When alighting on flowers or the bare ground, it holds its wings out at the sides, "sawing" them up and down several times.

Life Cycle. The eggs are laid in clusters on *Aster* leaves and related Compositae. These egg clusters may include up to two hundred eggs, in layers sometimes three deep. The mature larva is greenish and has bristly, blackish to yellow-brown tubercles. The blackish brown body has a yellow lateral stripe and yellow dots on the back. The gregarious larvae do not spin a web. The chrysalis is ornamented with short abdominal tubercles.

I have found seventy-six pairs *in copula* from 1970 to 1982. They have been found copulating every month from 14 May until 7 October (a late date for any species). Mating sometimes occurs in the early morning hours (9:00 to 10:00), but the great majority mated between 11:00 A.M. and 3:30 P.M. Only a few mated between 3:30 and 5:45 P.M.

In one pair courtship lasted only five minutes prior to copulation. Twice the female flew to a new location only to be pursued by the male. When the pair perched on a blade of grass, there were moments of wings rubbing and antennae touching. Then their caudal portions were joined, achieving copulation. When disturbed, the female, as is always the case in this species, flew a few feet carrying the male, which had its wings completely closed. The author watched another pair courting for one and one-half hours, but no mating occurred.

Temperatures recorded when mating *tharos* were observed ranged from 66°

to 90° F, with the majority of the records between the mid-70s and the mid-80s. Mating occurs in a variety of habitats—near margins of lakes, rivers, and streams, occasionally in an open lawn or field. Mating pairs were collected in Wabash, Kosciusko, Carroll, LaGrange, Noble, Union, and Warrick counties. *Tharos* has four, possibly five, broods in Indiana.

120. *Phyciodes batesii* (Reakirt). Tawny Crescentspot. Plate XXXVIII.

Description. The wingspread is 1.25 to 1.5 inches (32–38 mm). This species is very similar to *tharos*, and some specimens are difficult to identify. The VHW of *batesii* is almost an entirely unmarked yellow with the small brownish submarginal spots occupying the spaces between the veins (easily confused with the female *tharos* of the "*marcia*" seasonal form). The VFW of *batesii* has more extensive black coloring and the median line is complete or nearly so. The bar across the discal cell is usually clouded with orange-brown and is indistinct when compared with *tharos*.

Distribution and Habitat. The Tawny Crescentspot ranges from New England, Ontario, and Quebec west to Nebraska and south to Virginia.

Batesii has been recorded in only four widely scattered counties in Indiana. F. T. Hall of Crawfordsville first reported *P. batesii*, adding it to our state list (Hall, 1936). Shull and Badger (1971) found that what they had previously identified as *batesii* turned out to be aberrant *tharos*. Both species are known to coexist in the same habitat. Masters and Masters (1969) suggest that *batesii* may be widespread from Brown County northward. As yet, this has not proved to be the situation.

Life Cycle. The early stages are incompletely known. Reportedly, the larvae feed on *Aster*. It has one brood in late May or June.

Genus *Euphydryas* Scudder

121. *Euphydryas phaeton phaeton* (Drury). Baltimore. Plates XXXVIII and XXXIX.

Description. The Baltimore has a wingspread of 1.6 to 2.5 inches (41–64 mm). Dorsally, it is black with numerous cream-colored dots, with red-orange spots near the base of the wings and a border of red-orange half-moons. Ventrally, the colors are brighter. The female is considerably larger than the male. The Baltimore was selected for a stamp issued 6 June 1977.

Distribution and Habitat. *Phaeton* occurs in the Maritime Provinces, southern Quebec and Ontario, south to Virginia, Georgia, Illinois, Michigan, Minnesota, Wisconsin, eastern Kansas, and Iowa.

In Indiana the nominate subspecies is found in the northern counties from mid-June through July (one very exceptional record on 5 September 1975, in a wet meadow, North Manchester, Wabash County). The Baltimore is very local

PLATE XXXIX

Top row   Baltimore, *Euphydryas phaeton phaeton* UP♂. 12 July 1969, North Manchester, Wabash Co., IN.
E. p. phaeton UN♂. 12 June 1973, North Manchester, Wabash Co., IN.
E. p. phaeton UP♀. 12 June 1976, North Manchester, Wabash Co., IN.

Second row   *E. p. phaeton* UN♀. 22 July 1984, Pigeon River State Fish and Game Area, Mongo, LaGrange Co., IN.
E. p. phaeton UP♀. 22 July 1984, Pigeon River State Fish and Game Area, Mongo, LaGrange Co., IN.

Third row   Question Mark, *Polygonia interrogationis* UP♂. 3 August 1969, North Manchester, Wabash Co., IN.
P. interrogationis UN♂. 3 August 1969, North Manchester, Wabash Co., IN.

Fourth row   *P. interrogationis* UN♀. 14 August 1984, North Manchester, Wabash Co., IN.
P. interrogationis UN♀. 19 August 1984, North Manchester, Wabash Co., IN.

and usually uncommon to rare. The nominate subspecies seldom flies far from its larval foodplant, Turtlehead (*Chelone glabra*).

The most consistent way of separating the nominate subspecies from *Euphydryas phaeton ozarkae* seems to be by larval foodplant. According to Howe (1975), experiments show that young larvae feeding on *Chelone glabra* die when transferred to *Lonicera ciliata* and those feeding on *Lonicera ciliata* die when placed on *Chelone glabra*. Masters and Masters (1969) place the specimens from Brown County and other southcentral Indiana counties in the subspecies *ozarkae*; however, these may represent the gradual change in certain characteristics exhibited by members of a series of adjacent populations of the same species (a biological "cline"). In Indiana these two subspecies probably do not represent distinct populations.

On the other side, Irwin and Downey (1973) list both the nominate subspecies and *E. p. ozarkae* for Illinois and follow Masters's reasoning. Personally, I agree with Klots "that these poorly differentiated subspecies are really statistical gradations in a cline, and are still less noticeable because of variability" (Klots, 1951).

Life Cycle. The eggs are laid in clusters on the larval foodplants. Young larvae live in silk nests. The mature larva is black with orange lateral stripes and has numerous black, branching spines. The chrysalis is white, orange, and black. Its primary foodplant in northern Indiana is Turtlehead; however, Plantain (*Plantago lanceolata*), Ash (*Fraxinus*), Honeysuckle (*Lonicera*), Wistaria, and *Valeriana ciliata* may be eaten at times.

In Indiana I have found one pair of *Euphydryas phaeton in copula*: 15 June 1977, 12:20 P.M., 72° F, North Manchester, Wabash County. The pair was copulating on a shrub in a woodland marsh. After photographing them, I captured the pair. The female, carrying the male, flew up and down in the net bag (this behavior is a good way of determining the active flight partner). The Baltimore overwinters as a half-grown larva. It has one brood.

Subfamily Nymphalinae Swainson

Tribe Nymphalini Swainson

Genus *Polygonia* Hübner

Butterflies belonging to the genus *Polygonia* are popularly called "angle-wings" because of the ragged-looking outer margins of the wings. The mottled brown colors ventrally make them "dead leaf mimics" when perching with their wings held together over the back. In winter the adults "hibernate" in hollow trees, old barrels, and boxes. On warm, sunny winter days a few come out of "hibernation."

Seasonal dimorphism exists among the anglewings. Adults of the autumn brood are usually lighter in color; however, some similarly colored individuals may be produced among the summer populations. Sexual dimorphism also occurs, with females being somewhat paler above and more evenly and dully colored beneath. *Polygonia* are fond of sap and fruit juices, and generally they do not visit flowers freely. All species have a different comma or some other silver mark on the VHW.

122. *Polygonia interrogationis* (Fabricius). Question Mark. Plates XXXIX and XL.

Description. The Question Mark has a wingspread of 2.4 to 2.6 inches (60–67 mm). A distinctive characteristic is the silvery comma with an offset dot, forming a question mark on the VHW. This species has narrow tails and the wing margins are violet. *Interrogationis* has a dark spot in cell M_2 of the FW which is lacking in other species. The pale winter Question mark is called "*fabricii*" and the darker summer form "*umbrosa.*"

Distribution and Habitat. This species occurs in the Maritime Provinces, Quebec and Ontario, south throughout the entire United States into Mexico. It is common throughout the state of Indiana from March to November, appearing any month of the year when weather conditions are favorable.

The Question Mark is commonly a sap feeder. On 28 June 1980 I found dozens feeding on Willow (*Salix*) sap, which was heavily contaminated or inoculated with a form of yeast. On 8 August 1980 more were collected on the sap from *Salix*, along with other species of *Polygonia*, satyrids, and nymphalids. Sap-feeding may contribute to the longer flight periods of some butterflies, moths, and other insects.

Life Cycle. The light green, keg-shaped eggs are laid on the underside of leaves of the larval foodplants: Nettles (*Urtica*), Hops (*Humulus*), Hackberries (*Celtis*), Elms (*Ulmis*), Basswood (*Tilia*), and False Nettle (*Baehmeria*). The mature larva is reddish brown with irregular, lighter dots and patches and numerous branching spines. The angular grayish brown pupa occasionally has bright metallic spots on the sides. The pupa, as in all the Nymphalidae, hangs upside down from the branches of the foodplant or underneath wood fence railings. Even the twisted pupa suggests a question mark. It has two broods.

123. *Polygonia comma* (Harris). Comma; Hop Merchant. Plate XLI.

Description. The wingspread of the Comma measures 1.75 to 2.0 inches (44–51 mm). Its most distinctive characteristic is the silvery comma in the cell of the VHW which is usually enlarged or hooked at both ends. The HW tails of the *comma* are broader and shorter than in *interrogationis*. Around mid-July a dry-season form (called "*dryas*") appears. "*Dryas*" is fawn-colored on the ventral side.

Distribution and Habitat. The Comma ranges in the eastern United States and Canada, south in the mountains to the Carolinas and west to the Great

PLATE XL

Top row	Question Mark, *Polygonia interrogationis* UP♀. 3 August 1969, North Manchester, Wabash Co., IN. *P. interrogationis* UP♂. 19 August 1984, North Manchester, Wabash Co., IN. (on sugar/beer/banana mixture).
Second row	*P. interrogationis* UN♀. 19 August 1984, North Manchester, Wabash Co., IN. (on sugar/beer/banana mixture). *P. interrogationis* UN♂. 22 July 1984, North Manchester, Wabash Co., IN. (on sugar/beer/banana mixture).
Third row	*P. interrogationis* UP♂. 18 July 1984, North Manchester, Wabash Co., IN. (on sugar/beer/banana mixture). *P. interrogationis* UP♂. 12 June 1969, North Manchester, Wabash Co., IN.
Fourth row	*P. interrogationis* UP♀. 29 August 1982, Chain of Lakes State Park, Albion, Noble Co., IN. *P. interrogationis* UN♂. 18 August 1982, Silver Lake, Kosciusko Co., IN.

PLATE XLI

Top row
Comma or Hop Merchant, *Polygonia comma* UP♂. 3 October 1982, North Manchester, Wabash Co., IN.
P. comma UN♂. 26 September 1982, North Manchester, Wabash Co., IN.
P. comma UN♀: 29 August 1982, Chain of Lakes State Park, Albion, Noble Co., IN.

Second row
P. comma UP♂. 20 September 1984, North Manchester, Wabash Co., IN. (on sugar/beer/banana mixture).
P. comma UN♀, form "*dryas.*" 7 July 1984, Laketon, Wabash Co., IN.
P. comma UN♀. 10 September 1982, North Manchester, Wabash Co., IN. (on rotting apples).

Third row
P. comma UN♂. 18 September 1984, North Manchester, Wabash Co., IN. (on rotting wild cherries).
P. comma UP♀. 26 September 1982, North Manchester, Wabash Co., IN. (on rotten apples).
P. comma UN♂. 18 September 1982, North Manchester, Wabash Co., IN. (on rotten apples).

Fourth row
Satyr Anglewing, *Polygonia satyrus* UP♂. 25 July 1969, Silver Lake, Kosciusko Co., IN.
P. satyrus UN♂. 31 July 1969, Silver Lake, Kosciusko Co., IN.
P. satyrus UN♂. 5 May 1970, North Manchester, Wabash Co., IN.

Fifth row
Zephyr Anglewing, *Polygonia zephyrus* UN♀. 1 September 1975, Silver Lake, Kosciusko Co., IN. Det. Cyril F. dos Passos
P. zephyrus UP♂. 12 August 1974, Pole Mountains (8,500 ft.), Albany Co., WY.
Gray Comma, *Polygonia progne* UN♀. 18 September 1982, North Manchester, Wabash Co., IN. (on rotten wild cherries).

Plains. In Indiana *comma* occurs throughout the state from March to late November. Usually it is common, sometimes abundant, and may sometimes (but rarely) be seen on warm winter days any month of the year.

Like other *Polygonia* it is a sap-feeder. It also likes rotting fruits (apple and wild cherry) and is easily attracted to bait made of stale beer, brown sugar, syrup, and crushed bananas, smeared on tree trunks. After they have fed on this brew for a while, some adults can be captured with the fingers. The anglewings are all fast fliers, darting at birds, other butterflies, and the collector. The Comma occurs in forests, orchards, roadsides and clearings. After perching on a tree trunk or some other object, the wings are usually closed over the back, then opened and shut rhythmically.

Life Cycle. The eggs of the *comma* are similar to those of the above species, except that they are deposited in vertical columns. The larva is light green to brown with white spines. The brown pupa resembles a small piece of twisted dry wood. The dorsal tubercles have metallic gold or silver spots. The larval foodplants of *comma* are *Urtica, Baehmeria, Ulmus,* and *Humulus.* It has two broods.

124. *Polygonia satyrus* (Edwards). Satyr Anglewing. Plate XLI.

Description. *Satyrus* has a wingspread of 1.75 to 2.0 inches (44–51 mm). Dorsally, the HW has a dark border which is very narrow or almost absent. Ventrally, it is bright, warm brown, tending to yellowish brown. It is similar to *P. faunus,* a species found in Michigan but not yet recorded in Indiana. *P. progne,* another similar species, is gray beneath.

Distribution and Habitat. The Satyr Anglewing occurs in western North America, east to Minnesota, Michigan, New York, Ontario, Quebec, and Newfoundland.

On 25 June 1969 I collected this essentially western species in Kosciusko County in Indiana. Again, on 26 July 1969 I collected two in an open woods at Milford, Kosciusko County. On 30 May 1970 a few were found on a woodland trail near Silver Lake (Kosciusko County) and several more were found in a marshy woodland area near North Manchester in Wabash County. These are the first and only records for Indiana. Thus it was uncommon or rare for two years, from late May through July, in only two counties.

Life Cycle. In the west the larva feeds on Stinging Nettles (*Urtica*) and makes a crude nest. Reportedly, it has one brood.

125. *Polygonia zephyrus* (Edwards). Zephyr Anglewing. Plate XLI.

Description. The wingspread is 1.75 to 2.0 inches (44–51 mm). The silver comma on the VHW is tapered at both ends, not hooked or clubbed as in *P. comma* or *P. satyrus.* Ventrally, *zephyrus* is uniform gray or grayish brown. The longitudinal wing markings are subdued. Dorsally, it is light orange with a

narrow marginal brown band and a submarginal row of large pale yellow lunules.

Distribution and Habitat. It ranges from British Columbia to southern California in the Cascades and Sierra Nevada and east to Manitoba and New Mexico along the eastern Rockies.

On 1 September 1975 I collected a female in perfect condition just 3.5 miles east of Silver Lake (Kosciusko County) in a wooded area just off State Road 14 and the County Farm Road. It is a western species, so this is a very unusual Indiana state record. The specimen was identified by Cyril F. dos Passos of the American Museum of Natural History in New York. In the United States the normal range of *zephyrus* is west of the Great Plains.

According to Howe (1975), this species seldom flies below an altitude of 5,000 feet and is one of the few *Polygonia* that feed at flowers.

Life Cycle. The early stages are described in great detail in Howe (1975). The mature larva is one inch or more in length. The spines are variable, some reddish buff, others white, and still others black with chevrons. The slender pupa is lavender and marbled with salmon and has a series of a few silver spots on the upper tubercles of the abdomen. If larvae of *zephyrus* ever occur in Indiana, they should feed on garden Currants (*Ribes*) and Elm (*Ulmus*). *Zephyrus* overwinters in the adult stage.

126. *Polygonia progne* (Cramer). Gray Comma. Plates XLI and XLII.

Description. This is one of the smaller species of *Polygonia*, measuring 1.6 to 1.9 inches (41–48 mm). The dorsal HW has a broad dark brown border broken by small yellow dots. The VHW is transversed by thin blackish parallel lines and the silvery comma is tapered at both ends. *Progne* is dimorphic. The typical overwintering form is bright fulvous orange above, bordered with dark brown. The summer form, named "*l-argenteum*," is much darker above with darker scaling across the HW; the shape of the silvery comma suggests the letter "L."

Distribution and Habitat. The Gray Comma occurs from Nova Scotia south to Virginia and North Carolina and west to Illinois, Kansas, and Nebraska.

Blatchley (1891) reported that *progne* was found in six Indiana counties and scarce wherever found. I have found it common, uncommon, or absent some years from 24 June (early) to 1 November (late), primarily in the northeastern counties but also in Brown County State Park (rare). Its flight is short and it usually circles back to the very spot from whence it was disturbed. It frequents rocky ledges, shaded ravines, parking lots (where it basks in the sun), and the margins of dense woods.

On 14 September 1971 I collected several *progne* while they were feeding on sap oozing out of the holes in the trunk of a White Oak (*Quercus alba*) tree. When the wings of this species were closed and when their abdomens were distended with sap, I could collect them with my fingers.

Life Cycle. The egg is green and ribbed. The larva is variable, tan or rust marbled with dull green. It has short branching spines on the back. The larvae feed on Currants (*Ribes*). The pupae vary in color from dark brown to light buff streaked with black and brown. They hang suspended by the cremaster. The Gray Comma hibernates as an adult. There are two broods each year. Both Blatchley and Klots list Currant and Gooseberry (*Ribes*) and Elm (*Ulmus*) as larval foodplants.

Genus *Nymphalis* Kluk

127. *Nymphalis vau-album j-album* **(Boisduval and Leconte). Compton Tortoiseshell. Plate XLII.**

Description. The wingspread measures 2.5 to 2.9 inches (64–73 mm). Dorsally, it is rich, rusty-brown at the base, blending into golden crescents near the margin, with heavy black spotting on the FW. Ventrally, it is marbled gray (paler outwardly), usually with a small white "J" at the lower end of the cell of the HW.

Distribution and Habitat. The Compton Tortoiseshell occurs from Canada, south in the Canadian and Transition zones to North Carolina, Missouri, northern Michigan, and Iowa.

Blatchley (1891) found it to be rare in Vanderburgh, Decatur, and Lake counties in Indiana. I collected two specimens in August 1934 in an old pear and apple orchard (since destroyed by a housing project) in North Manchester, Wabash County. It visits rotting fruit, sap sources, and mud puddles. It is a strong flier.

Irwin and Downey (1973) report this species from several extreme northeastern Illinois counties. Because this species is periodic, it probably seldom appears in the state of Indiana. Recent records are lacking.

Life Cycle. This beautiful and rare butterfly probably does not breed in our area. The larva is greenish, speckled and striped with lighter shades. The pupa is brown with a horned head. Overwintering adults lay eggs in the spring. Where it breeds, the Compton Tortoiseshell has two broods.

128. *Nymphalis antiopa antiopa* **(Linnaeus). Mourning Cloak. Plate XLII.**

Description. The wingspread measures 2.9 to 3.4 inches (73–86 mm). This richly colored butterfly with its brownish maroon wings and distinct creamy-yellow borders needs little description. The blue spots inward from the yellow borders of both wings highlight the dorsal color pattern. Ventrally, the wings are darker.

Distribution and Habitat. The Mourning Cloak occurs from the Hudsonian Zone of Alaska and Canada south to the southern portions of the Temperate Zone.

In Indiana this species is common throughout the state, though it appears to be less common in the southern part. Adults may appear from their hibernation any month of the year when the days are warm and sunny. The majority of the adults fly from early April to late November. I lack records only for December and January.

In England this butterfly is called the Camberwell Beauty. Look for it along woodland trails and forest margins, in gardens, groves, and orchards, and near lakes, streams, and wet meadows. On 24 June 1972 I collected several feeding on yeast-contaminated sap which was accumulating on several Willow branches (*Salix*) in a marshy woodland near North Manchester, Wabash County. It was feeding on the sap along with several other nymphalid and satyrid butterfly species. The Mourning Cloak is a strong flier and sometimes difficult to catch. However, after feeding on the *Salix* sap it was easily netted.

Life Cycle. The pale egg becomes black before hatching. The larva is velvety black, speckled white, with a row of red spots on the back and several rows of branched black bristles. Its legs are rust-colored. The larvae feed in groups on many deciduous trees: Willow (*Salix*), Elm (*Ulmus*), Hackberry (*Celtis*), and Cottonwood (*Populus*). The tan to gray pupa has two horns on the head. Adults hibernate during the winter. It has two broods.

Genus *Aglais* Dalman

129. *Aglais milberti milberti* (Godart). Milbert's Tortoiseshell. Plate XLIII.

Description. The Milbert's Tortoiseshell has a wingspread of 1.75 to 2.0 inches (44–51 mm). The broad submarginal band of yellow and orange, as seen in the photographs, clearly identifies this butterfly.

Distribution and Habitat. It ranges from Newfoundland to the Canadian Pacific coast, south to West Virginia, Colorado, and California.

Milbert's Tortoiseshell probably occurs throughout Indiana, though only a few records from the lower third of the state have been reported. It is very common in northeastern Indiana. Adults fly from 15 February (early) to 26 October (late). Usually *milberti* are common from late April through September. They are attracted to meadow and garden flowers, on roadsides, streambeds, hillsides, and trails.

Life Cycle. The pale green eggs are deposited in clusters, which frequently contain as many as several hundred eggs. At first the larvae live in colonies in silken nests; then they become solitary leaf-folders. The larvae are variable, black with a lateral greenish yellow stripe and a subdorsal orange stripe. The larvae are sparsely covered with branching spines. The larval foodplants are chiefly Nettles (*Urtica*) and probably Willow (*Salix*). At least, adult butterflies frequently gather in the shade of these plants. The chrysalis is grayish or greenish. Adults overwinter.

PLATE XLII

PLATE XLIII

Genus *Vanessa* Fabricius

130. *Vanessa virginiensis* (Drury). American Painted Lady. Plate XLIII.

Description. The wingspread is 1.25 to 2.1 inches (44–54 mm). This butterfly is also known as "Hunter's Butterfly" and "Virginia Lady." The American Painted Lady has only two large postmedian ocelli on the VHW, instead of four or five smaller ones as found in other members of this genus.

Distribution and Habitat. It occurs from coast to coast and from southern Canada to Colombia. It has become established in Hawaii.

It is usually common throughout Indiana from 13 April to 23 October; however, in some years it is uncommon or absent. It is subject to periodic fluctuations in abundance. *Virginiensis* frequents open areas in woods and visits garden or roadside flowers, streambeds, riversides, and sandy shores. It is a strong and rapid flier.

Life Cycle. The yellowish green barrel-shaped eggs are laid singly. The larva (up to 35 mm) is black with yellow cross-bands and has white or rust-colored spots. It makes a solitary nest of leaves and silk on various species of Compositae. The lavender-brown chrysalis hangs upside down on Thistle (*Cirsium*) and a variety of Malvaceae and other plants.

In Indiana I have found one pair *in copula*: 10 July 1977, 3:20 P.M., 80° F, in a field of alfalfa and red clover, Silver Lake, Kosciusko County. The female was the active flight partner. It has two broods.

131. *Vanessa cardui* (Linnaeus). Painted Lady; Thistle Butterfly. Plate XLIII.

Description. The wingspread measures 2.0 to 2.25 inches (51–57 mm). The Painted Lady, or Thistle Butterfly, is also known as "Cosmopolite," because of its worldwide range. The additional ocelli on the VHW distinguish this species from *virginiensis*. In *cardui* the dorsal FW and the ventral FW have a distinct white bar running from the costa across the black patch near the tip.

Distribution and Habitat. The Painted Lady is cosmopolitan in the North American continent except for the Arctic. This highly migratory species occurs throughout the state of Indiana from mid-April to late October, being common to abundant in the counties where it has been found. *Cardui* show up almost anywhere, but they favor alfalfa/red clover fields, flowery meadows, state parks, and hilly country. Although this species is a strong flier, it is easily netted on flowers.

Life Cycle. The egg is pale green, barrel-shaped, and laid singly, as in the preceding species. The larva varies from chartreuse with black marbling to purplish with a yellow stripe on the back. It is covered with short spines. The bluntly beaked pupa is lavender-brown and hangs upside down. The larval foodplants are Thistle (*Cirsium*), Asteraceae, and Malvaceae. It probably has two broods in Indiana. It overwinters in the adult and pupa stages.

132. *Vanessa atalanta rubria* (Fruhstorfer). Red Admiral. Plate XLIV.

Description. The wingspread is 1.75 to 2.25 inches (44–57 mm). It can be easily identified from the photographs.

Distribution and Habitat. The subspecies *V. a. rubria* occurs in North America from the Atlantic to the Pacific and from northern Canada south to Florida and Guatamala. It has been naturalized in Hawaii.

In Indiana this subspecies is common throughout the state, having been recorded in most of the counties. Adults fly from March (early) through September (one was collected on 26 October 1970 at Silver Lake in Kosciusko County). In 1968 in Wabash County, for example, Red Admirals were abundant from 8 April through June.

This subspecies may occur almost everywhere, in fields, gardens, forest margins, hilly areas, trails, shorelines, barnyards, parks, roadsides, open woods, and even high (ten stories) on the window ledges and walls of city buildings. It could be called a "crepuscular" species, one that flies at twilight. On 30 May 1977 I found several feeding on Willow (*Salix*) sap in Silver Lake, Kosciusko County.

Life Cycle. The larvae are variable in color, warty and spiny. The brownish pupa is flecked with gold and has dull, short tubercles on the thorax; the abdomen is curved. The larval foodplants are Nettle (*Urtica*), Hops (*Humulus*), False Nettle (*Baehmeria*), and Pellitories (*Parietaria*). In mild areas, both adults and pupae overwinter; however, in Indiana, only adults hibernate. It has two broods.

Genus *Junonia* Hübner

133. *Junonia coenia* Hübner. Buckeye. Plate XLIV.

Description. The Buckeye has a wingspread of 2 to 2.5 inches (51–63 mm). The genus was known for many years as *Precis*. The Buckeye varies in size and color. A warm environment produces smaller adults with restricted ocelli and a lighter ground color than individuals inhabiting a cool, moist environment. In some autumn individuals, a beautiful "*rosa*" form develops, which is larger with pinkish undersides.

Distribution and Habitat. The Buckeye ranges from tropical America north to southern Canada. It is common or fairly common throughout Indiana. Adults fly from April (very early) to as late as 26 October, and rarely into early November. In autumn the species is highly migratory. When traveling by automobile, one should look for the Buckeye along the highways. It is a rapid and nervous flier. An expert dodger, it often escapes capture. The Buckeye is fond of flowers and mud puddles. It also occurs near waterways and in fields, meadows, swamps, woodland trails, and other places.

Life Cycle. The green-colored egg is stubby, ribbed, and flat. The larva

PLATE XLIV

Top row
Red Admiral, *Vanessa atalanta rubria* UP♂. 22 July 1984, North Manchester, Wabash Co., IN.
V. a. rubria UP♀. 27 August 1984, North Manchester, Wabash Co., IN.
V. a. rubria UN♂. 1 August 1984, North Manchester, Wabash Co., IN.

Second row
V. a. rubria UN♀. 22 July 1984, North Manchester, Wabash Co., IN.
Buckeye, *Junonia coenia* UP♂. 16 August 1981, North Manchester, Wabash Co., IN.
J. coenia UN♂. 1 August 1984, North Manchester, Wabash Co., IN.

Third row
J. coenia UP♀. 24 August 1981, North Manchester, Wabash Co., IN.
J. coenia UN♀. 16 August 1978, Kokomo, Howard Co., IN.
J. coenia UN♂, aberrant form. Note size of ocelli and variation in upper wings. 21 September 1971, North Manchester, Wabash Co., IN.

Fourth row
Red-spotted Purple, *Basilarchia arthemis astyanax* UP♂. 21 June 1969, Silver Lake, Kosciusko Co., IN.
B. a. astyanax UN♂. 11 August 1984, North Manchester, Wabash Co., IN.

shows various shades of green to blackish gray with orange and yellowish markings. The chrysalis is mottled pale brown.

Among the many recognized larval foodplants are Plantain (*Plantago*), Gerardia (*Gerardia*), Toadflax (*Linaria*), Snapdragon (*Antirrhinum*), False Loosestrife (*Ludvigia*), and Stonecrop (*Sedum*).

I have found two pairs *in copula*: 30 July 1970, 3:05 P.M., in a pasture field at Delphi, Carroll County; and 31 August 1970, 9:50 A.M., 60° F, North Manchester, Wabash County. When disturbed with the net handle, both pairs settled again in the deep grass. The females were the active flight partners. The Buckeye has one or two broods. Adults hibernate in winter.

Subfamily Limenitidinae Behr

ই

Tribe Limenitidini Behr

ই

Genus *Basilarchia* Scudder

134. *Basilarchia arthemis astyanax* (Fabricius). Red-spotted Purple. Plates XLIV, XLV.

Description. Howe (1975), Shull and Badger (1972), and many others placed this species in the genus *Limenitis*. Presently I am following Miller and Brown (1981). According to Platt and Brower (1968) *arthemis* and *astyanax* are not distinct species. Shull and Badger collected two specimens with indistinct white bands on 21 June 1969 in Wabash County. Perhaps some with more extensive white bands have been taken in a few northern counties. But after many years of research and collecting in all 92 counties, I have concluded that the nominate subspecies does not occur in Indiana, even though Blatchley (1891) reported that Worthington had found them in Lake County. Howe (1975) suggests that *arthemis* hybridizes with *astyanax* along a relatively narrow contact zone. The eastern Red-spotted Purple lacks the broad white bands of the nominate subspecies. Of the six categories of integration pictured by Platt and Brower (1968), my Indiana specimens fit category 3. That is not a strong argument for the nominate subspecies occurring in Indiana.

Distribution and Habitat. Our subspecies ranges from central and southern New England, New York, Pennsylvania, and Ohio west to Nebraska and south to Florida and Texas.

In Indiana, adults fly from mid-May to mid-October; however, they are more common from June through September. Look for them where a deciduous forest borders a meadow. They occur throughout the state of Indiana. From 16–19 August 1982 hundreds of Red-spotted Purples were resting on piles of horse manure on the trails in Brown County State Park, especially near Strahl Creek. On 24 June 1972 I found a few individuals feeding on Willow (*Salix*) sap, 88° F, North Manchester, Wabash County. *Astyanax* is usually a low flier, showing preference for the open forest and forest edges. It seldom visits flowers.

The Red-spotted Purple mimics the toxic Pipevine Swallowtail, thus gaining protection from birds, rodents, and other predators.

Life Cycle. The cream-colored larva has a postcephalic "saddlehorn" and prominent lateral wing cases. Its larval foodplants include Willows (*Salix*), Poplars and Aspens (*Populus*), Hawthorns (*Crataegus*), Cherries (*Prunus*), Apples (*Malus*), and Hornbeams (*Carpinus*). The species overwinters as a partly grown larva.

I have found two pairs *in copula*: 21 August 1969, 3:45 P.M., Silver Lake, Kosciusko County; and 7 June 1970, 2:25 P.M., Brown County State Park. When the last pair was disturbed, it flew into a tree at the edge of a meadow. The female carried the limp male. It has three broods.

135. *Basilarchia archippus archippus* (Cramer). Viceroy or Mimic. Plate XLV.

Description. The Viceroy has a wingspread of 2.6 to 3 inches (67–76 mm). It can be distinguished from the Monarch (which it closely resembles) by the postmedian dark line on the hindwing and by its smaller size. Dorsally, the Viceroy is a uniform orange-brown and the veins are dusted with black scales.

Distribution and Habitat. The Viceroy occurs over the entire United States east of the Rocky Mountains, from southern Canada and New England south to Georgia and Mississippi, and west to Colorado and Montana.

The nominate subspecies has been found in almost all Indiana counties. Adults fly from early June to mid-October. Look for the Viceroy along roadsides, edges of woods, in meadows, marshes, and along waterways.

Life Cycle. The caterpillar is mottled brown or olive with a saddle-shaped patch on its back. The pupa is brown and cream-colored, feeding chiefly at night. Its larval foodplants are Willows (*Salix*), Poplars and Aspens (*Populus*), Apples, Cherries, and Plums.

From 1970 through 1980 I have found nine pairs *in copula* in July, August, and September. The lowest mating temperature was 70° F and the highest 90° F. Mating occurred in the afternoons from 12:30 P.M. to 4:00 P.M. Copulating pairs were collected in Wabash, Kosciusko, and Carroll counties. The female was always the flight partner. It has two broods.

On 7 September 1971, 1:30 P.M., I watched the nominate *archippus* copulate with *B. arthemis astyanax* in a woods near North Manchester, Wabash County. I was unable to catch this mating pair because a dangerous bull was protecting his turf, where the copulating pair had flown. These two species rarely hybridize. The Viceroy overwinters as a partly grown larva.

PLATE XLV

Top row   Red-spotted Purple, *Basilarchia arthemis astyanax* UP♀. 14 August 1984, North Manchester, Wabash Co., IN.

B. a. astyanax UN♀. 11 August 1971, North Manchester, Wabash Co., IN.

Second row   *B. a. astyanax* hybrid, UN♀. Note partial light band in upper wings. 21 June 1969, North Manchester, Wabash Co., IN.

Viceroy or Mimic, *Basilarchia archippus archippus* UP♂. 6 June 1971, North Manchester, Wabash Co., IN.

Third row   *B. a. archippus* UN♂. 21 June 1969, North Manchester, Wabash Co., IN.

B. a. archippus UP♀. 13 June 1970, North Manchester, Wabash Co., IN.

Family Apaturidae Boisduval
૨&
Subfamily Charaxinae Guen'ee
૨&
Genus *Anaea* Hübner

136. *Anaea andria* Scudder. Goatweed Butterfly. Plate XLVI.

Description. *Andria* has a wingspread of 2.4 to 3 inches (60–76 mm). Specimens vary considerably in wing color, patterns, and seasonal differences. Colors vary from orange-red to buff, some females being very pale. The pattern may be boldly marked or almost obliterated. Summer specimens are usually more lightly marked.

Distribution and Habitat. According to William Phillips Comstock (1961), there are records from West Virginia, North Carolina, Ohio, Illinois, Colorado, and Texas, and one record from Jalapa, Mexico. It is common in Missouri, Kansas, Alabama, and Louisiana.

In Indiana there are scattered records, chiefly from the central and southern counties, in April, July, and August. It was found in July in Orange County and in August in Wabash County. On 3 July 1981, I collected one by a stream bordered by trees and shrubs near Corydon, Harrison County. This was the first *andria* I had found in Indiana since 1934. Look for it along country roads, fallow fields, canals, streams, edges of woods, and prairie groves. The Goatweed Butterfly, with its mottled brown colors, pointed wing tips, and stemlike tails, is an almost perfect mimic of a dead leaf. *Anaea andria* is exceedingly rare in Indiana.

Life Cycle. The grayish green larva tapers posteriorly and is covered with numerous raised points. The head has small tubercles. The larva folds the leaf of the host plant into a protective cover and ties it with silk. The pupa is blunt and thick. Its larval foodplants are Crotons or Goatweeds (*Croton capitatus* and *C. monanthogynus*). Adults overwinter. It has two broods.

Subfamily Apaturinae Boisduval
૨&
Genus *Asterocampa* Röber

137. *Asterocampa celtis* (Boisduval and Leconte). Hackberry Butterfly. Plate XLVI.

Description. The wingspread of the Hackberry Butterfly measures 2 to 2.5 inches (51–64 mm). The males vary from grayish olive to olive-brown. The females are larger and paler in ground color than the males. In both sexes albinic and melanic forms occur. The two basal spots in the discal cell and the dorsal zigzag bar of ocelli in the upper FW are obvious diagnostic features.

Distribution and Habitat. *A. celtis* occurs throughout North America wherever Hackberry (*Celtis*) trees grow. They range from central New England to southern Minnesota, southward to northern Florida and eastern Texas.

In Indiana the Hackberry Butterfly is common and sometimes abundant throughout the state from late May to late August or early September. Adults seldom fly far from Hackberry trees; they perch on the trunks and branches of these trees and on nearby shrubbery. They do not visit flowers but feed on rotting fruit, fermenting tree sap (30 May 1977, on *Salix* sap, Wabash County), animal excrement, and carcasses. Adults, especially males, pugnaciously defend their territory, even landing on the collector's head or chest. This butterfly is often crepuscular.

On 22 August 1975 I found thousands of these butterflies in the Salamonie River State Forest in Wabash County. Drivers of vehicles stopped to ask me what these insects were, for many of them had flown into the open windows of the cars. On 14 June 1979, I again found a big association of *celtis*. Hundreds were perched on the roads and plants in the Morgan-Monroe State Forest.

Life Cycle. The spherical pale green egg hatches into a bright grass-green larva with yellow and chartreuse longitudinal stripes. The bluish green pupa is sharply horned. The only foodplant of the Hackberry Butterfly is the leaves of the Hackberry tree (*Celtis*). It has two broods. It overwinters as a half-grown larva.

138. *Asterocampa clyton* (Boisduval and Leconte). Tawny Emperor. Plate XLVI.

Description. This species has a wingspread of 2 to 2.6 inches (51–67 mm). The dorsal FW of *clyton* lacks the prominent submarginal, round, black or ocellate spot in cell Cu$_1$ found in both *celtis* and *leila*. Dorsally, *clyton* has two solid zigzag bars; in *celtis* the basal bar is broken into two spots. The Tawny Emperor is tawnier and has larger ocelli (black spots circled with orange) than *celtis*.

Distribution and Habitat. *Clyton* ranges from southern New England and New York west to Nebraska and Wisconsin and south to eastern Texas and southern Georgia.

The Tawny Emperor is common throughout the state of Indiana but less so than the Hackberry Butterfly. Adults fly from late May to late August. This butterfly prefers deciduous woods where Hackberry trees abound. On 22 August 1975 when I saw thousands of *A. celtis* in the Salamonie River State Forest, dozens of the Tawny Emperors were also present, especially on an unused road through the forest. Look for *clyton* on decaying animals killed on country roads. They like shaded woodland paths and trails.

Life Cycle. The light green eggs are laid in clusters. The larva is striped with green, yellow, and white; it has two tail-like projections at the posterior

PLATE XLVI

Top row   Goatweed Butterfly, *Anaea andria* UP♂. Mid-August, 1934, North Manchester, Wabash Co., IN.

A. *andria* UP♀. Mid-August, 1934, North Manchester, Wabash Co., IN.

Second row   A. *andria* UN♀. 3 July 1981, Corydon, Harrison Co., IN.

Hackberry Butterfly, *Asterocampa celtis* UP♂. 16 August 1978, Burlington, Howard Co., IN.

A. *celtis* UN♂. 11 August 1984, North Manchester, Wabash Co., IN.

Third row   A. *celtis* UP♀. 16 August 1984, Burlington, Howard Co., IN.

A. *celtis* UN♀. 14 August 1984, North Manchester, Wabash Co., IN.

Tawny Emperor, *Asterocampa clyton* UP♂. 25 July 1978, Camp Mack, Milford, Kosciusko Co., IN.

Fourth row   A. *clyton* UN♂. 20 July 1977, Camp Mack, Milford, Kosciusko Co., IN.

A. *clyton* UP♀. 25 August 1978, Camp Mack, Milford, Kosciusko Co., IN.

A. *clyton* UP♀. 20 July 1978, Camp Mack, Milford, Kosciusko Co., IN.

end. The head bears large antlerlike protuberances. The chrysalis is blue-green with a sawtoothed ridge on the back. The only larval foodplant of *clyton* is Hackberry leaves (*Celtis*). The Tawny Emperor hibernates as a half-grown larva. It has only one brood in our area.

Family Satyridae Boisduval

The majority of the Satyrs, or Wood Nymphs, are dull brown or blackish butterflies of moderate size. The wings are usually short and broad and marked with eyelike spots (ocelli) in interesting patterns above and below. The VHW are beautifully variegated with protective color patterns. The forelegs of both sexes are poorly developed and useless for walking. The cells of both wings are closed and the veins of the forewings are usually swollen at the base. Frequently the males have patches of androconial scales on the forewings or hindwings, or both.

The members of this family are not migratory and they seldom wander far from the area where they hatched. Except for some *Cercyonis* (especially *C. alope*), they seldom visit flowers. When adult satyrids close the upper wings over the lower wings and settle in the grass or on the trunk of a tree, they are well hidden from predators.

Subfamily Elymniinae Herrich-Schäffer
Tribe Parargini Tutt
Genus *Enodia* Hübner

139. *Enodia anthedon* A. H. Clark. Northern Pearly Eye. Plate XLVII.

Description. The wingspread measures 1.6 to 2 inches (41–51 mm). Formerly this species was known as *Lethe portlandia anthedon* in our area. Recently, *portlandia* and *anthedon* have been separated into two distinct species. Dorsally, the wings of *anthedon* are light brown with dark brown zigzag lines across the wings. On the HW above there is a prominent row of submarginal brownish black spots. Ventrally, the ocelli are an opalescent gray, light brown, or lilac (lilac predominates in fresh specimens). The four FW ocelli and the seven (usually) present on the HW all have pupils.

Distribution and Habitat. It occurs from Manitoba and northern Arkansas east to Maine and Virginia.

In Indiana the Northern Pearly Eye is probably more widespread than indicated by the county records. Adults are usually uncommon from early June to late August. *Anthedon* may be found along the edges of forests and on woodland trails and paths. When disturbed, it flies into the trees where its colors conceal its whereabouts. Occasionally individuals alight on the ground. This pugnacious species chases other butterflies from its territory, and males often fight each other.

Life Cycle. The yellowish green larva has red-tipped protuberances at both ends. The larvae feed on forest grasses. *Anthedon* is probably single-brooded in our area. It hibernates as a partly grown larva.

140. *Enodia creola* (Skinner). Creole Pearly Eye. Plate XLVII.

Description. The wingspread is 2 to 2.25 inches (51–57 mm). For a long time this species was known as *Lethe creola*. The male of this species is easy to recognize by the more extended apical region of the FW and the conspicuous androconial patches on the upper FW, which are absent in *E. portlandia*. The identification of females is more difficult. In *creola* the costal portion of the postmedian line to M_3 is irregularly convex, and the segment in M_1 and M_2 is strongly convex. Also, *creola* usually has a subterminal ocellus below vein Cu_2 on the VFW.

Distribution and Habitat. *Enodia creola* ranges from southern Illinois and southeastern Virginia south to east Texas and Georgia.

In Indiana the Creole Pearly Eye has been recorded in only two counties, LaGrange and Brown. Howe (1975) includes southern Indiana in its range. In the early 1930s, it was rare in the wooded area of our family farm in Girard, Illinois. Irwin and Downey (1973) restrict *creola* to southern Illinois where it is associated with Cane (*Arundinaria*). Klots (1951) includes Illinois and Michigan in its range. Many *creola* have been confused with *portlandia* until recently. *Creola* prefers shaded woods and is highly crepuscular, flying after other butterflies have gone to sleep. This species is very rare, or absent, in late May and June and again in August and September. It is a fast flier and often alights on tree trunks.

Life Cycle. The early stages remain unrecorded. Its larval foodplant is Cane (*Arundinaria*). Reportedly, it has two broods.

Genus *Satyrodes* Scudder

141. *Satyrodes eurydice eurydice* (Johansson). Eyed Brown. Plate XLVII.

Description. Its wingspread is 1.6 to 2 inches (41–51 mm). *Satyrodes* (formerly *Lethe eurydice appalachia* R. L. Chermock) has recently been separated into two separate species, *eurydice* and *appalachia*. The morphological differences between them are not great, but color and pattern characters justify separation. In *eurydice* the most constant and distinguishing characteristic is the shape of the postmedian lines on the underside of both wings, which

PLATE XLVII

Top row
Northern Pearly Eye, *Enodia anthedon* UP♂. 20 August 1984, Strahl Creek, Brown County State Park, Nashville, IN.

E. anthedon UN♂. 20 August 1984, Strahl Creek, Brown County State Park, Nashville, IN.

E. anthedon UP♀. 21 August 1984, Strahl Creek, Brown County State Park, Nashville, IN.

Second row
E. anthedon UN♀. 21 August 1984, Strahl Creek, Brown County State Park, Nashville, IN.

Creole Pearly Eye, *Enodia creola* UP♂. 16 June 1976, Jackson Co., IL. Det. R. T. Arbogast

E. creola UP♀. 4 July 1976, Benedictine School, Savannah, GA. Det. R. T. Arbogast

Third row
Eyed Brown, *Satyrodes eurydice eurydice* UP♂. 9 July 1973, North Manchester, Wabash Co., IN.

S. e. eurydice UN♂. 22 July 1984, Mongo Tamarack Bog, LaGrange Co., IN.

S. e. eurydice UP♀. 4 July 1978, Mongo Tamarack Bog, LaGrange Co., IN.

Fourth row
S. e. eurydice UN♀. 10 July 1984, North Manchester, Wabash Co., IN.

Appalachian Brown, *Satyrodes appalachia leeuwi* UP♂. 22 July 1984, Nasby Fen, Mongo, LaGrange Co., IN.

S. a. leeuwi UN♀. 22 July 1984, Nasby Fen, Mongo, LaGrange Co., IN.

Fifth row
Gemmed Satyr, *Cyllopsis gemma gemma* UN♂. 20 June 1983, woods east of Goonee Lake, Green Co., GA.

Mitchell's Satyr, *Neonympha mitchellii* UP♂. 6 July 1956, Cedar Lake Bog, LaGrange Co., IN. Coll. H. F. Price

N. mitchellii UN♂. 6 July 1956, Cedar Lake Bog, LaGrange Co., IN. Coll. H. F. Price

are jagged with sharp points, especially near the angle of the secondaries; in *appalachia* the postmedian lines are straighter (less jagged). The dorsal ground color of *eurydice* is pale brown; ventrally it is somewhat yellowish. The ground color of *appalachia* is darker, mousy brown or grayish with the underside tinged with purple or lilac.

Distribution and Habitat. The nominate subspecies ranges from Delaware westward to northern Illinois and northwestward to Great Slave Lake, Northwest Territories.

In Indiana, this Eyed Brown is common some years, uncommon other years, from May 20 (early), June through August, occasionally into September. It occurs in our northern and central counties, with no records south of Brown County. *Eurydice* usually occurs in open sedge marshes and wet meadows, occasionally in dry grassy areas.

Howe (1975) and Miller and Brown (1981) list a larger, darker subspecies indigenous to the prairie states, named *S. eurydice fumosa* (Leussier). D. Oosting (1980) reported *fumosa* from Lake County from 24 June to 6 July 1980. It is now extirpated in many parts of its range. Both size and color variations are so great in specimens from our northeastern counties that some entomologists are reluctant to accept these differences as taxonomically significant. Opler (1984), however, makes *fumosa* a separate species.

Life Cycle. The slender, light green larva has dark green longitudinal stripes, with red-tipped horns on both head and tail. The green chrysalis has a small, blunt hook on its head.

I collected one pair of the nominate subspecies *in copula*: 29 July 1972, 12:30 P.M., 68° F, in an open woodland marsh, North Manchester, Wabash County. The female was the active flight partner. It has one brood.

142. *Satyrodes appalachia leeuwi* (Gatrelle and Arbogast). Appalachian Brown. Plate XLVII.

Description. The wingspread of *appalachia* measures 1.6 to 2 inches (41–51 mm), identical in size to *eurydice*. The differences between the two species were described under the former butterfly.

Distribution and Habitat. The Appalachian Brown and the Eyed Brown are sibling species, which are similar in appearance and occur in many of the same localities, as they do in Indiana. Irwin Leeuw, for whom this species was named by Gatrelle and Arbogast, mailed a perfect pair of *leeuwi* to me. Arbogast (personal communication) has confirmed my *Lethe appalachia* to be *leeuwi*.

The habitat distinctions, as claimed by some experts, are not always as clearly delineated as claimed; nevertheless, most *appalachia* are found in woodland swamps or along streams through woods, and in the borders of shaded bogs. I have collected most of my specimens of *leeuwi* just inside the tamarack bog, Mongo, LaGrange County, from June through August. The topotype was collected by Irwin Leeuw on 4 July 1975, in the vicinity of Wakelee, Cass

County, Michigan. In Indiana, *appalachia* is not as common or as widespread as *eurydice*.

Life Cycle. Howe says that the larvae of *appalachia* are like those of *eurydice*, but the red side stripes on the head capsule do not extend ventrally below the bases of the horns. The larval foodplants are Sedges (*Carex*).

Subfamily Satyrinae Boisduval

Tribe Euptychiini Müller

Genus *Cyllopsis* R. Felder

143. *Cyllopsis gemma gemma* (Hübner). Gemmed Satyr. Plate XLVII.

Description. The wingspread of the Gemmed Satyr is 1.25 to 1.4 inches (32–35 mm). This species was formerly placed in the genus *Euptychia*. The VHW of *gemma* is brightly silvered and has small ocelli grouped in a large sub-marginal gray patch. Its ground color is yellow-brown.

Distribution and Habitat. The nominate subspecies ranges from southern Illinois to Virginia, south to central Florida and the Gulf states.

The only Indiana records are those of Masters and Masters (1969), who found them in Perry County. They took a number of specimens in a deep ravine on their winter farm. They found them in late April and early May and again in July. The Masters suggest that a third brood may occur in late September and early October, as it does in northeast Arkansas and southeast Missouri. Masters and Masters should be complimented for these state records.

Look for the Gemmed Satyr in moist, shaded, grassy areas, along streams and ponds in open woods, and in wet meadows. This species is very local and is apparently quite rare.

Life Cycle. The globular egg is covered with a network of lines. The larva is green in early summer and light brown in the fall. Both forms are striped with darker lines. There are two long, hornlike tubercles on the head and two on the anal segment. The pupa is green or brown and distinctly bifid at the head. Its larval foodplants are Bermuda Grass (*Cynodon dactylon*) in Texas and other grasses (Poaceae) which grow in Indiana.

Genus *Neonympha* Hübner

144. *Neonympha mitchellii* French. Mitchell's Satyr. Plate XLVII.

Description. The wingspread of *mitchellii* is 1.5 to 1.75 inches (38–44 mm). The greater number of ocelli distinguish this species from other similar species. It has a row of four ocelli in the VFW and six more in the VHW.

Distribution and Habitat. Mitchell's Satyr inhabits the bogs in southern Michigan, Ohio, and Indiana and perhaps in northern New Jersey.

In Indiana *mitchellii* has been found only in Steuben and LaGrange counties in July. Homer Price (personal communication) of Payne, Ohio, regularly found *mitchellii* in the 1950s in a quaking bog on the east side of Cedar Lake in LaGrange County. On 6 July 1956 he collected twenty-one specimens from the north bog at Cedar Lake. This species has also been found in Steuben County. However, I was unable to find it in either county until recently.

Lee Casebere, Assistant Director of the Indiana Division of Nature Preserves, gave me a damaged *mitchellii* which had been collected on 11 July 1980, in the Cedar Lake bog. Concern for the survival of this endangered species in Indiana has increased because of recent landfills and the building of more cabins around Cedar Lake. Although the species seems to be holding its own in southern Michigan, habitat destruction may cause its extirpation in Indiana.

An encouraging note is that David Eiler (personal communication) found another *mitchellii* on 7 July 1981 in the Cedar Lake bog. Their inaccessibility may be their greatest protection. The flight period seldom extends beyond two weeks.

Life Cycle. The larvae of Mitchell's Satyr have six instars (molts). Both the egg and the larva are pale green. The larva has contrasting stripes and two fleshy horns extending on the caudal portions. Its larval foodplant is probably Sedges (*Carex*). The greenish-lime chrysalis has a large bump protruding from the back of the head and small horns in front. *Mitchellii* has only one brood.

Genus *Megisto* Hübner

145. *Megisto cymela cymela* (Cramer). Little Wood Satyr. Plate XLVIII.

Description. This nominate subspecies has a wingspread of 1.75 to 1.9 inches (44–48 mm). Formerly this butterfly was placed in the genus *Euptychia*. Dorsally, the ground color is dull brown and the FW has two ocelli. Ventrally, the wings are dull brown to tan and crossed with darker brown lines. There are two eyespots in the VFW, and two larger eyespots, encircled with yellow, with some smaller ocelli in between the larger black ocelli, on the VHW. Sometimes the smaller ocelli are obscure.

Distribution and Habitat. This species ranges throughout the eastern United States and southeastern Canada.

In Indiana the Little Wood Nymph is common and widespread from May through July and, rarely, into early August. It prefers open deciduous forests and wet meadows, especially meadows bordered by woods and containing considerable shrubbery. Catching *cymela* is not easy, because they fly rapidly among the trees and shrubs.

Life Cycle. The egg is pale yellowish green. The greenish brown larva is covered with fine hairs and has narrow longitudinal stripes. The tubercles on the head and body are whitish. Its larval foodplants are grasses (Poaceae) and probably sedges (Cyperaceae). The pupa is rounded and curved near the rear. It hibernates as a partly grown larva.

I have found five pairs *in copula*: two pairs on 6 June 1969, 1:00 P.M. and 1:15 P.M., Mongo, LaGrange County; 1 July 1969, 4:10 P.M., Silver Lake, Kosciusko County; 22 June 1970, 1:05 P.M., North Manchester, Wabash County; and 4 July 1978, 11:50 A.M., 76° F, Mongo, in a woods near the tamarack bog. The female was always the active flight partner. Temperatures, not always recorded, were generally in the 70s. It has one brood.

Tribe Maniolini Grote

Genus *Cercyonis* Scudder

The Nearctic genus *Cercyonis* has long been a difficult group to identify with certainty. The subspecies of *C. pegala* and its integrating forms raise some serious problems, especially of range limits and stable populations. As Klots (1951) stated, "Actually no clear-cut boundaries exist between contiguous forms but instead, blend zones of varying width in which many intermediate forms occur." He suggests that it might be better to "lump" them all into one broadly distributed clinal species. All of the forty-two mating pairs of *Cercyonis* that I have collected in Indiana from 1970 through 1982 were *Cercyonis pegala alope*. *C. p. olympus* and *C. p. nephele* (and even some specimens with *texana*-like and *boopis*-like characters) also occur in Indiana, but I have never found them *in copula*. Enough research has been completed to justify listing three subspecies of *C. pegala* for Indiana. David Hess (personal communication) has examined my collection several times and concurs with this conclusion. Ferris and Brown (1981), Irwin and Downey (1973), and Miller and Brown (1981) also follow the practice of separating *Cercyonis pegala* into several subspecies.

146. *Cercyonis pegala alope* (Fabricius). Wood Nymph or Grayling. Plate XLVIII.

Description. *C. p. alope* is the largest subspecies found in Indiana. It has a wingspread of 2.1 to 2.9 inches (54–73 mm). The female is much larger than the male. The FW, above and below, has a large patch or unbroken band, which is distinctly yellow. Two large black ocelli with whitish-purple centers are present in the FW. The ocellus in the secondaries (not always present) is much smaller than the eyespots in the FW. The VHW eyespots are variable, sometimes pale and indistinct, and sometimes so prominent that they show *texana*-like characters.

Distribution and Habitat. *Alope* occurs in the Midwest. This species has

PLATE XLVIII

Top row   Little Wood Satyr, *Megisto cymela cymela* UP♂. 1 July 1969, Silver Lake, Kosciusko Co., IN. This specimen was mating with the next one.
M. c. cymela UP♀. 1 July 1969, Silver Lake, Kosciusko Co., IN.
M. c. cymela UN♂. 6 June 1969, Pigeon River State Fish and Game Area, LaGrange Co., IN.

Second row   Wood Nymph or Grayling, *Cercyonis pegala alope* UP♂. 16 July 1983, Whitewater Memorial State Park, Union Co., IN.
C. p. alope UN♂. 31 July 1983, Laketon Wildlife Sanctuary, Wabash Co., IN.
C. p. alope UP♀. 6 August 1983, North Manchester, Wabash Co., IN.

Third row   *C. p. alope* UN♂. 25 July 1983, Silver Lake, Kosciusko Co., IN. This specimen was mating with the next one.
C. p. alope UN♀. 25 July 1983, Silver Lake, Kosciusko Co., IN.
C. p. alope UP♀. 25 July 1983, Lake Waubee Bog, Milford, Kosciusko Co., IN.

Fourth row   *C. p. alope* UP♀. Note large ocelli in upper forewing. 21 July 1969, North Manchester, Wabash Co., IN.
C. p. alope UN♀. 5 August 1978, Pigeon River State Fish and Game Area, Mongo, LaGrange Co., IN.
C. p. alope UP♂. 25 August 1983, Lake Waubee Bog, Milford, Kosciusko Co., IN.

Fifth row   *C. p. alope* UP♂. 26 July 1969, Camp Mack, Milford, Kosciusko Co., IN.
C. p. alope UN♂. Note ocelli near border of lower wings. 19 July 1969, North Manchester, Wabash Co., IN.
C. p. alope UP♂. 1 July 1981, Madison, Jefferson Co., IN.

been recorded in Ohio, Illinois, and Indiana. Blatchley (1891) listed the Wood Nymph as *Satyrus alope* (Fabricius), the Alope Butterfly or the Blue-eyed Grayling, certainly an appropriate common name.

The Wood Nymph is found primarily in the northeastern counties of Indiana, but it also occurs in Union, Franklin, Jefferson, and Switzerland counties. Until recently it had not been found south of Kokomo (Howard County), but on 19–20 July 1980 I found a colony in the Whitewater Memorial State Park in Union County and several more in Franklin County. (20 July 1980). It was not unexpected to find it in Jefferson and Switzerland counties along the Ohio River. A few were taken in Switzerland County and in Clifty Falls State Park near Madison, Jefferson County, on 1 July 1981. Wood Nymphs can be very difficult to catch when they fly among the branches of shrubbery; however, when resting on flowers or mating, they are easily captured.

Life Cycle. All *Cercyonis* have one brood. *Alope* adults fly from 26 May (early) to 21 September (very late). The greatest numbers are active in July and August. Its larval foodplants are grasses.

In Indiana I have found forty-two pairs of *Cercyonis pegala alope in copula*, all having the large yellow patches or bands, with the characteristic *alope* (or *alope*-like) markings. Mating begins in late July and has continued until 25 August (a late date), reaching its peak around mid-August. Pairs *in copula* have been collected as early as 9:05 A.M. and as late as 5:20 P.M. Normally mating occurred between 11:00 A.M. and 3:00 P.M. Temperatures ranged from 65° to 80° F, but the 70s dominated. Most of the pairs were observed in a meadow bordering a woods, in Wabash and Kosciusko counties. One pair was found *in copula* on 23 July 1981, 10:00 A.M., 68° F, in the Whitewater Memorial State Park, Union County, at the edge of a woods and in low grasses, where Red Cedars and Hackberries dotted the landscape. The larger female is always the active sex partner, carrying the limp male with his wings folded together. A mating pair does not fly far when disturbed.

147. *Cercyonis pegala nephele* (Kirby). Nephele Wood Nymph. Plate XLIX.

Description. *Nephele* is smaller than *alope*, measuring 1.75 to 2 inches (44–51 mm). This subspecies lacks the yellow patch or band and the ocelli are much smaller. Irwin and Downey (1973) believe that *C. p. olympus* and *C. p. nephele* are separable only by larval characters. However, the *olympus* in my collection can be separated from *nephele* by the FW ocelli and difference in size and color.

Distribution and Habitat. I have found *nephele* in only three Indiana counties, LaGrange, Wabash, and Kosciusko. Its broader distribution range has not been determined, probably because many experts still consider it to be only another form of *C. pegala* and not a valid subspecies. Adults fly in July and August.

Life Cycle. Unknown for Indiana, but similar to other members of the genus *Cercyonis*.

148. *Cercyonis pegala olympus* (Edwards). Olympian Wood Nymph. Plate XLIX.

Description. The wingspread measures from 2 to 2.25 inches (51–57 mm). The Olympian is a uniform brown butterfly with somewhat restricted ocellation on the VHW. The two dorsal FW ocelli are large and separated, with only a trace of a yellow patch.

Distribution and Habitat. According to Irwin and Downey (1973), *olympus* is the most common and widely distributed subspecies in Illinois. In Indiana *olympus* is most common in the northern counties; however, I found a few on 23 July 1981 in the Whitewater Memorial State Park in Union County. These were close to a rather large colony of *C. p. alope*. I have collected *olympus* from July 5 through September 21 (a very late date). They are fairly common in July, especially in our far north border counties. One specimen resembled the Ox-eyed Wood Nymph (*C. p. boopis*). It was not identified as this form but was only considered "*boopis*-like." It was collected on 20 August 1974 at Mongo in LaGrange County and was examined by David Hess.

Life Cycle. Unknown for Indiana. The larval foodplants are grasses. It has one brood. The males emerge first, because it takes the females longer to develop. Thus, it is quite noticeable that the smaller males arrive two or even three weeks before the females.

Family Danaidae Duponchel

 è▲

Subfamily Danainae Duponchel

è▲

Genus *Danaus* Kluk

149. *Danaus plexippus* (Linnaeus). Monarch Butterfly. Plates XLIX, L.

Description. The Monarch has a wingspread of 3.5 to 4 inches (89–102 mm). Dorsally, the bright fulvous color of the wings and the strong black veins separate this species from others of the genus. The black borders of the wings display two rows of white and whitish yellow dots. The only similar butterfly in Indiana is the Viceroy, but the Monarch is larger and lacks the narrow postmedial line in the HW of the Viceroy.

Distribution and Habitat. The Monarch ranges over most of North America from south of Hudson Bay through South America. It is not found in Alaska and the Pacific Northwest coast, but it is established in the Hawaiian Islands and Australia. Reports of *D. plexippus* from India, Sri Lanka, and Burma should be referred to *D. genutia* (Option 282, International Commission on Zoological Nomenclature).

PLATE XLIX

Top row

Nephele Wood Nymph, *Cercyonis pegala nephele* UP♂. 22 August 1984, Nasby Fen, Mongo, LaGrange Co., IN.

C. p. nephele UN♂. 22 August 1984, Nasby Fen, Mongo, LaGrange Co., IN.

C. p. nephele UN♂. 22 August 1984, Nasby Fen, Mongo, LaGrange Co., IN.

Second row

Olympian Wood Nymph, *Cercyonis pegala olympus* UP♂. 20 August 1984, Nasby Fen, Mongo, LaGrange Co., IN.

C. p. olympus UN♂. Note ocelli. 25 August 1970, Pigeon River State Fish and Game Area, Mongo, LaGrange Co., IN.

C. p. olympus UN♂. 25 July 1978, Pigeon River State Fish and Game Area, Mongo, LaGrange Co., IN.

Third row

C. p. olympus UP♀. 25 July 1978, Pigeon River State Fish and Game Area, Mongo, LaGrange Co., IN.

C. p. olympus UN♀. 11 August 1981, Pigeon River State Fish and Game Area, Mongo, LaGrange Co., IN.

C. p. olympus UN♀. Note small ocellus below basal ocellus on upper wing, called "crying eye" or "tear." 5 August 1978, Pigeon River State Fish and Game Area, Mongo, LaGrange Co., IN.

Fourth row

Monarch Butterfly, *Danaus plexippus* UP♀. 20 July 1969, North Manchester, Wabash Co., IN.

PLATE L

Monarch, *Danaus plexippus* UP♂. 13 September 1984, North Manchester, Wabash Co., IN.

D. plexippus UN♂. 13 August 1984, North Manchester, Wabash Co., IN.

The Monarch, or Milkweed Butterfly, occurs throughout the state of Indiana. It is one of our best known butterflies, probably because of its large size, bright colors, great migrations, and presence everywhere, in town, country, and city. The earliest date for *plexippus* in Indiana is 22 March 1976, when I found an adult resting near the wall of a big barn, which protected it from cold and wind, at North Manchester, Wabash County. It may have been a hibernating adult which never migrated to the south. On 8 November 1969 (a very late date), I found several Monarchs in a grassy field in the midst of a housing development project in the city of Indianapolis, Marion County—that find again suggests that a few Monarchs may hibernate as adults or as pupae. The majority of Monarchs occur from April through September, showing great preference for the flowers of the Milkweeds (*Asclepias*) and Dogbane (*Apocynum*); however, they visit many other flowers, both wild and cultivated.

In late July and early August the Monarchs begin to congregate in the forests and groves, preparing for their long flight southward. In the coastal city of Pacific Grove, California (called "Butterfly Town, U.S.A." by the residents), thousands, even millions, of these beautiful insects cluster in groves of pine, cypress, and eucalyptus trees to spend the winter as hibernating or semi-hibernating adults. These are mostly western broods. Many Monarchs from the Midwest and East migrate to the Sierra Madre of middle Mexico, where they hang on the branches of fir trees at high altitudes. C. B. Williams and Paul A. Zahl have described these fascinating migrations in several issues of the *National Geographic Magazine*.

Nearly every year a few Monarchs can be seen in their autumnal migratory flights, but it takes an observant eye. They are not always in huge bands. More frequently they fly one after the other, or a few moving together in one direction above the cars on our highways. On 17 September 1983 thousands flew into the tops of the trees on the Saint Francis College campus (in Fort Wayne), where they spent the night, only to continue their long flight the next morning.

Life Cycle. The egg is greenish and ovate-conical in shape. The larva is bright green or greenish yellow, banded with shining black, and has threadlike appendages at both ends. The chrysalis is pale green and spotted with gold. The pupae are usually found on the host plants, but I found one hanging from the underside of wood siding of a building in Kosciusko County. The larval food-plants are Milkweeds and Dogbane.

In Indiana I have found 66 pairs of the Monarch *in copula*. The male was always the active flight partner; however, Pronin (1964) reported the female as the active flight partner, a dubious record. With the exception of five pairs mating in June (6th to 30th), the remaining 61 pairs mated in July and August. One pair mated 22 August 1977, 9:45 A.M., at a cold 59° F, Silver Lake, Kosciusko County. The male could not fly when released. Its wings were spread open toward the sun, a process of thermoregulation prior to morning flight. Other pairs were mating between 70° F and 92° F, the great majority mating in the mid-70s and mid-80s. Mating usually takes place from late morning to late evening (11:00 A.M. to 6:45 P.M.), the greatest number mating between 2:00 P.M. and 4:30 P.M. A few pairs may remain *in copula* throughout the night. The author has seen mating pairs resting in the treetops at sunset. Courtship between the male and female Monarch is usually of short duration. The male's sweet-smelling sex cells (androconia) soon attract a willing female. I have found mating pairs in Wabash, Kosciusko, LaGrange, Randolph, Delaware, and Allen counties. *Plexippus* has three to four broods.

The Monarch is the model for the Viceroy or Mimic. The larval foodplants of the Monarch make the adults bad-tasting to would-be predators. The Viceroy is edible, but protected by its Monarch-like color pattern.

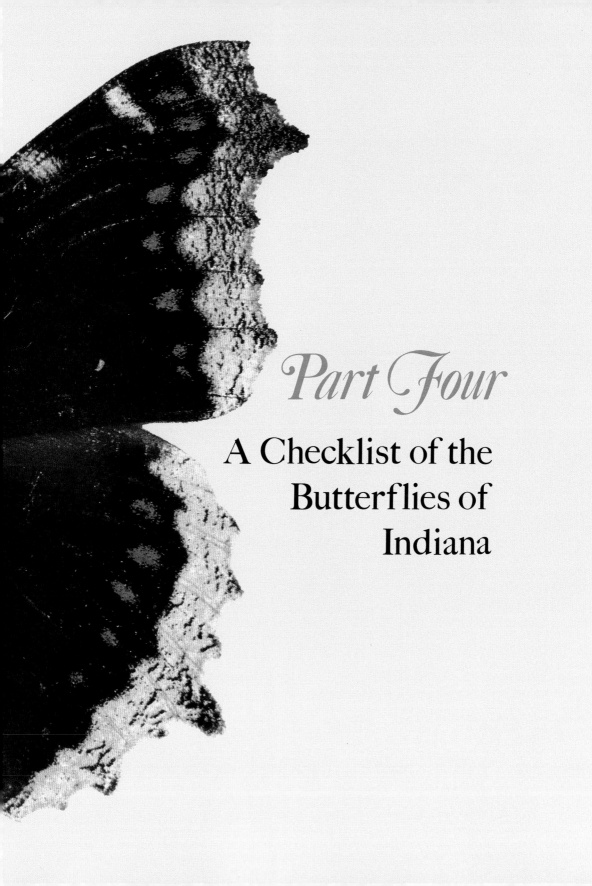

Part Four

A Checklist of the Butterflies of Indiana

Superfamily Hesperioidea

*

Family Hesperiidae

*

Subfamily Pyrginae

1. *Epargyreus clarus clarus*, Silver-spotted Skipper
2. *Autochton cellus*, Golden-banded Skipper
3. *Achalarus lyciades*, Hoary Edge
4. *Thorybes bathyllus*, Southern Cloudywing
5. *Thorybes pylades*, Northern Cloudywing
6. *Thorybes confusis*, Eastern Cloudywing
7. *Staphylus hayhurstii*, Scalloped Sootywing
8. *Erynnis icelus*, Dreamy Duskywing
9. *Erynnis brizo brizo*, Sleepy Duskywing
10. *Erynnis juvenalis juvenalis*, Juvenal's Duskywing
11. *Erynnis horatius*, Horace's Duskywing
12. *Erynnis martialis*, Mottled Duskywing
13. *Erynnis zarucco*, Zarucco Duskywing
14. *Erynnis funeralis*, Funeral Duskywing
15. *Erynnis lucilius*, Columbine Duskywing
16. *Erynnis baptisiae*, Wild Indigo Duskywing
17. *Erynnis persius*, Persius Duskywing
18. *Pyrgus communis*, Common Checkered Skipper
19. *Pholisora catullus*, Common Sootywing

Subfamily Hesperiinae

20. *Nastra lherminier*, Swarthy Skipper
21. *Lerema accius*, Clouded Skipper
22. *Ancyloxypha numitor*, Least Skipper
23. *Oarisma powesheik*, Powesheik Skipper
24. *Thymelicus lineola*, European Skipper
25. *Hylephila phyleus*, Fiery Skipper
26. *Hesperia ottoe*, Ottoe Skipper
27. *Hesperia leonardus*, Leonardus Skipper
28. *Hesperia metea*, Cobweb Skipper
29. *Hesperia sassacus*, Indian Skipper
30. *Polites coras*, Peck's Skipper

*=Authentic recent records are needed to keep these species on the Indiana list.

31. *Polites themistocles,* Tawny-edged Skipper
32. *Polites origenes origenes,* Crossline Skipper
33. *Polites mystic,* Long Dash
34. *Wallengrenia egeremet,* Northern Broken Dash
35. *Pompeius verna,* Little Glassywing
36. *Atalopedes campestris,* Sachem or Field Skipper
37. *Atrytone logan logan,* Delaware Skipper
38. *Problema byssus,* Byssus Skipper
39. *Poanes massasoit,* Mulberry Wing Skipper
40. *Poanes hobomok,* Hobomok Skipper
41. *Poanes zabulon,* Zabulon Skipper
42. *Poanes viator,* Broad-winged Skipper
43. *Euphyes dion,* Sedge Skipper
44. *Euphyes dukesi,* Scarce Swamp Skipper
45. *Euphyes conspicua conspicua,* Black Dash
46. *Euphyes bimacula,* Two-spotted Skipper
47. *Euphyes ruricola metacomet,* Dun Skipper
48. *Atrytonopsis hianna,* Dusted Skipper
49. *Amblyscirtes hegon,* Pepper-and-Salt Skipper
50. *Amblyscirtes vialis,* Roadside Skipper
51. *Amblyscirtes belli,* Bell's Roadside Skipper
52. *Lerodea eufala,* Eufala Skipper
53. *Panoquina ocola,* Long-winged Skipper

Superfamily Papilionoidea

Family Papilionidae

Subfamily Papilioninae

54. *Battus philenor philenor,* Pipevine Swallowtail
55. *Eurytides marcellus,* Zebra Swallowtail
56. *Papilio polyxenes asterius,* Eastern Black Swallowtail
57. *Heraclides cresphontes,* Giant Swallowtail
58. *Pterourus glaucus glaucus,* Tiger Swallowtail
59. *Pterourus troilus troilus,* Spicebush Swallowtail

Family Pieridae
Subfamily Pierinae

60. *Pontia protodice,* Checkered White
61. *Artogeia napi oleracea,* Veined White or Mustard White
62. *Artogeia rapae,* Cabbage White

Subfamily Anthocharinae

63. *Euchloe olympia,* Olympia Marblewing
64. *Falcapica midea midea,* Falcate Orangetip

Subfamily Coliadinae

65. *Colias philodice philodice,* Common Sulphur
66. *Colias eurytheme,* Orange Sulphur or Alfalfa Butterfly
67. *Zerene cesonia,* Dogface Butterfly
68. *Phoebis sennae eubule,* Cloudless Giant Sulphur
69. *Phoebis philea,* Orange-barred Giant Sulphur
70. *Eurema mexicana,* Mexican Yellow or Yellow Sulphur
71. *Pyrisitia lisa lisa,* Little Yellow
72. *Abaeis nicippe,* Sleepy Orange
73. *Nathalis iole,* Dwarf Yellow or Dainty Sulphur

Family Lycaenidae
Subfamily Miletinae

74. *Feniseca tarquinius tarquinius,* Harvester

Subfamily Lycaenidae

75. *Lycaena phlaeas americana,* American Copper
76. *Hyllolycaena hyllus,* Bronze Copper
77. *Epidemia epixanthe,** Bog Copper
78. *Epidemia dorcas dorcas,* Dorcas Copper
79. *Epidemia helloides,* Purplish Copper
80. *Atlides halesus halesus,* Great Purple Hairstreak
81. *Harkenclenus titus titus,* Coral Hairstreak

82. *Satyrium acadica acadica*, Acadian Hairstreak
83. *Satyrium edwardsii*, Edwards' Hairstreak
84. *Satyrium calanus falacer*, Banded Hairstreak
85. *Satyrium caryaevorum*, Hickory Hairstreak
86. *Satyrium liparops strigosum*, Striped Hairstreak
87. *Calycopis cecrops*, Red-banded Hairstreak
88. *Mitoura gryneus gryneus*, Olive Hairstreak
89. *Incisalia polios*, Hoary Elfin
90. *Incisalia irus irus*, Frosted Elfin
91. *Incisalia henrici turneri*, Henry's Elfin
92. *Incisalia niphon clarki*, Eastern Pine Elfin
93. *Euristrymon ontario ontario*, Northern Hairstreak
94. *Parrhasius m-album*, White M Hairstreak
95. *Strymon melinus humuli*, Gray Hairstreak

Subfamily Polyommatinae

96. *Leptotes marina*, Marine Blue
97. *Hemiargus isola*, Reakirt's Blue
98. *Everes comyntas comyntas*, Eastern Tailed Blue
99. *Celastrina ladon ladon*, Spring Azure
100. *Celastrina ebenina*, Sooty Azure
101. *Glaucopsyche lygamus couperi*, Silvery Blue
102. *Lycaeides melissa samuelis*, Karner Blue

Family Riodinidae
ે₂
Subfamily Riodininae

103. *Calephelis borealis*, Northern Metalmark
104. *Calephelis muticum*, Swamp Metalmark

Family Libytheidae

105. *Libytheana bachmanii bachmanii*, Snout Butterfly

Family Heliconiidae
ે₂
Subfamily Heliconiinae

106. *Agraulis vanillae,** Gulf Fritillary

Family Nymphalidae

Subfamily Argynninae

107. *Euptoieta claudia*, Variegated Fritillary
108. *Speyeria diana*, Diana
109. *Speyeria cybele cybele*, Great Spangled Fritillary
110. *Speyeria aphrodite aphrodite*, Aphrodite
111. *Speyeria aphrodite alcestis*, Ruddy Silverspot
112. *Speyeria idalia*, Regal Fritillary
113. *Speyeria atlantis*, Atlantis Fritillary
114. *Clossiana selene*, Silver-bordered Fritillary
115. *Clossiana bellona bellona*, Meadow Fritillary

Subfamily Melitaeinae

116. *Charidryas gorgone carlota*, Gorgone Checkerspot
117. *Charidryas nycteis nycteis*, Silvery Checkerspot
118. *Charidryas harrisii*, Harris' Checkerspot
119. *Phyciodes tharos tharos*, Pearly Crescentspot or Pearl Crescent
120. *Phyciodes batesii*, Tawny Crescentspot
121. *Euphydryas phaeton phaeton*, Baltimore

Subfamily Nymphalinae

122. *Polygonia interrogationis*, Question Mark
123. *Polygonia comma*, Comma or Hop Merchant
124. *Polygonia satyrus*, Satyr Anglewing
125. *Polygonia zephyrus*, Zephyr Anglewing
126. *Polygonia progne*, Gray Comma
127. *Nymphalis vau-album j-album*, Compton Tortoiseshell
128. *Nymphalis antiopa antiopa*, Mourning Cloak
129. *Aglais milberti milberti*, Milbert's Tortoiseshell
130. *Vanessa virginiensis*, American Painted Lady
131. *Vanessa cardui*, Painted Lady or Thistle Butterfly
132. *Vanessa atalanta rubria*, Red Admiral
133. *Junonia coenia*, Buckeye

Subfamily Limenitidinae

134. *Basilarchia arthemis astyanax*, Red-spotted Purple
135. *Basilarchia archippus archippus*, Viceroy or Mimic

Family Apaturidae

❧

Subfamily Charaxinae

136. *Anaea andria*, Goatweed Butterfly

Subfamily Apaturinae

137. *Asterocampa celtis*, Hackberry Butterfly
138. *Asterocampa clyton*, Tawny Emperor

Family Satyridae

❧

Subfamily Elymniinae

139. *Enodia anthedon*, Northern Pearly Eye
140. *Enodia creola*, Creole Pearly Eye
141. *Satyrodes eurydice eurydice*, Eyed Brown
142. *Satyrodes appalachia leeuwi*, Appalachian Brown

Subfamily Satyrinae

143. *Cyllopsis gemma gemma*, Gemmed Satyr
144. *Neonympha mitchellii*, Mitchell's Satyr
145. *Megisto cymela cymela*, Little Wood Satyr
146. *Cercyonis pegala alope*, Wood Nymph or Grayling
147. *Cercyonis pegala nephele*, Nephele Wood Nymph
148. *Cercyonis pegala olympus*, Olympian Wood Nymph

Family Danaidae

❧

Subfamily Danainae

149. *Danaus plexippus*, Monarch Butterfly

Hypothetical List

Blatchley (1891) reported only 108 species of butterflies for Indiana. He also included Edwards's list of 23 more species that might occur in Indiana or in territory adjacent to Indiana. Fifteen of the "possibles" have already been found in our state, but a few in his list probably will never occur here.

Since the Shull and Badger list (1972), the status of many species has changed considerably. Following is a revised list of species that might be expected to occur in Indiana. The serious collector should look for them.

Family Hesperiidae

Pyrgus centaureae (Rambur). Grizzled Skipper.

Occurs from New York to Colorado. The subspecies *P. c. wyandot* (W. H. Edwards) has been reported from Illinois.

Hesperia uncas W. H. Edwards. Uncas Skipper.

Uncas is a western prairie species that sometimes enters the eastern area. There are several subspecies.

Hesperia attalus (W. H. Edwards). Dotted Skipper.

Klots (1951) gives the range as "Florida to Texas, n. to Massachusetts, Ohio, Wisconsin, and Nebraska." Irwin and Downey (1973) expect to find it in Illinois. It should occur in Indiana.

Polites vibex (Geyer). Whirlabout.

According to Howe (1975), the "nominate *vibex* is the most widespread in the United States, ranging from Connecticut to Florida and west to Arkansas and Texas." Irwin and Downey say that it "may occur northward at least as far as southern Illinois."

Atrytone arogos (Boisduval and Leconte). Arogos Skipper.

Arogos ranges from Florida and Texas northward to New Jersey, Iowa, Minnesota, and Nebraska. Irwin and Downey have never found this species in Illinois, but if found, it may be of the subspecies *A. a. iowa* (Scudder). It eventually may appear as a casual in Indiana.

Family Pieridae

***Colias interior* Scudder. Pink-edged Sulphur.**

This is a Canadian Zone species ranging nearly across the continent. One of the three subspecies may occur in Indiana, but so far *interior* has been found no closer than in Michigan.

***Phoebis agarithe* Boisduval. Large Orange Sulphur.**

The subspecies *P. a. maxima* (Neumoegen) is usually found in southern Florida, but strays occasionally wander as far as Kansas, Arizona, Texas, and Illinois.

***Kricogonia lyside* (Godart). Lyside.**

Klots (1951) reported that this southern butterfly strays to northern Illinois. This highly migratory species may eventually appear in Indiana.

Family Lycaenidae

***Gaeides xanthoides* (Boisduval). Great Copper.**

It occurs in the upper Mississippi Valley, Kansas north through Nebraska, Minnesota, and northern Illinois. Irwin and Downey (1973) report that the subspecies *G. x. dione* (Scudder) is increasing in numbers and distribution in Illinois. Thus this butterfly should be looked for in the prairie meadows of Indiana.

***Satyrium kingi* (Klots and Clench). King's Hairstreak.**

Harry K. Clench (personal communication) has suggested that this hairstreak should be found in the same habitat as *Lethe creola* (=*Enodia creola*). Thus, it is very possible that *S. kingi* will be found in Indiana.

***Plebejus saepiolus* Boisduval. Greenish Blue.**

According to Howe (1975), this species occurs in isolated pockets throughout southern Canada eastward to Maine and southward into the Great Lakes states. One of its many subspecies should be found in Indiana.

***Incisalia augustus* (W. Kirby). Brown Elfin.**

Klots (1951) gives the range as "Newfoundland w. to Manitoba, s. to Virginia, West Virginia, Illinois, and Michigan." One of its several subspecies may possibly occur in Indiana.

Family Riodinidae

Calephelis virginiensis (Cuérin-Mén'eville). Little Metalmark.

This species ranges from southern Florida, the Gulf states, and southern Texas north to Virginia and Ohio. Likely it will be found in Indiana.

Family Nymphalidae

Proclossiana eunomia (Esper). Bog Fritillary.

This species (formerly *Boloria eunomia*) occurs in Michigan. There is a remote possibility that it may occur in the acid bogs of northern Indiana.

Polygonia faunus (W. H. Edwards). Green Comma.

This species ranges from Canada south to Georgia and Iowa. Irwin and Downey (1973) mention a few records (some recent) from Illinois, where it rarely occurs in the extreme northern portions. All *Polygonia* are strong fliers, known to move long distances. *P. faunus* could stray into Indiana.

Glossary

Abdomen. The last of the three major divisions of an insect body.

Anal spot. Spot at the anal angle of the hindwing.

Androconia. Specialized scent scales or patch on wings of male Lepidoptera.

Antennae. Jointed appendages between the eyes, known as "feelers."

Apex. The wing tip: the angle of the wing between the costa and the termen.

Apiculus. The recurved segment of the antenna.

Author. The person who first described and named a species.

Basal. Pertaining to the base of the point nearest the main body.

Bifid. Cleft or forked.

Chrysalis. Third stage in the life cycle of Lepidoptera.

Cilia. The hairlike fringe edging the wings or tails.

Clasp. A process of the valva.

Conspecific. Belonging to the same species.

Costa. The thickened anterior margin of a wing; the dorsal margin of the valva of the male genitalia.

Crepuscular. Active at twilight or at dusk.

Cubitus. Fifth vein of a wing.

Dentate. Having tooth-like projections.

Dimorphism. Difference in form or appearance in members of the same species, whether seasonal or sexual.

Distal. Toward the free end of an appendage; farthest from the main body.

Diurnal. Active during the day.

Dorsal. Upper, as opposed to under (ventral), surface of the wings and other parts.

Emarginate. Notched.

Foodplant. The plant on which the caterpillar feeds.

Fringe. An even row of scales or hairs projecting beyond the membrane of the margin of the wing.

Genitalia. The apparatus for reproduction at the end of the abdomen.

Genus. A scientific group designated to incorporate closely related species.

Ground color. The color occupying the largest area of the wing.

Gynandromorph. An individual exhibiting morphological characters of both sexes.

Head. The first of the three major divisions of an insect body.

Instar. The period between two larval molts.

Interspace. The numbered areas on the wing between veins.

Larva. Caterpillar; stage after the egg in the life cycle of a butterfly.

Lepidoptera. The major group or order to which scale-winged insects belong (butterflies and moths).

Margin. The area between the termen and the disc.

Mimicry. Among certain Lepidoptera there is a protective resemblance that may benefit one sex only (the female) or both sexes of the mimicking species. The bad-tasting species are called the models and the edible species the mimics.

Ocellus. A colored spot surrounded by a ring of another color.

Palp. The labial palp, an organ projecting in front of the face.

Polymorphism. Multi-variation in form of a species.

Proboscis. The external coiled feeding tube of an adult Lepidopteran.

Pupa. The third stage of the butterfly life cycle, sometimes called the chrysalis.

Species. A distinct group of animals that mate with one another and closely resemble their own kind.

Subfamily. A group of related genera or tribes.

Subspecies. A stable, geographically or topographically isolated variety of a species, also called a race.

Superfamily. A group of related families.

Thorax. The second of three major divisions of the butterfly body, bearing the wings and legs.

Tornus. Anal angle or inner part of a wing.

Tribe. A group of related genera or subtribes.

Truncate. Cut off square, used especially of the wing apex.

Valva. Paired appendages of the male genitalia, commonly called "claspers."

Veins. Tubes that strengthen the wing membrane through which blood and air can be pumped for flying and thermoregulation. The pattern of tubes or veins on the wing.

Literature Cited

Anonymous. 1972. *J. Lepid. Soc.* 25(1):18.

———. 1980. Season Summary. *News Lepid. Soc.*, No. 2.

Badger, F. S. 1958. *Euptychia mitchellii* (Satyridae) in Michigan and Indiana tamarack bogs. *Lepid. News* 12:41–46.

Barnes, W. B. 1952. Zoogeographic regions of Indiana. *Amer. Midland Naturalist* 48: 694–99.

Blatchley, W. S. 1886. Some southern Indiana butterflies. *Hoosier Naturalist* 2(4):42–43 (November) and 2(5):62–63 (December).

———. 1891. Catalogue of the butterflies known to occur in Indiana. *Ann. Rept. Indiana Dept. Geol. Natural History* 17:365–408.

Bowden, S. R. 1979. Subspecific variation in butterflies: adaptation and dissected polymorphism in *Pieris (Artogeia)* (Pieridae). *J. Lepid. Soc.* 33:77–111.

Brewer, Jo. 1982. A visit with 200 million monarchs and Monarch roosts: will Mexico preserve them? *Defenders of Wildlife* 57(2):13–20.

Brown, F. Martin. 1966. The authorship of *Polites mystic*, Edwards or Scudder? (Hesperiidae). *J. Lepid. Soc.* 20:237–42.

Burns, John M. 1964. Evolution of skipper butterflies in the genus *Erynnis*. *Univ. Calif. Publ. Entomology* 37:1–216.

———. 1968. Mating frequency in natural populations of skippers and butterflies as determined by spermatophore counts. *Proc. Nat. Acad. Science* 61:852–59.

Carde, Ring T., Arthur M. Shapiro, and Harry K. Clench. 1970. Sibling species in the *eurydice* group of *Lethe* (Lepidoptera: Satyridae). *Psyche* 77:70–103.

Clench, Harry K. 1966. Behavioral thermoregulation in butterflies. *Ecology* 47:1001–1034.

———. 1967. Temporal dissociation and population regulation in certain Hesperiinae butterflies. *Ecology* 48:1000–1006.

———. 1970. Communal roosting in *Colias* and *Phoebis* (Pieridae). *J. Lepid. Soc.* 24: 117–20.

———. 1972. *Celetrina ebenina*, a new species of Lycaenidae (Lepidoptera) from the eastern United States. *Ann. Carnegie Mus.* 44:33–44.

——— and Lee D. Miller. 1980. *Papilio ladon* Cramer vs. *Argus pseudargiolus* Boisduval and Leconte (Lycaenidae): A nomenclatorial nightmare. *J. Lepid. Soc.* 34(2):103–19.

——— and Theodore Sargent, eds. 1977. *The Lepidopterist Society Commemorative Volume (1945–1973)*.

Comstock, William Phillips. 1961. *Butterflies of the American tropics, the genus Anaea, Lepidoptera Nymphalidae*. New York: American Museum of Natural History.

Cooper, R. H. 1938. A breeding record for the Red-barred Sulphur (*Callidryas philea* Linn.) from Indiana. *Ent. News* 49:261.

Crovello, Theodore J., Clifton A. Keller, and John T. Kartesz. 1983. *The vascular plants of Indiana: a computer based checklist*. Amer. Midland Naturalist. Notre Dame and London: University of Notre Dame Press.

dos Passos, Cyril F. 1964. A synonymic list of the Nearctic Rhopalocera. *Lepid. Soc. Mem.* 1.

———. 1969. A revised synonymic list of the Nearctic Melitaeinae with taxonomic notes (Nymphalidae). *J. Lepid. Soc.* 23:115–25.

———. 1970. A revised synonymic catalogue with taxonomic notes on some Nearctic Lycaenidae. *J. Lepid. Soc.* 24:26–38.

Ehrlich, Paul R., and Anne H. Ehrlich. 1961. *How to know the butterflies*. Dubuque, Iowa: Wm. C. Brown.

———. 1965. The color patterns of butterflies and moths. *Scientific American* 245(5):140–51.

———. 1982. Butterfly retreat, some North American butterflies in trouble. *Defenders of Wildlife* 57(2):13–16.

Ehrlich, Paul R., and Peter H. Raven. 1965. Butterflies and plants: a study in coevolution. *Evolution* 18(4):538–605.

———. 1969. Differentiation of populations. *Science* 165:1128–231.

Eliot, J. N. 1973. The higher classification of the Lycaenidae: A tentative arrangement. *Bull. British Museum (N.H.)* 28(6):371–505.

Ferris, Clifford, and F. Martin Brown. 1980. *Butterflies of the Rocky Mountain states*. Norman: University of Oklahoma Press.

Field, William D., Cyril F. dos Passos, and John M. Masters. 1974. *A bibliography of the catalogs, lists, faunal and other papers on the butterflies of North America north of Mexico arranged by state and province (Lepidoptera: Rhopalocera)*. Smithsonian Contributions to Zoology, No. 157. Smithsonian Institution Press.

Hall, F. T. 1936. The occurrence of unusual Rhopalocera in Indiana. *Proc. Indiana Academy Science* 45:272–74.

Harris, Lucien, Jr. 1972. *Butterflies of Georgia*. Norman: University of Oklahoma Press.

Holland, W. J. 1940. *The butterfly book*. New York: Doubleday.

Howe, William H. 1975. *The butterflies of North America*. Garden City, New York: Doubleday.

Irwin, Roderick R., and John C. Downey. 1973. Annotated check list of the butterflies of Illinois. *Biol. Notes* 81 (Illinois Natur. Hist. Survey, Urbana).

Jaques, H. E. 1947. *How to know the insects*. Dubuque, Iowa: Wm. C. Brown.

Klots, Alexander B. 1951. *A field guide to the butterflies*. Boston: Houghton Mifflin Co.

———. 1957. *The world of butterflies and moths*. New York: McGraw-Hill.

Kohler, Steve. 1977. Revision of North American *Boloria selene* (Nymphalidae) with description of new subspecies. *J. Lepid. Soc.* 31:243–68.

Lindsey, Alton A. ed. 1966. *Natural features of Indiana*. Indianapolis: Indiana Academy of Science.

Masters, J. H., and Wilma L. Masters. 1969. An annotated list of the butterflies of Perry County and a contribution to the knowledge of Lepidoptera in Indiana. Mid-Continent Lepidoptera Series No. 6.

McAlpine, Wilbur S., Stephen P. Hubbel, and Thomas E. Pliske. 1960. The distribution, habits, and life history of *Euptychia mitchellii* (Satyridae). *J. Lepid. Soc.* 14:209–26.

McDunnough, James H. 1938. *Check list of the lepidoptera of Canada and the United States of America. Part I. Macrolepidoptera*. Mem. So. California Academy Science.

———. 1939. *Check list of the Lepidoptera of Canada and the United States of America. Part II. Microlepidoptera*. Mem. So. California Academy Science.

Michener, Charles D. 1942. A generic revision of the Heliconiinae (Lepidoptera: Nymphalidae). American Museum of Natural History, Novitate 1197.

Miller, Lee D. 1968. The higher classification, phylogeny, and zoogeography of the Satyridae (Lepidoptera). *Mem. Amer. Entomol. Soc.* 24(6).

Miller, Lee D., and F. Martin Brown. 1981. *A catalogue/checklist of the butterflies of America north of Mexico.* Mem. Lepid. Soc. No. 2.

Miller, Lee D., and Harry K. Clench. 1968. Some aspects of mating behavior in butterflies. *J. Lepid. Soc.* 22:125–31.

Mitchell, Robert T., and Herbert S. Zim. 1962. *Butterflies and moths. A Golden Guide.* Racine, Wisconsin: Western Publishing Co.

Montgomery, R. W. 1931. Preliminary list of the butterflies of Indiana. *Proc. Indiana Academy Science* 40:357–59.

Necomb, William W. 1911. The life history of *Chrysophanus dorcas* Kirby. *Canad. Entomol.* 43:160–68.

Nielsen, Morgan C. 1970. Distributional maps for Michigan butterflies. Part I. Skippers. Mid-Continent Lepidoptera Series No. 16.

Niering, William A., and Nancy C. Olmstead. 1979. *The Audubon Society field guide to North American wildflowers.* New York: Alfred A. Knopf.

Nijhout, H. Frederik. 1981. The color patterns of butterflies and moths. *Scientific American* 245(5):140–51.

Oosting, D. 1980. Season Summary No. 2. *News Lepid. Soc.*

Opler, Paul A., and George O. Krizek. 1984. *Butterflies east of the Great Plains.* Baltimore: Johns Hopkins University Press.

Peterson, Roger Tory, and Margaret McKenny. 1968. *A field guide to wild flowers of northeastern and north central North America.* Boston: Houghton Mifflin Co.

Platt, Austin P., and Lincoln P. Brower. 1968. Mimetic versus disruptive coloration in integrating populations of *Limenitis arthemis* and *astyanax* butterflies. *Evolution* 22:699–718.

Price, Homer F., and Ernest M. Shull. 1969. Uncommon butterflies of northeastern Indiana. *J. Lepid. Soc.* 23:186–88.

Pronin, J. D. 1964. The mating behavior of Lepidoptera. *J. Lepid. Soc.* 18:35–41.

Pyle, Robert Michael. 1981. *The Audubon Society field guide to North American butterflies.* New York: Alfred A. Knopf.

Remington, Jeanne, and Charles L. Remington. 1957. Mimicry, a test of evolutionary theory. *Yale Scientific Magazine* 32(1):8. Gibbs Research Lab., Yale University.

Shapiro, Arthur M. 1965. Ecological and behavioral notes on *Hesperia metea* and *Atrytonopsis hianna* (Hesperiidae). *J. Lepid. Soc.* 19:215–21.

Shull, E. M. 1968. *Thymelicus lineola* (Hesperiidae) in Indiana. *J. Lepid. Soc.* 22:20.

Shull, Ernest M. 1972. Indiana state records and notes on some rare butterflies and skippers in the state. *Proc. Indiana Academy Science* 81:175–76.

———. 1975. *Erynnis funeralis* (Lepidoptera: Hesperiidae) and *Polygonia zephyrus* (Lepidoptera: Nymphalidae) in Indiana: new state records. *Great Lakes Entomol.* 9:207.

———. 1977. Colony of *Pieris napi oleracea* (Pieridae) in Indiana. *J. Lepid. Soc.* 31:68–70.

———. 1979. Mating behavior of butterflies (Papilionoidea) and skippers (Hesperioidea) in Indiana. *Proc. Indiana Academy Science* 88:200–208.

———. 1981. Indiana state records and notes on some rare and endangered Lepidoptera in the state (1972–1980). *Proc. Indiana Academy Science* 91:309–12.

Shull, Ernest M., and F. Sidney Badger. 1972. Annotated list of the butterflies of Indiana. *J. Lepid. Soc.* 26:13–24.

Sutherland, Douglas W. S. 1978. *Common names of insects and related organisms.* Special Pub. 78-1, Entomol. Soc. America. College Park, Maryland.

Urquhart, Fred A. 1960. *The Monarch butterfly.* Toronto: University of Toronto Press.

———. 1976. Found at last—the monarch's winter home. *National Geographic,* August, 161–73.

Williams, C. B. 1930. *The migration of butterflies.* Edinburgh: Oliver and Boyd.

———. 1937. Butterfly travelers. *National Geographic,* May, 568–85.

Wright, David M. 1983. Life history of the immature stages of the Bog Copper butterfly *Lycaena epixanthe* (Bsd. & Le C.) (Lepidoptera: Lycaenidae). *J. Res. Lepid.* 22(1):47–100.

Foodplant Index

General Index

ERNEST M. SHULL, Professor of Sociology at St. Francis College
in Fort Wayne, Indiana, until his recent retirement,
has studied and collected butterflies since his
boyhood. He has taken about 70,000
specimens, most of which are
in museum collections.

Editor
≿
Lynn Lightfoot

Book designer
≿
Sharon L. Sklar

Jacket designer
≿
Sharon L. Sklar

Production coordinator
≿
Harriet Curry

Typeface
≿
Caslon 224

Compositor
≿
G&S Typesetters, Inc.

Printer
≿
Toppan Printing Co., Inc.